De Quincey's Art
of Autobiography

De Quincey's Art of Autobiography

EDMUND BAXTER

EDINBURGH UNIVERSITY PRESS

© Edmund Baxter 1990
Edinburgh University Press
22 George Square, Edinburgh

Set in Palatino on the Telos Text Composition System,
Printed in Great Britain by
Page Brothers, Norwich.

British Library Cataloguing
  in Publication Data
Baxter, Edmund
  De Quincey's art of autobiography
  1. Prose in English.   De Quincey, Thomas, 1785–1859
  I. Title
  828.808

ISBN   0 7486 0138 4
       0 7486 0181 3 pbk

Contents

	Acknowledgments	vi
	Bibliographical Note and Short Titles List	vii
	Introduction	1
1	*Confessions of an English Opium-Eater*	12
2	Autobiographical Essays	36
3	Biographical Interventions: sketches of Coleridge and Wordsworth; and 'Sir William Hamilton'	64
4	Fictions	93
5	'The English Mail-Coach' and De Quincey's political works	121
6	*The Logic of Political Economy* and related works	153
	Notes	186
	Bibliography	200
	Index	212

Acknowledgments

Without the help of numerous people, this work would not have been written. I should like to acknowledge the help of the staff of the following institutions: The British Library; University of London Library; King's College, London, Department of English; Cambridge University Library; National Library of Scotland – in particular the staff of the NLS Manuscript Collection for providing me with immediate access to a vast number of texts. Thanks also to the staff of Edinburgh University Press.

Many people provided me with encouragement, ideas and sustenance over the last few years – they know who they are and will doubtless be content to be silently thanked here. Particular thanks to Cyril Baxter, Patricia Baxter, Barry Symonds, Chris Baxter, Fiona Train, Nick Baxter, Andy Hopton and Kate Hardy, all of whom helped me in various ways to continue this project. Finally, I wish to thank most emphatically John Woolford. I hope all those concerned one way or another think it was worth the effort.

This work is dedicated to the memory of Dorothy Wells.

Bibliographical Note

Unless otherwise stated, all references are to Thomas De Quincey, *Selections Grave and Gay, from Writings, Published and Unpublished, of Thomas De Quincey, Revised and Arranged by Himself*, 14 vols (Edinburgh: James Hogg, 1853–60). Citations from this work are designated parenthetically in the text by volume and page number (e.g. 5: 227).

All manuscripts cited are from the collection of the National Library of Scotland (abbreviated in this work to NLS). Citations from these manuscripts are designated by volume and folio (e.g. NLS MS 4717 fo. 36).

Short titles list

Quotations from the following works, which supplement De Quincey's edition of his writings, are identified in the text by the appropriate abbreviation and page number (e.g. *L* 79).

Blackwood's: *Blackwood's Edinburgh Magazine*.

L: *Confessions of an English Opium-Eater and Other Writings* ed. Grevel Lindop (London: Oxford University Press, 1985).

Logic: *The Logic of Political Economy* (Edinburgh and London: William Blackwood and Sons, 1844).

PW: *Posthumous Works of Thomas De Quincey* ed. A. H. Japp (London: Heinemann, 1891) 2 vols.

SG: *The Stranger's Grave* ed. Edmund Baxter (London: Aporia Press 1988).

Tait's: *Tait's Edinburgh Magazine*.

Tave: *New Essays by De Quincey: His contributions to the* Edinburgh Saturday Post *and the* Edinburgh Evening Post *1827-1828* ed. Stuart M. Tave (Princeton, New Jersey: Princeton University Press, 1966).

TC: *The Caçadore: A story of the Peninsular War* ed. Edmund Baxter (London: Aporia Press 1988).

UW: *Uncollected Writings of Thomas De Quincey* ed. James Hogg (London: Swan Sonnenschein, 1890).

Writings: *The Collected Writings of Thomas De Quincey* ed. David Masson (Edinburgh: Adam and Charles Black, 1889-90) 14 vols.

Introduction

An adequate text of De Quincey's writings, the first requirement of a truly thorough study, would reprint all his articles in chronological sequence, using the original text (including punctuation) and, in a very few cases, following the original page lay-out. The numerous revisions of his essays would fall in their proper place. No such edition exists. Instead, the student of De Quincey is obliged to refer to numerous sources: newspapers, journals, annuals, anthologies and De Quincey's own edition of his works, *Selections Grave and Gay* (hereafter *Selections*), which I have used as my main source throughout this work.[1] The *Selections* (published 1853–60) provides the only strictly accurate version of those of De Quincey's works which it does contain.[2] In using this edition, I have broken with the practice of recent De Quincey scholarship, the general tendency of which has been to use David Masson's edition of the *Writings*, ordinarily considered the standard text.[3] Masson's text, however, which is by no means complete, has several disadvantages which disqualify it from being accepted as definitive. First, where he reprints versions of De Quincey's revised essays, Masson does not follow De Quincey's punctuation with any degree of accuracy. De Quincey's reference in the revised *Confessions* to 'crotchety authors, superstitiously fastidious in matters of punctuation' (5: 175) – a reference to his own care in this matter – ought surely to warrant some attention. Secondly, Masson chops entire articles into pieces and occasionally removes whole sections of prose (the most glaring example being the case of 'Hannah More' in vol. 14 of the *Writings*: Axon rightly comments that Masson's reasons for omitting parts of this work are 'quite insufficient'.[4]) Masson also fails to follow De Quincey's text on occasion. For example, De Quincey writes as follows:

In a moment I saw too plainly that I was not Monsieur^2. I might be *Monsieur*, but not *Monsieur to the second power* (5: 79).

Masson omits the *squared* sign ('Monsieur$^{2\prime}$), an omission which makes the sentences senseless ('[. . .] I was not Monsieur. I might be *Monsieur*, but not *Monsieur to the second power*').[5] Such inaccuracies necessitate using the author's edition of his writings wherever possible; and, where De Quincey did not supervise or oversee matters such as punctuation, using the original printed version of the text. It is necessary to supplement the *Selections*. Several dozen pieces were not revised by De Quincey, among them the important series of (chiefly political) articles written for *Blackwood's Edinburgh Magazine*; all of De Quincey's fictions; and numerous shorter pieces, some of which have been published in Tave's *New Essays*.[6] Many of these works were also neglected by Masson.

For the original versions of the 'Confessions' (1821), 'The English Mail-Coach' (1849) and 'Suspiria De Profundis' (1845), I have used Grevel Lindop's convenient and accurate edition of these works; for the texts of *The Stranger's Grave* and 'The Caçadore' I have used my own editions.[7] In most other instances I refer to the original source for De Quincey's writings: in the main, *Blackwood's Edinburgh Magazine* and *Tait's Edinburgh Magazine*. Some other sources have also been used: these are listed in my Short Titles List. Occasionally, where (for instance) the original magazine page lay-out has relevance to my argument (as in the case of 'Sir William Hamilton' discussed in Chapter 3), I have referred to the original (unrevised) version of a particular text. As the original and revised versions of many of De Quincey's articles often differ considerably, I have in some instances given *two* references for any one quotation. The second reference should be understood as providing the parallel version of the quotation, the wording of which may differ from that reproduced in my study.

At all stages, the De Quinceyan text seems to be problematic. Masson's edition of the *Writings* compounds a process begun by De Quincey's earlier editors (William Tait and Robert Blackwood especially) who were prone to alter De Quincey's copy as they saw fit. I might add that the compositor would not necessarily follow De Quincey's manuscript exactly (given that some words such as 'and' would ordinarily be indicated only by a cross in the manuscript – and also, obviously, glaring mistakes in sense would be silently corrected); while De Quincey's correction of his proofs in some cases would be only an approximation to his manuscript work. The process of publication, then, diverges from the original work. Given that comparatively few manuscripts survive, the publication must be accepted as the definitive trace, the sole evidence. The work is never De Quincey's alone: it is a trace of the publication process, of interference, of error and compromise, of the author's lack of control over his material and his alienation from his labours.

In the course of my research I have attempted to read all of De Quincey's published writings; and have also consulted as many unpublished manuscripts and letters as I could. It is not necessary for the interested reader to have read all the essays to which I refer, though some knowledge of at least the main works is presupposed. Inevitably, I comment on only a very small portion of these materials.

Introduction

In a study such as this, it is not possible to offer much more than an overview of what seem to me to be the most lucid and eloquent of De Quincey's writings. Taking De Quincey's output into consideration, the essays I do *not* deal with directly far outnumber those analysed here – but I believe that the themes I outline in this study will illuminate De Quincey's oeuvre in its entirety. Some readers will not, perhaps, be much surprised to find little mention of De Quincey's translations, or his historical sketches. Some may consider my commentary (or lack of) on such well-known works as 'On Murder Considered as One of the Fine Arts' inadequate or unfocussed and that on obscure pieces such as 'Animal Magnetism' excessive. It is as well therefore to declare now that this work is an attempt to reassess De Quincey's writings and, as such, of necessity pays unequal attention to his numerous works – each of which contains information which might usefully be adumbrated and analysed. I have tried to suggest the range of material that *could* usefully be discussed while simultaneously keeping in focus the key themes which, to my mind, make of De Quincey's disparate works a unified whole. In this study I contend that his writings may be defined as a single work – an autobiographical work. I attempt to outline formal patterns in a variety of De Quincey's essays which support such a contention. Inevitably, while my argument avoids the temptation, so often implied in contemporary criticism, to dismiss out of hand most of De Quincey's work, it does tend to reduce his writings to a reiteration of these formal patterns. I am aware of this tendency, though I have not sought to check it since it may help to focus attention on what I consider the important aspects of a vast body of writing. I cannot pretend that the present work provides much more than a bare outline.

It is appropriate at this juncture to site my own intervention more precisely in the context of recent academic criticism. The present work takes note of all the major studies of De Quincey published over the last three decades (if only in passing) and many miscellaneous works going back to the last century. My approach draws on a variety of critical materials, which I have used to enable an exposition of the possible meaning of the De Quinceyan text. I have not followed one single critical method rigorously, nor sought to locate my text in the framework provided by any single study. Instead, I have used the works of various critics as tools. My argument revolves around an area of anxiety, of doubt; and in interpreting the text, in claiming a specific meaning for it, I raise questions about the status of any text, about the nature of the work which it does and, implicitly, about interventions such as my own.

The analyses of De Quincey by Maniquis, Goldman and Heinzelmann provide the most obvious sources of my lines of enquiry; while numerous other essays contain information and ideas that have, either positively or negatively, determined the course of my argument.[8] It is fair to say that until recently De Quincey's writings have been generally neglected; and the student or scholar has been obliged to proceed with comparatively little in the way of a critical tradition that might indicate which elements of De Quincey's work are of significance. Symptomatic of the current state of De Quincey scholarship is the 1985 *Thomas De Quincey Bicentenary Studies* volume, which provides numerous visions of 'the opium-eater'.[9] The volume's editor, Robert Lance Snyder, states quite correctly that our understanding of De Quincey 'must hinge upon an unbiased and close scrutiny of his texts', a comment which implies that approaches to De Quincey have so far tended to avoid such a scrutiny, while his hope that *Bicentenary Studies* will 'lay the foundation for a fresh recognition of De Quincey's achievement' is similarly indicative of the relative lack of attention paid to De Quincey's work and the largely negative reactions it has provoked.[10]

The present work is intended as a piece of constructive (if also deconstructive) and affirmative criticism. It is my contention that De Quincey's writings have been misunderstood to a great extent. I do not suppose that the remarks which comprise the rest of this introduction will be popular, nor is it necessary for readers to agree with them entirely. If I overstate my case, so be it: such a redefinition of the subject is surely requisite. As well as the fact that the De Quinceyan text has scarcely been meticulously scrutinised – the *Bicentenary Studies* volume opts for Masson's edition without questioning its accuracy – there are three major obstacles, as I see it, which have prevented and retarded the kind of 'unbiased' analysis that Snyder mentions. These are, put crudely, the notion of De Quincey's writing as psychoanalytic evidence; the notion of De Quincey as a drug addict who wrote; and the notion of De Quincey's text as intrinsically flawed. I do not deny that much useful work has of course been done, work which this study acknowledges; but so often are De Quincey's writings obscured by one or other of the aforementioned assumptions that it is necessary to call attention to them here.

The general psychoanalytical approach to De Quincey's works is of limited use. It tends to reduce all his writing (or at least that part which conveniently fits the bill) to a prefiguration and proof of Freudian theory and presupposes precisely definable and permanent states of human life, states 'scientifically' observed. The reader is led away from De Quincey's texts into areas which have very little to do with literature by comments such as this, made by Charles L. Proudfit in a recent essay, 'Thomas De Quincey and Sigmund Freud':

> De Quincey, unlike Freud and others, was not a trained psychologist seeking scientific answers to scientific questions, yet

Introduction 5

many of his nursery observations and reflections have been validated in clinical settings.[11]

Such observations about the scientific validity of De Quincey's 'observations' are at best beside the point. Worse are those critics who take the presuppositions of psychoanalysis for granted and are led into profound absurdities. An example is Sundelson's essay on 'The English Mail-Coach', 'Evading the Crocodile'. Sundelson conceives of psychoanalytical criticism as a tool with which 'we can see a coherent pattern of threats and defenses in his prose, instead of turning in despair to terms like "repetitious, digressive" and "shapeless"' – terms employed by Alvarez in his edition of the *Confessions* (New York, NAL 1966).[12] Certainly, Alvarez's criticisms are inadequate; but Sundelson's method of redeeming De Quincey's text is to define it as a manifestation of a Freudian master-code. This leads him to statements like the following:

> I believe that this cycle of euphoria and despair or terror is the product of De Quincey's attempts to gratify sexual wishes within a peculiarly destructive context.[13]

The critic's reading of the text attempts to substantiate this belief. He concludes that 'Psychoanalysis enables us to recognise De Quincey's restless prose style as the mirror of his poignant attempts now to confront, now to evade deeply disturbing fears and wishes that are never more than partly conscious'.[14] This is simply not so. Psychoanalysis allows us to *define* De Quincey's prose as this. Turning away from despair, Sundelson clings to a deceptive and not particularly useful construct provided by psychoanalysis. He does not consider it necessary to explain this construct, nor to point to the nature of its limitations.

This example is by no means unique, but it is rare when compared the numerous definitions of De Quincey as a neurotic 'drug addict' who wrote to excuse his 'addiction' – a characterisation which likewise severely limits an appreciation of his literary endeavours, subordinating the writings to the projected biological (as well as psychological) habits of the writer. The terms 'addict' and 'addiction' are used repeatedly in essays about De Quincey, often loaded with disproportionate, unquestioned and unexplained significance. Thus, Michael Haltresht asserts that the female in the 'Dream-Fugue' (in 'The English Mail-Coach') represents 'all those women whom De Quincey felt he ruined by his very passivity; that is, by his drug addiction'.[15] He comments further:

> Utterly helpless in his addiction, he could extort female solicitude indefinitely – and, at the same time, wreak his passive-aggressive revenge on the Woman for expelling him into this world and then failing to fulfill his needs. Under the effect of the drug, it was *not* 'too late' for him to indulge his sexual and hostile fantasies and, at the same time, by his misery and

terror, expiate for all past and future sins, and earn his way into paradise. Is it any wonder that, having fallen under the spell of opium, De Quincey could never be free again?'[16]

This criticism supposes that the writing is little more than evidence of the writer's addiction, which addiction supposedly resolves psychological difficulties and sexual problems – things we can really know nothing about. Such commentaries can only detract from De Quincey's writings. Bilsland writes in like fashion: De Quincey became an 'addict' because of his 'instability'; his relation to his brother William (recounted in the *Hogg's Instructor* 'A Sketch from Childhood' papers) was, in Bilsland's view, 'quite abnormal'; and childhood habits paved the way for adult deviant behaviour: 'by the time he first used laudanum, therefore, he was a ripe candidate for addiction'.[17] This is quite simply nonsense, in refutation of which I need only cite De Luca, who sensibly comments that De Quincey depicts in 'A Sketch' a 'typical boyhood world of strife, in which his aggressive brother reigns'.[18]

Opium was 'the one key fact of his existence', according to Snyder, and De Quincey was unable 'to escape self-reproach for his own addiction'.[19] Evidently the fact of De Quincey's writing was secondary to his use of the drug – a view which can hardly be supported. As with Haltresht, the text is interpreted (one might even argue misquoted) primarily as evidence of addiction:

> Pre-eminently intellectual and scholarly, he was yet forced to mortgage his talents to the periodical press to maintain a meager livelihood. Such exigencies, coupled with 'the oppression of inexpiable guilt' (3: 446) over his opium addiction, occasionally led him to the brink of despair.[20]

De Quincey does not state that he feels guilty about his use of opium in the phrase from the *Confessions* cited above. Snyder's interpretation articulates the very thing he claims to want to avoid, for on the same page he writes:

> Too often critical response to his writing has succumbed to the fallacy of identifying his dramatic personae or self-projections with the man himself, of naïvely assuming that a single and generally sensational stereotype is an accurate representation of his abilities as a writer.[21]

The stereotyped 'addict' is the primary naïve assumption made in connection to De Quincey, one which Snyder himself instinctively adopts. It is a stereotype which has a long history. 'Addiction' is specifically a medico-legal term which defines a certain type of behaviour as 'illness'. The addict's behaviour is supposedly harmful to others, a 'social disease'. It is a term which Szasz styles 'promotive rhetoric' and as such should be treated with some suspicion, or at least caution.[22] 'Addiction' also suggests vice and crime. The addict's is a socially stigmatised role.

Opium was used as a cure in De Quincey's time; but it was known that the drug was poisonous in large doses, as one of De Quincey's contemporaries, the doctor Robert Christison, points out. Christison calls opium 'the most common drug in medical practice'.[23] Since the 1820s, use of the drug has become defined as an 'illness': addiction. The history of this reversal need not be rehearsed here, but it may be worth pointing out that the link between medicine, the study of insanity, and the concept of 'vice' was already operational in De Quincey's lifetime. Isaac Ray's *Treatise on Insanity* (1838) describes the 'vice' of drunkenness in terms which echo those used by De Quincey to describe his nightmares in the *Confessions*:

> One of the most common hallucinations, is, to be constantly seeing devils, snakes, vermin, and all manner of unclean things around him and about him, and peopling every nook and corner of his apartment with these loathsome objects.[24]

It would be easy to define De Quincey's dream-visions (especially those which feature crocodiles, etc.; see 5: 268-9) as evidence of similar 'pathological' delusions. The terms 'addict' and 'addiction' have often been used to 'explain' De Quincey's work – usually without questioning their meaning or implications.

Berridge has traced the development of the concept of addiction as disease and as vice, and has provided some useful comments on the formation of the attitudes that shaped the stigmatisation of the addict:

> Addiction was not seen as a pressing social problem in England, nor did it become a matter of public policy until 1916, but in the nineteenth century attitudes had already been formed which helped justify the eventual introduction of full-scale legislative control of opiates and their uses.[25]

The addict is one who has passed under control – supposedly of a drug, but more properly of the law and of social pressures. The recognition of the nature and scope of addiction was and is a *definition* of drug usage *as a problem*. The addict represents the 'anti-social' element in a society which is enabled to retain a sense of unity, by excluding certain 'deviants', and a sense of power, by oppressing said 'deviants'. Szasz, commenting on the stigmatisation of groups of people who engage in such 'anti-social' activities, observes that 'What all of these persecutions have in common is that the victims are harassed by the majority not because they engage in overtly aggressive or destructive acts, like theft or murder, but because their conduct or appearance offends a group intolerant to and threatened by human differences'.[26]

De Quincey has been used as a representative of this (recently created) class of 'addict' and more.[27] Hayter's criticism of De Quincey is a case in point. In *Opium and the Romantic Imagination*, she writes that De Quincey 'is often blamed, and rightly, for the terrible fascination of his masterpiece in drawing others to follow his example, but he is not often given credit for the impetus which his book undoubtedly gave to the scientific investigations which have helped and saved other addicts'.[28] Such remarks need some comment. First, Hayter seems to damn De Quincey for publicising opium; secondly, and in the same sentence, she seems to praise De Quincey for spurring on the medical investigation of addiction. De Quincey's text generates addicts and the saviours of addicts. The text takes the place of the so-called disease which others have caught, but is also the inoculation by which they are 'saved'. Such reasoning is surely mistaken. De Quincey can neither be blamed for addiction nor be praised for the cure of addiction. In fact, the relation of addiction to the *Confessions* or to De Quincey is inapposite, unless one analyses it in terms of social relations, power, the law and so forth. A text cannot act contagiously, nor is the use of drugs something one 'catches' either, but a social habit. To use medico-legal terminology in this casual way is, I think, unwarranted and foolish. One might as well argue that the *Confessions* could draw others to follow De Quincey's example in writing about themselves – which, as dealing with literature, would at least be more to the point.

While it cannot be denied that De Quincey seems to provide suitable material which would allow one to cast him in the role of addict, this is surely not the task of the critic, who should rather analyse than make glib judgments. Yet much criticism relies heavily on such judgments. De Quincey is depicted as a drug addict who wrote, not a writer who used (and became dependent on) opium. Spengemann, in his analysis of the *Confessions*, states that 'each apparent statement about addiction is in fact a symptom of addiction'.[29] Aside from the fact that De Quincey does not make any statements about 'addiction' as such, but about 'opium-eating' (which has quite different connotations in his writings), this comment implies that the writing in question is secondary to the biological dependency, rather than of primary concern to the critic. I find it difficult to square Spengemann's pertinent conclusion that 'the creator of the work is in fact its creation'[30] with his assertions that opium provides 'the ground of the addict's [i.e. De Quincey's] true being' and that De Quincey's 'inability to escape the interminable and seemingly pointless sufferings of addiction prevented him from formulating some final, clear opinion about the shape and meaning of his life'.[31] The *writing about the drug*, if anything, provides a ground of being and a ground of meaning (and even this is debatable, as I shall argue in the course of this study). Writing produces the autobiographer: it is an on-going process which does not allow for 'final opinions'. Other examples abound: Whale speaks of De Quincey's 'personal authority as an addict'; Michael Cochise Young comments, bizarrely, that De Quincey refused 'to accept responsibility for his addiction' and writes of his 'projected audience of addicts' (!); while Martin Bock argues that 'much of De Quincey's work is an apologia that serves to explain the nature and causes of his opium addiction' – a comment which may be negated by the blank assertion that the vast majority of De Quincey's writings have no concern whatsoever with opium.[32]

Janzow usefully comments on the supposed manifestations of addiction and its relation to De Quincey's work:

> But none of the evidences for the "pains of opium" during De Quincey's editorship [of the *Westmoreland Gazette*] and for their hampering effect can negate the visible concrete evidences for his many contributions at various levels to his journal.[33]

One may apply this refreshingly sensible comment to his writing career as a whole. Opium did not prevent De Quincey from working. There are no 'evidences' provided by others - merely conjecture and a critical reading of his text which distorts De Quincey's achievements. To search for the effects of opiate-use on De Quincey's output strikes me as needless, whether it is thought opium helped or hindered his writing.

My concern here is first and foremost with *writing* and not with extra-literary behaviour, the conjectured biological existence and habits of the writer. The autobiographical writings of De Quincey perhaps inevitably suggest to the critic the imaginative recreation of the real-life De Quincey (and indeed this may be impossible to avoid one way or another), but this relation of text to historical events, for the actuality of which in many instances De Quincey's writing provides the only indication, lies outside my study. Such problems as the existence or non-existence of, say, Ann in the *Confessions of an English Opium-Eater* or the reality of the various experiences recounted by De Quincey are only of secondary importance to me. The text is the object of my scrutiny.

It will be appreciated from the attention I pay to much of De Quincey's neglected works – the political and economic commentaries, his fictions – and from my attempt to set these works in a context of his writings as a unified body, that I do not countenance the third, and most widespread, critical commonplace that De Quincey is a sporadically brilliant writer, the unevenness of whose writing allows the critic to ignore all but a handful of texts or, worse, all but a few passages from these select texts. Many critics write of De Quincey's 'faults' and characterise much of his work as 'flawed'. I reject this idea of a flawed text outright, since it implies that somehow De Quincey's writing can be changed or improved – presumably by the critic, following Masson's example with 'Hannah More'. Inevitably, a critical reading will involve a matter of selection: one could not and need not comment on everything. To select, however, may also be to ignore – and to ignore the important. The definition of De Quincey as a 'flawed' writer, perhaps the greatest obstacle to a thorough critical appraisal of his writings, appears in several guises. All assume that a stable ground of value, universally accepted and known, exists: that the exercise of the critical faculty is fundamentally the deployment of individual taste, rather than being an analysis of information. Thus, Virginia Woolf's criticism of De Quincey's autobiographical writings selects and dismisses at whim. Woolf does not analyse the writing at hand, but instead alludes to its 'great defects'[34] and ultimately gives up on it:

> Sometimes he makes a joke – it is generally painful. Sometimes he tells a story – it is always irrelevant. Most often he spreads himself out in a waste of verbosity, where any interest that there may have been peters out dismally and loses itself in the sand. We can read no more.[35]

Similar attitudes are reproduced in other critical texts. Whale, for instance, approves of Woolf's 'refreshing' criticism in general.[36] To my mind it is quite inadequate.

Woolf's criticism is symptomatically important for a related reason. In claiming that 'prose writer though he is, it is for his poetry that we read him and not for his prose',[37] she implies that the critic may somehow extract from the 'bad' prose a 'good' poem – a poem which, if one accepts and uses such terms accurately, simply does not exist. The critic creates this pseudo-poem in lieu of analysing the text. Woolf's curious notions prefigure De Luca's recent reading of De Quincey's works 'as if they were in fact poems'.[38] Yet De Luca comments that De Quincey had 'scant leisure for pursuing the usual avenues of imaginative literature – poetry, fiction, and drama – and, as is quite likely, had little aptitude for them'.[39] Thus, De Quincey, who had little aptitude for poetry, is treated as a writer of (presumably failed) poems (or at least, possibly successful prose-poems embedded in extraneous contexts). I can see little use in such a reading. De Quincey did not write poems. To treat his works as if they were poems is severely limiting. What is one to make, for instance, of his political commentaries, his economic essays, his reviews and so forth? The answer is, that a large amount of De Quincey's writings are consigned to oblivion. De Luca continues Woolf's work and divides De Quincey's writing into two more or less easily discernible parts, the visionary and the hack-work:

> In too much of De Quincey's writing the visionary impulse is found awash in a sea of prose, prose written under anxiety to meet a printer's deadline and to please an undiscriminating periodical readership. Vision sinks into prose, becomes masked in chatter, details, the prosaic.[40]

This blinkered approach has been rightly criticised by Maniquis, who (in a generally excellent monograph) nevertheless himself writes of De Quincey's 'faults': 'Despite his faults, he fascinated Baudelaire, and still he draws admiring echoes from Jorge Luis Borges, another wanderer in the realm of the self'.[41] While he rejects a view which separates De Quincey's writings, Maniquis still indulges, at least implicitly, in the idea of a 'flawed' De Quincey who can somehow be improved, an idea I reject. The notion of 'faults' implies an aesthetic absolute: it allows the critic to dismiss what (s)he does not like or approve of out of hand. De Quincey has been repeatedly defined as faulty, though sometimes this is meant to suggest something more positive. Thus Goldman (whose work is useful) describes him as 'a man eager to borrow but balked by his own ineptness and carelessness, and almost compelled to be "original"'.[42] Evidently De Quincey's inability as a writer produces an able text, a notion echoed by E. Michael Thron who begins an essay extravagantly entitled 'A New Introduction for Thomas De Quincey' by turning the idea of 'fault' to De Quincey's advantage: 'It is easy,' he writes, 'to like a writer with so many faults as Thomas De Quincey'.[43] I need hardly add that retaining the 'fault' schema does nothing to add to our knowledge or appreciation of De Quincey's writings. It is necessary to state this clearly here, for I want to differentiate between the *failure* of De Quincey's text, as I define it, and the generally accepted critical idea of the 'flawed' text. By *failure* I wish to signify the text's inadequacy to operate as the author would wish (not as the critic would wish): how it breaks down in a *productive* way, producing meanings other than (and often as well as) those intended. Writing produces both more than it promises - and this more is qualitatively distinct – and less than it promises. Thus, in autobiography it promises a semblance of a self (De Quincey's, for example): instead, it produces a partial version of this, plus it produces signs of *itself*. An element of doubt creeps in here. In the same spirit of scepticism, I diverge from those critics who write as if all was stable and immediately knowable. My work is a hypothesis, a proposal which attempts to say something about writing using De Quincey's text as a beginning.

   I do not intend to apologise for or defend De Quincey here. Speaking personally, I find a fair proportion of his jokes crass and the bulk of his political and religious beliefs entirely distasteful. But this does not mean that I shall ignore them: instead, my task is, I think, to attempt to elucidate the material by applying some understanding. A defence or apology would fall flat: for instance, it would be futile to deny that De Quincey's writing is often tedious and digressive. But this is not a 'fault' (and it might even be the opposite). Rather it is a particular aspect of his writing, a tactic or strategy which ought to be criticised in an open frame of mind. That I am not merely indulging in perversity, saying that for 'flaws' read 'good points' will, I hope, be demonstrated in the main body of this study.

Confessions of an English Opium-Eater

The 'Confessions of an English Opium-Eater' was originally published in the *London Magazine* in 1821; in 1822 this text subsequently appeared, in a slightly modified form, as a book.[1] The work was extensively revised and expanded by De Quincey in 1856 for the fifth volume of his *Selections*. In this chapter I am primarily concerned with aspects of the revised work, though necessarily a proportion of my analysis can be applied to aspects of the original version as well, and many of the points I raise apply to both. The *Confessions* remains the central De Quinceyan text: the fact that that title indicates two (being pedantic, we could say three) different works is indicative of the problematic nature of De Quincey's oeuvre. In concentrating on the revision, I do not intend in any way to make a value judgment that consigns the original text to second-rate status. Rather, my intention is to suggest the interdependence of the two works – and the interdependence of the vast number of De Quincey's writings that lie between them.

Aberrance / the conflation of errors

> I was, I had been long a captive: I was in a house of bondage: one fulminating word – *Let there be freedom* – spoken from some hidden recess in my own will, had as by an earthquake rent asunder my prison gates. At any minute I could walk out (5: 70).

De Quincey's abscondence from school constitutes the crucial event in both versions of the *Confessions* (1821, 1856). This act, he insists, determines the course of much of his future life. De Quincey describes the morning of his abscondence as that 'which was to launch me into the world; that morning from which, and from its consequences, my whole succeeding life has, in many important points, taken its colouring' (5: 89). One of the 'consequences' attributed to this primary error is that of writing. In itself apparently simple, the error of quitting school has a complex significance.

De Quincey's writing constitutes a form of labour for which he is paid. He produces a commodity to be marketed and consumed. Leaving school has, ultimately, obliged him to enter the labour market. The error of leaving is also the 'error' of having grown up – of working or having to work, of *writing*. The crucial action of abscondence dramatically represents the action of writing. In the *Confessions*, the text which examines the apparent necessity of his wilful abscondence, De Quincey repeatedly articulates his having-to-write.

There is an element of absurdity in De Quincey's insistence upon 'error' in the *Confessions*. Growing up is not a matter of choice (although one may choose not to grow up, as it were, by committing suicide), it is a biological occurrence. However, it is also a social event: other people choose for you when you grow up, or they allow you to do so. De Quincey's error is to take responsibility for his own development. He does so without realising that the trap of childhood is in many respects identical to the trap of adulthood. There can be no 'freedom' such as he desires. Analytical self-consciousness alone, which separates childhood from adulthood and makes of the self two (or more) identities – child judged by adult, adult determined by child – prevents an escape. The entrance into adulthood involves the recreation of childhood. Being in one state necessitates a knowledge of the other from which one is separated. The two states thus tend to define one another. The error lies not in having grown up or even in having determined to grow up in one's own time, but in the *representation* of adulthood and childhood as exclusive but interdependent states. More than analytical self-consciousness is involved in De Quincey's definition of the complementary states of childhood and adulthood, since he produces in the autobiographical text an artefact which apparently attests to a stable state of selfhood – a *self* in which child and adult differences are resolved. The production of the written text compounds the error of representation, since it posits a singular identity in the artefact (the *Confessions*). De Quincey's relation to this work is ambiguous: it is a commodity over which – after a certain time, at a certain point in the production process – he has no control. The consumption of the *Confessions* – of the text of De Quincey's self – does not necessarily entail an accurate appreciation of the writer's intent. Misinterpretation by the reader must always be considered, not only as a possibility, but as a likelihood. The text is evidence of the distance between reader and writer – even in the case of these being the same entity (the reviser De Quincey). De Quincey acknowledges this state of affairs:

> The reader indeed – that great idea! – is very often a more important person towards the fortune of an essay than the writer (7: 311).

Given this estrangement of the writer from his audience, it is necessary for De Quincey to produce a text which in turn *produces* a reader fully equipped to read 'correctly'. De Quincey must impart a large amount of information, explicit or otherwise, if his work is to be understood precisely. In the revision of his writings, then, he has to be sure of what he originally meant to write: but this would require (following the logic of the ideal production process already outlined) that the original text produced an 'aware' reviser in De Quincey – something which its incompleteness, its need to be revised, suggests is not possible. Clearly, this problem cannot be simply resolved.

The possibility of error plagues De Quincey. In his revision of the *Confessions* he apologises in advance for any mistakes he might have made in the text. His prefatory apology negates the declared purpose of improving and making more coherent the writing in question:

> The press has groaned under the chronic visitation; the compositors shudder at the sight of my handwriting, though not objectionable on the score of legibility; and I have much reason to fear that, on days when the pressure of my complaint has been heaviest, I may have so far given way to it, as to have suffered greatly in clearness of critical vision. Sometimes I may have overlooked blunders, mis-statements, or repetitions, implicit or even express. But more often I may have failed to appreciate the true effects from faulty management of style and its colourings. Sometimes, for instance, a heavy or too intricate arrangement of sentences may have defeated the tendency of what, under its natural presentation, would have been affecting; or it is possible enough that, by unseasonable levity at other times, I may have repelled the sympathy of my readers – all or some. Endless are the openings for such kinds of mistake – that is, of mistakes not fully seen *as* such. But, even in a case of unequivocal mistake, seen and acknowledged, yet when it is open to remedy only through a sudden and energetic act, then or never, – the press being for twenty minutes, suppose, free to receive an alteration, but beyond that time closed and sealed inexorably: such being supposed the circumstances, the humane reader will allow for the infirmity which even wilfully and consciously surrenders itself to the error, acquiescing in it deliberately, rather than face the cruel exertion of correcting it most elaborately at a moment of sickening misery, and with the prevision that the main correction must draw after it half-a-dozen others for the sake of decent consistency. I am not speaking under any present consciousness of such a case existing against myself: I believe there *is* none such. But I choose to suppose an extreme case of even conscious error, in order that the venial cases of oversight may, under shelter of such an *outside* license, find toleration from a liberal critic. To fight up against the wearing siege of an abiding sickness, imposes a fiery combat. I attempt no description of this combat, knowing

the unintelligibility and the repulsiveness of all attempts to communicate the Incommunicable (5: xii–xiii).

This pre-emptive apology is enormously significant. It constitutes a veiled explanation on De Quincey's part of the process he is involved in – of the means of production which delimit his art. The 'error' which he wishes to explain is grounded in the fact that he has chosen to embark on the revision.

The link which is made in this apology between the paradigmatic error from which the *Confessions* seems to emanate, his abscondence from school, and the process of writing as a hit-and-miss affair for which De Quincey would like equally to be excused, calls into question the relation between the real events recounted in the autobiographical text(s) and the representation of these events. Is it that the error of leaving school prefigures the errors involved in the process of writing and publishing? Or that the errors of composing a complex piece of writing determine the negative characterisation of what is represented as the crucial action in life? The latter interpretation is surely pertinent. Although De Quincey implies that, if he had not quit school, he would be better off, a different person – one with money, respect and no need to write for a living – it may also be argued that, if he had not started to write, his past experiences would not necessarily have been 'errors'. The linear connection between the fateful day and (any) present-time of composition for De Quincey, which demands that the *Confessions* has a fundamental hold on all subsequent writings (revisionary interventions such as the 'Suspiria' notwithstanding), is itself an error in that it involves a misreading on De Quincey's part. This misreading, which his massive overhaul of the *Confessions* at once corrects and augments, is the paradigm of writing for De Quincey.

Despite the negative characterisation implied in the definition of experience as error, De Quincey is enabled to overcome the threat to the meaning of his words by the endless extension made possible by having erred. The mistake, if it is such, can be articulated but never fully explained away. There is thus always something held in reserve, something extra which remains to be written. The aberrance of representation is decisively productive: it generates text. Having begun to write, the process seems apparently to extend itself, possibly for ever. There is an element of irony in De Quincey's complaint about the Press. First, its appearance in print suggests that the Press allows for error by letting the writer declare his lack of control. Secondly, the complaint is undercut by the revisions executed on the writing before publication in its final form. The characteristic De Quinceyan footnotes, and his footnotes to footnotes, imply that the Press is not as 'inexorable' as he claims and that the translation of script into print is part of a more complex problem that cannot be 'solved' by any amount of correction. The problem provokes De Quincey strategically to characterise himself as a martyr to the process of writing – to the entire process of production and consumption – to dealing in the performative present of composition with the *future* status of the text in its printed form. De Quincey works within and under the pressure of the machinery of the Press.

The Press

De Quincey's self-characterisation as a 'martyr' may be understood in terms of the archetypal shaman, who undergoes traumatic experiences in an 'underworld' from which he rises renewed. The formal patterns of these and related experiences, as manifested in various cultures, have been remarked by Rogan P. Taylor.[2] Crudely put, they consist of first, an apparent death; secondly, various trials in an underworld; the dismemberment of the body; and finally a mystical flight and return to the world of the living. It will be readily appreciated that De Quincey's Opium-Eater corresponds roughly to this crude paradigm (the dealing with 'forbidden substances' provides another correspondence). The Opium-Eater plunges into a nightmare world where he is tortured and annihilated before waking. The experience of suffering in the nightmare world produces value in the form of a radically transformed self or sense of perception (of the world, of the self, and so forth). The dream is a form of initiation, like those rites which 'consist in a simulation of death and resurrection'.[3] Opium extracts the 'soul', as it were, of the Opium-Eater: an exchange of life between opium and Opium-Eater takes place, by which the Opium-Eater invests in the drug. To put it another way, De Quincey claims that opium produces value – even though it is he, the Opium-Eater, who does the producing via this text.

In the *Confessions* and other texts De Quincey recounts various trials – at school, in London, and in his dreams – which have produced value in his life. He passes through a variety of areas of painful activity which he survives. Past experience is one such area, the remembrance of the actual experience is yet another. Remembrance asserts De Quincey's identity. Through memory he lends meaning to his existence. To remember the actual suffering is itself a form of torture and again produces value. These trials of remembered experience are secondary to a future trial which, in contrast to the comparatively secure and stable basis offered by the remembrance of suffering, is utterly insecure and quite out of De Quincey's control and which threatens to distort and dismantle his value system. The Press, in the context of which his work is conducted, constitutes the critically problematic future which De Quincey must face. His entrance into a working relationship with the Press is again a form of initiation rite, one of critical significance. The Press is an 'underworld' of traumatic experiences from which the charismatic Opium-Eater must rise. The problem he is obliged to face is whether or not he will survive intact. Will he emerge alive? The Press, 'closed and sealed inexorably', is a type of grave from which it is De Quincey's task to rise. He must be given by his writing, must self-resurrect. In this context, then, resurrection is a mundane and even banal affair; it is *the tolerance of a set of social relations* which oppress and figuratively 'kill' one. Obviously De Quincey cannot control this set of relations effectually, as he admits. His characterisation of it emphasises its destructive effect. The question this characterisation raises is, can one resurrect even if one *fails* (as one must inevitably) to take control of this set of social relations – if one is crushed by the Press? De Quincey answers this question in the affirmative, though this affirmation is conditional.

In an important letter written during the revision of the *Confessions* for his collected edition, De Quincey remarks the difficulty which pertains to his task as a writer. These difficulties are grounded in the ambiguities of language, ambiguities which allow for error and for the *extra* meaning, for a potentially infinite process of re-interpretation:

> To the Press
> I am much afraid – that in consequence of the very imperfect means for communicating with the Press which I now possess or ever *have* possessed (being at all times reduced to the single resource of *writing* – which, to evade misinterpretation and constant ambiguity, requires a redundancy of words – and, after all that is done on *my* part, requires in addition a *Reader* that is not only singularly attentive, but also that has a surplus stock of *leisure time*[)] – *Premising* all this, I am and *have* been at all stages of this nominal reprint (but virtually *rifacimento*) of the Confessions, in terror of mutual misunderstandings – consequently [sic] of each party unintentionally thwarting or embarrassing the other by movements at *cross purposes*.[4]

The Press, as this letter indicates, is obviously more than a printing-machine: it is a specific set of power relations – of the author to the compositor, to the publisher or journal proprietor; of the author to the reader or market; of the author to his writing, to his own product. De Quincey disowns responsibility for his inability to take effectual control of the Press, as well he might given that he necessarily *belongs* to capital, is constricted and controlled by a machinery which, existing as a historical fact, defines and delimits his own role and involvement in it. His lack of control is in this sense very real; his alienation from his labour is real; he represents himself as the victim of the social relations: they oppress him. He is obliged to suffer them. The relation of language to the Press is problematic: does language represent accurately the social relations which oppress De Quincey? or do the social relations represent a property of language? For De

Quincey the relation of Press to language is not as important as the relation of himself to their combined force. Through the publication of his writings, he is obliged to produce an autobiographical self. The idea of the Press – of social relations – of 'others' – provides an excuse for the inadequacy of the self. If 'I' am unique, how can I hope to communicate? In uniqueness and privacy, everything becomes incommunicable. Communication of any sort becomes an attempt, as De Quincey suggests in the revised *Confessions*, to 'communicate the Incommunicable'. Thus De Quincey complains in the revised *Confessions* that he was unable to communicate with his mother because they operated in separate, private 'realities'. 'If in this world there is one misery having no relief,' he remarks, 'it is the pressure on the heart from the *Incommunicable*' (5: 114). Both De Quincey and his mother shared an experiential reality (a reality such as a text, then), but their interpretation of this was contradictory: 'She and I were contemplating the very same act; but she from one centre, I from another' (5: 114-15). What De Quincey is most afraid of is an inadequate or unself-conscious reader – of his being misunderstood because the reader does not share *his* perspective and cannot appreciate the difficulties involved in the management of language and of dealing with the Press. De Quincey cannot surmount the idea of his labour failing. He knows it must and will fail. De Quincey will be misunderstood, his work will not function as he desires. Together the Press and language provide him with an alibi – the work was never De Quincey's own, it was always an inflexion of the 'necessary' set of relations.

De Quincey articulates a precise and singular reaction to the Press. It is not analytical. Instead, it posits the author as victim: one obliged to cope with a hostile set of social relations which do not acknowledge him as a human being, but instead tend always to reduce his labour to the homogeneous level of all saleable labour. In effect, the machinery of the Press asserts his utter insignificance, his ordinariness, his unimportance. In these terms, he is a hack, though his self-characterisation (as a privileged, suffering artist) tends to limit his insignificance. That is to say, through hyperbole he retains a vestige of individuality. His reaction is not radical, but rather recalcitrant. He implicitly (and sometimes explicitly) supports the power relations by which the capitalist (Blackwood, say) exploits the worker (De Quincey), because this power relation sites him – it gives him a *formal* role.

De Quincey has to deal in the performative present – while he is writing – with the text as a publishable article (in a journal, a book, etc.), with his own work as a saleable commodity. The unknown and therefore distressing future, the how and where it is published and how and where it is consumed, impinges upon and forms the present of writing. Given the mass of material concerned specifically with past events, one might mistakenly overlook the formative influence on the fate of De Quincey's writing of its future. Yet the writing does not occur in a vacuum, and indeed De Quincey displays a great awareness in his works of the status of the text.

In a sketch entitled 'Walking Stewart' (1840), which deals with Stewart and (rather harshly and provocatively) with Wordsworth, De Quincey addresses the reader in a passage that prefigures the long apology at the opening of the revised *Confessions*. Here he explains that the published version of his sketches diverges from the manuscript version. The passing of time has obliterated his memory of his original text, so he must rely to a great extent on a possibly faulty proof. The Press oppresses him and only the sheer volume of published material acts as a compensation:

> In these sketches (written with so much hurry as, in no one instance that I remember, to have allowed me time for once reading over a single paragraph of what I had written,) I have usually thought it best, in the few cases where I had afterwards an opportunity of correcting the press errors, simply to restore the word which it was probable or apparent that I had originally written; or which, at least, I must have meant to write. Changes more extensive than this it could not be advisable to make, in a case where I had no opening for a thorough recast of the whole. Even in those instances where a thought, or an expression, or a statement of facts, might be calculated to do me some little injury, unless it were expanded, or accompanied with an explanation, or more cautiously restricted, I thought it better, on the whole, to abide the hazard; placing my reliance for the redress of any harsh judgment on the absolute certainty that each successive month washes out of the public mind every trace of what may have occupied it in any previous month (*Tait's*, vol.VII [October 1840], p. 636).

This published explanation echoes De Quincey's objections to the publisher William Tait, voiced in a letter (written in the third person) of 16 December 1839. Here he writes that the task of correcting the proofs of his work is difficult 'especially because in some places unguided by the MS. he is left totally at a loss to conjecture what might be the original words or sense' (NLS MS 1670 fos.63-4). A footnote in the letter adds that he was, in a sense, always at a disadvanatage:

> *'at a loss to conjecture:'* – Let it be remembered that this whole series of papers was written about $1^3/_4$ years ago, or near 2 years: and generally speaking without the benefit of *once* reading over (NLS MS 1670 fos. 63-4).

De Quincey's complaint is contradicted by a letter from Tait to a Mrs Johnstone (dated 22 August 1840).[5] Tait asks if he is 'regarded as responsible, more than the author, for anything objectionable in the published Autobiography?' and calls into question De Quincey's gloss on his 'Sketches':

> Look at the addition Mr De Quincey has made to the article we are printing. The explanation he gives is not correct. His memory has strangely deceived him. Every piece of MS belonging to the Autobiography which he put into my hands bore many, very many proofs of having been carefully read over and corrected (NLS MS 1670 fos. 73–5).

Tait reinforces his objections by adding that De Quincey is a slow writer who has had plenty of time to correct the proofs, 'sometimes even months'. De Quincey elsewhere remarks that he always writes slowly: '[. . .]in any state of health, I do not write with rapidity' (*Tait's*, vol. V [June 1838], p. 358): how thorough his proof-reading was at any period of his career must be primarily a matter of conjecture.

In the apology in the revised *Confessions* De Quincey writes that he is not conscious of any actual errors in the text, but has chosen to 'suppose an extreme case of even conscious error' (5: xiii). He supposedly *chooses* to enter into relations with the machinery of the Press. But how far is it a matter of choice? How can he ever be understood as he would wish? Clearly, there can not and will not be an absolute understanding of the text. There can be no coincidence of identity between the text as written and the text as read, between the manuscript version and the proof, or between the writer and the reader (even where they are the same entity, De Quincey). The relation of text-as-written to text-as-read is one of productivity: one produces the other. On the one hand, the text-as-written may suggest itself, the possibility of its having existed, within the text-as-read. On the other hand, in the written text may be articulated the possibility of the writing being read in a particular way. The text-as-read produces the *semblance* of the text-as-written: all the evidence for the text having been written in a particular way exists within the text-as-read. To characterise the finished, readable and published text as essentially faulty compensates for the autobiographer's inability to give himself through writing. Thus, the apology in 'Walking Stewart', like that in the *Confessions*, is grounded in an appreciation of the means of production of the De Quinceyan text. The text's consumption is deferred endlessly: as it is consumed (read) it reproduces its own generation. The writing produces a reading which is always a revision, a rewriting.

The essential contingency of De Quincey's writings generates a characterisation of all his experience as contingent. The representation of the self and the representation of the self-in-writing are coincident acts. Everything is necessarily incomplete for De Quincey. (Thus even the desired 'recast of the whole' which he implies is necessary in 'Walking Stewart' would be inadequate. There can be no 'whole' – as J. Hillis Miller has remarked, 'none of De Quincey's essays can be definitive or exhaustive'.⁶) The production of the text and the recalcitrance shown towards its publication – its translation into a definitive, economically determined literary form – inform his definition of reality. In the revised *Confessions* the journal form of the paper (as originally published in the *London Magazine* in 1821) and of its sequels, the 'Autobiographic Sketches', 'Suspiria de Profundis' and 'A Sketch from Childhood', – the 'sealed' form – is broken open. The revisionary process of textual production informs De Quincey's reflections on the formation of his individual self:

> In fact, every intricate and untried path in life, where it was from the first a matter of arbitrary choice to enter upon it or avoid it, is effectually a path through a vast Hercynian forest, unexplored and unmapped, where each several turn in your advance leaves you open to new anticipations of what is next to be expected, and consequently open to altered valuations of all that has been already traversed. Even the character of your own absolute experience, past and gone, which (if anything in this world) you might surely answer for as sealed and settled for ever – even this you must submit to hold in suspense, as a thing conditional and contingent upon what is yet to come – liable to have its provisional character affirmed or reversed, according to the new combinations into which it may enter with elements only yet perhaps in the earliest stages of development (5: 113–14).

De Quincey, a suspended or hanging entity, whose self is conditional upon 'what is to come' – an interpretation by others – is lived by and lives through the process of revision. He is the process, the process is his 'self'.⁷ Everything is produced at once in a revolving 'present' of production: everything is of the production process.

'[. . .] some irresistible agency'

The contingent narrative of De Quincey's works suggests that something exists outside or beyond it: that a process of pointing beyond itself operates outside and inside the narrative. The autobiographical narrative points to a 'self' not given, and to a kind of life. What lies beyond De Quincey's autobiographical narrative is not only his self, which is in the past, his past self, but the fate of his text in the Press. Revision formally articulates the desire for a resurrection in spite of De Quincey's failure to communicate effectually and as he would wish. This failure, grounded in his relation to language and to the Press, is inevitable and necessary. It consists of his want of control, his non-existence, the lack of De Quincey's self. Revision is conducted within the confines of the Press, but it still implies the possibility of revising the marks made by the Press. De Quincey's collected edition re-locates his essays, sites them in a context of posterity, a posterity which represents the possibility of resurrection. He writes that his audience is a readership at one or two generations' remove from the time of composition and publication: 'The fact is, I imagine myself writing at a distance of twenty – thirty – fifty years ahead of this present moment, either for the satisfaction of the few who may then retain any interest in myself, or of the many [. . .] who will take an inextinguishable interest in the mysterious powers of opium' [5: 233]. He wants to survive and the 'literature of power' is the means by which he may be enabled to achieve an afterlife. Of Ovid, De Quincey writes: 'This man's people and their monuments are dust; but *he* is alive: he has survived them, as he told us that he had it in his commission to do, by a thousand years; "and shall a thousand more"' (9: 10).

The disorder of De Quincey's *Selections* allows the reader to re-order the texts. His collected edition is a contingent arrangement which readers can seemingly rearrange at will. Indeed, its apparently random ordering of writings makes some sort of re-ordering almost a necessity. De Quincey's texts inform one another. Thus, the *Confessions* is mentioned at the beginning of the 'Autobiographic Sketches' as if it had already been read; and again within a chapter ('The Priory') as if the 'Sketches' preceded it. The *Confessions* is a text which penetrates De Quincey's other works, a *deciphering figure* like the Opium-Eater himself. De Quincey destroys the historical actuality of the publication of his texts in journal form by repeatedly referring to other works as if they had still to be completed. The disorder of his collected edition reflects the disruptive process which characterises his autobiographical intervention. The destruction of a given historical actuality (that the work has been once and for all published in a specific form) articulates De Quincey's reaction to the Press: within his work he attempts to subvert the way the Press tends to render his writing permanent and finished. This destructive action of course constitutes a historical actuality itself.

In his description of the Indian Summer he witnesses in the revised *Confessions*, De Quincey figures the possibility of a resurrection – one which might occur, the destruction of his self and his lack of personal power notwithstanding. This resurrection is elusive and ends, ironically, with death triumphant:

> It is that last brief resurrection of summer in its most brilliant memorials, a resurrection that has no root in the past, nor steady hold upon the future, like the lambent and fitful gleams from an expiring lamp, mimicking what is called the 'lightning before death' in sick patients, when close upon their end. There is the feeling of a conflict that has been going on between the lingering powers of summer and the strengthening powers of winter, not unlike that which moves by antagonist forces in some deadly inflammation hurrying forwards through fierce struggles into the final repose of mortification. For a time the

> equilibrium has been maintained between the hostile forces; but at last the antagonism is overthrown; the victory is accomplished for the powers that fight on the side of death; simultaneously with the conflict, the pain of conflict has departed: and thenceforward the gentle process of collapsing life, no longer fretted by countermovements, slips away with holy peace into the noiseless depths of the Infinite. So sweet, so ghostly, in its soft, golden smiles silent as a dream, and quiet as the dying trance of a saint, faded through all its stages this departing day, along the whole length of which I bade farewell for many year to Wales, and farewell to summer. In the very aspect and the sepulchral stillness of the motionless day, as solemnly it wore away through morning, noontide, afternoon, to meet the darkness that was hurrying to swallow up its beauty, I had a fantastic feeling as though I read the very language of resignation when bending before some irresistible agency. (5: 149–50)

The crucial day, which echoes the day of De Quincey's abscondence, fades: meaning itself is destroyed – which is to say, the revision of the *Confessions* becomes historically sited. The darkness of history swallows up the beauty of the timeless moment. After all is said and done, the revision of Press relations is always conducted within these relations. The Press is an 'irresistible agency' to the powers of which De Quincey is resigned. The text which would articulate a sense of the Infinite, of an ahistorical process, of the possibility of resurrection, is necessarily bound by the form of its publication. De Quincey evidently has no choice in this matter: the conditions of production restrict his actions. The restrictions imposed upon his labour, and upon what it can signify, can nevertheless be exploited.

Choice and contradiction

> Compared with its own former self, the book must certainly tend, by its very principle of change, whatever should be the *execution* of that change, to become better (5: xi-xii).

Although he reasons that the revised version of the *Confessions* must necessarily be an improvement on the original text, De Quincey displays some measure of ambivalence towards the task of rewriting and correcting his work. Thus, in the revision, describing his change of attitude towards opium over the course of fifty years, he admits that in his earlier writing he had given a false impression of the drug's effects, but fails to correct this impression entirely:

> The reader will infer, from what I have now said, that all passages, written at an earlier period under cloudy and uncorrected views of the evil agencies presumable in opium, stand retracted; although, shrinking from the labour of altering an error diffused so widely under my own early

misconceptions of the truth, I have suffered them to remain as they were (5: 252).

De Quincey's revised test does not entail a complete readjustment of the original *Confessions*. Previous errors are suffered to remain and are compounded in the new work. The failure of the text to communicate in a thorough and deliberate way the true ideas of the author is accepted as inevitable. Past errors are allowed to stand in the finished text, even though they are contradicted by (extra-textual) experience. In this way, De Quincey undermines the whole concept of giving the 'truth' in his work. In its place stands the possibility that any representation of reality may be aberrant; that a principle of inevitable error operates, producing a value system in which the *actual* is measured against an *ideal* from which it always falls away. In De Quincey's scheme of revolving error, actual experience is deliberately undervalued. That is, it is conceived of as incomplete, necessarily mutable, always requiring some sort of additional information. It only begins to make sense when compared with an imaginary future, a future in which the deferred payment of the sense of what is valuable may finally be realised and an appreciation of the 'proper' state of things comprehended.

By insisting upon error so forcefully, De Quincey also insists upon the possibility of an absolute, coherent and 'proper' state from which he has diverged and to which he may yet return. However, this state of integration and completion is only ever *inferred*: it cannot be delineated. More than this, it is inevitably open to question for, as a future state, it has yet to be experienced. Analogous states may have been experienced, moments in which past actualities apparently made sense, but such moments are necessarily governed by the possible effects of a future moment in which the given meaning of experience may be refuted. There is always the chance of ultimate reinterpretation to be considered. This is a source of constant (productive) anxiety.

Rather than attempt to take positive control of his situation, De Quincey invests in error and chooses to err: at least, such is his claim. The constituents of this choice are figured in the complementary episodes of his youthful visits to the Whispering Gallery of St Paul's and to Altrincham. The visit to the Gallery is recounted as an experience which informs De Quincey's decision to quit school. As such, it amplifies the central error of the *Confessions*. This episode is representative, therefore, of one aspect of the process of revision. The amplification of details in the revised text at once continues what has gone before (in his earlier writings), even if the details were incorrect or open to misconstruction; and, paradoxically, seems to negate what De Quincey had written, by throwing into relief the supposedly negative aspects of having erred. The original error is compounded, but the value attached to it is simultaneously called into question: for, if error itself is open to misconstruction, it may cease to be 'error' at all. Though it is not possible to escape from error totally, the possibility of *having erred in defining experience in terms of error* always threatens to undercut the basis for De Quincey's vision of experience. Error, then, is nothing if not productive. By choosing to characterise the crucial events in his life (quitting school; starting to write) as errors, De Quincey ensures that the quality of his life is ever open to new interpretations, which may suddenly be revealed (or created). Thus, while the connotations of the Gallery experience reinforce the sense of foreboding which he feels on quitting school, the *suddenness* with which the memory strikes him hints at unforseen, mysterious possibilities. An element of chance throws into relief the 'fixed' definition of experience. The sense of fatality and inevitability which accompany the fatal choice (one known to have been made already) is undercut by the ever-imminent possibility that at any time a novel construction may be placed upon the past. Thus, De Quincey writes that as he had stood in the Gallery he 'had suddenly been surprised by a dream [. . .] in which a thought that often had persecuted me figured triumphantly' (5: 91). He goes on to explain:

> This thought turned upon the fatality that must attend an evil choice. As an oracle of fear I remembered that great Roman warning, *Nescit vox missa reverti* (that a word once uttered is irrevocable), a freezing arrest upon the motions of hope too sanguine, that haunted me in many shapes. Long before that fifteenth year of mine, I had noticed, as a worm lying at the heart of life and fretting its security, the fact that innumerable acts of choice change countenance and are variously appraised at varying stages of life – shift with the shifting hours. Already, at fifteen, I had become deeply ashamed of judgments which I had once pronounced, of idle hopes that I had once encouraged, false admirations or contempts with which once I had sympathised. And as to acts which I surveyed with any doubts at all, I never felt sure that after some succession of years I might not feel withering doubts about them, both as to principle and as to inevitable results.
>
> This sentiment of nervous recoil from any word or deed that could not be recalled had been suddenly re-awakened on that London morning, by the impressive experience of the Whispering Gallery (5: 91).

In the context of making a problematic choice, De Quincey focuses on the 'word or deed that could not be recalled'. In terms of the writing of the autobiographical text, the inability to 'recall' the significant details of the past suggests two things: can the past be *remembered*? and can it be *altered*? The scene in the Gallery dramatises the inability of the autobiographer to recollect (and in recollection, imaginatively to transform) the justificatory details of his life. Labouring under the threat of 'a freezing arrest upon the motions' of his text, De Quincey is obliged to gloss that other 'word [...] that could not be recalled' – the original *Confessions*, which still exists as itself in spite of the revision.

Revision entails a contradiction of what has already been written, a displacement of experience, including the experience of writing and defining previous experience (e.g., in the original *Confessions*). This displacement is far-reaching: indeed, *everything* is displaced – there can be no centring of meaning. Thus, having located so precisely (as it appears) the ground of error in the Whispering Gallery scene, having established so forcefully the existence of a principle of inescapable fatality, De Quincey subverts his own vision by citing the case of his visit to Altrincham. If the Gallery episode articulates De Quincey's doubts about the quality of the revision, and about the relation of the two versions of the *Confessions*, then the parallel episode in Altrincham suggests that the original and revised texts, are, after all, an integral unit. De Quincey's experience in Altrincham largely contradicts that of the Whispering Gallery: the suggestion here is that it is possible for De Quincey to return to some places without resentment or anxiety – which is to say, that some parts of the *Confessions* may be rewritten with ease. In Altrincham, the passing of time has had no effect: 'Nothing had altered' (5: 96). De Quincey's blunt comment on the absence of change – 'All places, it seems, are not Whispering Galleries' (5: 96) – radically modifies the elaborately explained, and apparently decisive, negative implications faced in the Gallery.

Although the Gallery and Altrincham seem to offer contradictory views, they are similar in that both are suggestive of the validity of a definable and permanent state, one which lies 'beyond revision'. On the one hand, the Whispering Gallery scene seemingly defines De Quincey's personality in terms of the irrevocable word which cannot be escaped; on the other hand, Altrincham, though peaceful and reassuring, also conveys to the autobiographer a kind of permanence. The two scenes are suggestive of types of finality – one through change, one in spite of change; one in which the future is mostly uncertain, one in which the future is likely to be exactly the same as the past. What both visions share is a belief in the concept of a properly realised state. Whether a repetition or a radical departure from what is already known, this state is felt to be impending. Though De Quincey may predict the form of this future state, like the 'solemn truth' uttered in the Whispering Gallery it is not directly articulated in the *Confessions*. Indeed, given that his autobiographical intervention must always be a prelude to the realisation of an integrated 'proper self', De Quincey cannot know, and therefore cannot write directly of, this future state – which is at once the state of 'death' and, when death is invested in life, of 'resurrection'.

Peoples' relationship with death, Ariès writes, 'depends on the unknown state of the beyond, the solidity or ephemerality of survival, the persistence of memory, the erosion of fame, and the intervention of supernatural beings. Between the moment of death and the end of survival there is an interval that Christianity, like the other religions of salvation, has extended to eternity'.[8] The anxious desire for an extension of this moment, for liberated time and for a state of existence different from that of life, is articulated as a death-wish – a confused and confusing desire for negation which is also a desire for an ideal state of being.

The opposition of death to life is called into question by the possible conflation of the two states. Ariès writes of the nineteenth-century conviction, implicit in widespread fears of being buried alive, 'that there is an impure and reversible state that partakes of both life and death'.[9] When he reduces his ingestion of opium, De Quincey's state is one which conflates the equally painful states of life and death:

> Lord Bacon conjectures that it may be as painful to be born as to die. That seems probable; and, during the whole period of diminishing the opium, I had the torments of a man passing out of one mode of existence into another, and liable to the mixed or the alternate pains of birth and death (5: 275).

Being born and dying are qualitatively analogous, the difference between them is blurred. The experience of near-death and the consciousness of having been born, of being alive *as* a conscious entity which is aware of its existence – and therefore of the possibility of a termination of this existence – produce anxiety. Such anxiety is a by-product of the intermittent nature of the self and of self-reproduction (by which I mean both physical survival on a day-to-day basis and psychological survival, the maintenance of one's identity, which under capitalist relations entails the maintenance of one's separation from others). The possibility of death-in-life and life-in-death (the intrusion of semi-domesticated nature, reasserted by death, into a solid and secure culture on one hand; and the sense of entrapment in a permanent and suffocating society on the other) results in a feeling of crisis in which consciousness is defined by extremes. When the anxiety which is the immediate manifestation of this feeling is rationalised, a state of *fascination* is produced.

The formal pattern of De Quincey's writings consists of a movement between the complementary states of fascinated procrastination, calm, or delay and anxious extremity or crisis. By extremity (a term used by De Quincey on several occasions) I mean a state of heightened experience, such as a near-death experience.[10] Extremity and procrastination inform one another. The calm defers the crisis, but it also defines and prefigures the crisis. There can be no decisive break from this pattern, in which contradictory forces prove to be interdependent. Rather, a revolving moment of disintegration that 'is and is not' occurs. De Quincey's writing provides an area in which the struggle between life and death is enacted, but only locally resolved. An observation of Derrida's is relevant here:

> I renounce my present life, my present and concrete existence in order to make myself known in the ideality of truth and value. A well-known schema. The battle by which I wish to raise myself above my life even while I retain it, in order to enjoy recognition, is in this case *within myself*, and writing is indeed the phenomenon of this battle.[11] (My italics.)

Elsewhere Derrida writes:

> Writing in the common sense is the dead letter, it is the carrier of death. It exhausts life. On the other hand, on the other face of the same proposition, writing in the metaphoric sense, natural, divine, and living writing, is venerated; it is equal in dignity to the origin of value, to the voice of conscience as divine law, to the heart, to sentiment, and so forth.[12]

In writing is an impure state analogous to that which makes resurrection and the reversal of life and death possible. The mechanics of the death-wish and the mechanics of writing are analogous. In writing the alienated self becomes acclimatised to its non-existence; and this acclimatisation is a concomitant of the social relations which produce the individual being. Writing idealises, memorialises and exhumes the supposed self of the writer.

Property and the production of the proper

De Quincey's desire for 'freedom' in the *Confessions* leads him to quit school and travel to Wales. For a while, travelling without property allows him the freedom he had wished. Without property, he writes, 'Where I pleased, and *when* I pleased, I could call a halt' (5: 144). Writing is such a travelling without property. It allows for infinite freedom of movement; but, just as De Quincey's journey exhausts his resources and obliges him to acknowledge the demands of property – in the capital, London – so too the autobiographical text consists of the consumption of the past self and the acknowledgment of the propriety of the proper (future) self (mediated through the Press).

De Quincey's sense of freedom alters when he visits the inn before departing on the last stage of his journey to London. He pays the 'entrance-money' which signifies that he is now 'a man *comme il faut*' (5: 151) – a *proper* man, a man of property. The entrance into a new stage of existence means acknowledging – or creating – the sense of the proper. Ironically, and typically, De Quincey's acknowledgment is undercut by the fact of his poverty and distress in London. Here he lacks economic property: the wealth he ought eventually to inherit is out of reach. He is obliged to borrow the property of others. The fugitive self requires a creditor if it is to survive. The payment and subsequent entrance into the 'kingdom' of the enormous ball-room at the inn figures the achievement of an apparently full and proper identity, against which De Quincey sets the utter lack of identity he experiences in the capital. His proper self ironically is impoverished, lacking in present property and, indeed, is obliged to feed off a sense of what he *will* be – which is what interests his creditors (the money-lenders; and the reader).[13]

In the sense that resurrection consists of the realisation of a proper self, the revision of the *Confessions* at once attests to the validity of the concept of 'the proper' and implies the impossibility of fully achieving it in actuality. De Quincey's revision consists of a self-consuming activity which is both destructive and productive. He wastes himself in work, wastes his life in the evasion of death (see Chapter 6). The production of the proper self entails the consumption of the writer's present existence: life is used up so that another, more 'essential' life may be produced. The revision implies that the task of the autobiographical narrative can be completed from a new vantage of 'properness' in which the previous assertions of the autobiographer can be placed in their correct and fully amplified context. But as De Quincey's Preface asserts, with its apology for errors that might occur in the revised text, in actuality there is no proper state. From the vantage of an appreciation of the proper, the proper is destroyed and reprojected once more in the future. While the ability to cope with the original text of the *Confessions* implies that De Quincey has already achieved, in the present of revisionary composition, an integrated state of selfhood, the very fact of the revision necessitates the erasure of this state. Like the original autobiographical text, this supplementary work entails the 'death' of the writer. The original *Confessions* suggests that there is a sense in which this 'death' has already happened. In the notice to the reader with which the work opens, De Quincey writes of the limits imposed on his writing by his sense of propriety:

> I have for many months hesitated about the propriety of allowing this, or any part of my narrative, to come before the public eye, until after my death (when, for many reasons, the whole will be published)(*L*1).

This comment is repeated in the revision of 1856, a repetition which implies several things: first, that the writer's death has indeed occurred (since the revision promises to tell the whole story); further, that this death had already happened from the moment he started writing – and that this is always the case; and, again, that the revised and completed *Confessions* is itself open to revision, cannot be completed until the actual death of the autobiographer.

De Quincey deals with the problem of his own death, real and imagined, at length in the *Confessions*. The revised version attests to the survival of the writer of the work of 1821 and claims to be the testament of one who has cheated death: 'Thirty-five years ago, beyond all doubt, I should have been in my grave' (5: 235). This death is apparently the 'inevitable' biological result of ingesting an excess of opium, itself taken to ward off death from pulmonary consumption: 'Either way it seemed as though death had, in military language, "thrown himself astride my path"' (5: 273). The likely result is deferred by a painstaking review of De Quincey's use of the drug:

> Such an effort I made: every step by which I had gone astray did I patiently unthread. And thus I fought off the natural and spontaneous catastrophe, whatever that might be, which mighty Nature would else have let loose for redressing the wrongs offered to herself (5: 237–8).

Through analysis of the progress of his life, De Quincey has survived the probability (as he sees it) of spontaneous human combustion or a similar destruction. The 'natural and spontaneous catastrophe' has been deferred; but the cultural and predeliberated catastrophe of writing must be met continually. The latter catastrophe delays the former: it constitutes a mechanism by which the writer can self-reproduce or self-resurrect. The unthreading of past errors – a revision of experience – removes De Quincey from immediate danger. De Quincey's writings, which are traces of multiple revision (written revisions of mnemonic revisions; revisions of these works, first at proof stage, then in the revision for his collected edition), constitute an elaborate continuation of a process grounded in a consciousness of death, self-consciousness. Self-consciousness has removed the infant from a 'natural' state and, in an analogous action (by which consciousness of self-consciousness operates), has removed the young adult from a state of childhood. The child De Quincey – the entity which the autobiographer is no longer – has become the *property* of the adult De Quincey.

Each stage in this productive series of experiences is ambivalent, but also entirely necessary. At each stage, there can be no 'going back' to the relinquished state. The relation of the stages in the development of the self to the concept of the production of *individual property* may be appreciated from Locke's conception of Nature as the source of proprietorship:

> It being by him removed from the common state nature placed it in, hath by this *labour* something annexed to it, that excludes the common right of other Men. For this *Labour* being the unquestionable Property of the Labourer, no man but he can have a right to what is once joyned to, at least where there is enough, and as good left in common for others.[14]

What I want to underline here is, first, the idea of a struggle against Nature; and secondly, the idea of *exclusion* in terms of which the property of the individual is defined. The self is that which has been wrested in a violent movement from 'others' (in De Quincey's case, from the control of Lawson *et alia* at school). The individual's identity is grounded in a concept of self-possession, of rightful ownership of one's proper state (a state of *removal*). In the *Confessions* De Quincey delineates the anxious struggle to assert his identity as he is led astray – from an absolute and knowable self to an inadequate and bankrupt self. De Quincey's observation on the state of resourcelessness which is selfhood is simultaneously a comment on the problem of producing the autobiographical writing. The revision of the text and the assertion of the self are complementary actions, the relation of which is one of mutual production:

> 'It comes then to this,' thought I, 'that in myself only there lurks any arrear of help:' as always for every man the ultimate reliance should be on himself. But this *self* of mine seemed absolutely bankrupt; bankrupt of counsel or device – of effort in the way of action, or of suggestion in the way of plan (5: 66).

Like the autobiographical text, which seems to De Quincey to require amplification and modification, the self always needs something more, another figure which might allow it to function despite its untenable nature. The text of the *Confessions* is itself such a figure (a figure of work); De Quincey as a reviser is another, as is the analogous figure of the reader. In short, what is required is a compensatory figure, the function of which is to interpret the self properly, a creditor of some sort to provide it with some *vital property*. This figure in turn requires another figure of compensation, or else needs be of such a quality as to over-ride the economies of proper-self-production.

I now wish to turn my attention to two examples of De Quincey's strategies of self-preservation and self-production.[15] First, I shall analyse the scene on the Cop, which dramatises many of the issues typical of the De Quinceyan autobiographical narrative. Secondly, I shall analyse the significance of opium as a figure of compensation and an agent of resurrection.

'In some way I must contrive to restore the letter' (5: 98)

In the revised *Confessions* De Quincey receives a letter before he quits school, addressed to a 'Monsieur Monsieur De Quincey'. The letter proves problematic. De Quincey cannot decipher its meaning, though he ascertains that it is designed to repay a sum of forty guineas (5: 78). He carries the letter off with him, not willing to be implicated by its possession and yet unable to give it up to the post-office. Finally, he gives it to the woman he encounters on the Cop after witnessing the cataclysmic progress of a Bore. She takes the letter to the post-office, freeing De Quincey from any responsibility and providing a sort of alibi. (It is not really pertinent whether or not this episode of the letter actually took place. What is interesting is how it functions as a figure of the process of the revision of the *Confessions* and of the *self*.)

De Quincey writes that he is translated into a self-multiplied 'Monsieur Monsieur' *by the touch of the pen*. In his autobiographical writings this is precisely what happens: he reproduces himself, creating a doppelgänger which asserts its own identity, an identity which is not *his*: 'I was astonished to find myself translated by a touch of the pen not only into a *Monsieur*, but even into a self-multiplied *Monsieur*' (5: 79). The process of writing reveals to the writer that he is separate from his writing, from the letter which carries his name. While he might claim to be himself (his 'proper' self), he is *not* the self he represents:

> Prophet of evil I ever am to myself: forced for ever into sorrowful auguries that I have no power to hide from my own heart, no, not through one night's solitary dreams. In a moment I saw too plainly that I was not Monsieur[2]. I might be *Monsieur*, but not *Monsieur to the second power*. Who indeed could be *my* debtor to the amount of forty guineas? If there really *was* such a person, why had he been so many years in liquidating his debt? (5: 79)

The hypothetical debtor, whose 'dreadful procrastination' (5: 79) in repaying 'Monsieur Monsieur' is remarked by De Quincey, is a figure of an adequate reader, specifically of De Quincey himself as reader-reviser. Later in the narrative he becomes indebted to the woman he meets on the Cop, who carries the embarrassing letter for him to the post-office. The complex drama with the letter in the *Confessions* constitutes an imaginative, symbolic attempt to resolve difficulties of communication. De Quincey's writing attempts to create a semblance of the freedom he has vainly sought. The letter significantly embarrasses his movements:

> The odious responsibility, thrust upon me in connexion with this letter, was now becoming every hour more irritating, because every hour more embarrassing to the freedom of my own movements, since it must by this time have drawn the post-office into the ranks of my pursuers (5: 98).

De Quincey requires figures such as the woman on the Cop for his version of 'freedom' to function. In effect, freedom entails a dependency on others – on figures of redemption (such as Ann in the *Confessions* or Elizabeth in the 'Autobiographic Sketches': see Chapter 2) or of compensation (economically charged figures such as the capitalist and murderer: see Chapter 6). The figure of redemption enables De Quincey to continue freely. De Quincey runs for his life with the woman on the Cop (the text is grounded in extremity, under threat of the Bore.[16]) The woman subsequently carries the letter away: she intervenes between the fearful fugitive De Quincey (the figure of a fugitive self) and the powerful authority of the post-office (representing the Press, the depository of letters). The woman functions as a figure of a possibly fear-free writing, a text that would work as De Quincey would wish. She carries off the letter, which is an image of the original *Confessions*. She is a figure of a painless revision, one who allows De Quincey to resurrect: he uses her as a messenger, as a carrier of the letter which carries his name. In other words she is a figure of a rewriting of the accusing letter, of the revisionary process of rewriting the original confession: she is a figure of the revised *Confessions*, which seeks to exculpate its author where the original text had failed. The woman resolves symbolically the dilemma which exists between the fugitive self and the Press-controlled autobiographical text.

Opium and the luxury of self-possession

In his description of his attitude when listening to music, De Quincey offers a vision of an immediate present-time experience in which he does not have to cope with the past or the future, with the present mediated through the past or (as life is through the fact of his death) through the future. He comments that music has a special effect upon his consciousness, that 'it is sufficient to say that a chorus, &c., of elaborate harmony displayed before me, as in a piece of arras-work, the whole of my past life – not as if recalled by an act of memory, but as if present and incarnated in the music; no longer painful to dwell upon, but the detail of its incidents removed, or blended in some hazy abstraction, and its passions exalted, spiritualised, and sublimed' (5: 207). This apparent realisation of presence is delusive, since the 'proper self' which it seems to suggest is 'incarnated' not in De Quincey but in the music which he hears. Elsewhere De Quincey analyses the unreality of presence, commenting in the 'Suspiria' that although the present is that 'which only man possesses' (L 159) through self-consciousness, this is in a sense a *false* consciousness since the 'possessed' present does not actually exist:

> The time which *is*, contracts into a mathematic point; and even that point perishes a thousand times before we can utter its birth (L 159).

Since he can have no purchase on a present which is always being consumed by the past, De Quincey can never truly possess himself, nor write of himself, in the *now* of imaginary being. He is obliged rather somehow to suggest the possibility of self-possession in a future state. His belief in an afterlife, intermittingly expressed throughout his autobiographical intervention, offers him such a state. The effect of opium ('this luxury' [5: 203]) similarly holds the promise of selfhood, the luxury of self-possession:

> Wine robs a man of his self-possession; opium sustains and restores it (5: 197).

Opium is the agent of a resurrection in life ('So shall he rise again *before* he dies' [L 153]), a figure of self-belonging, of everything having fallen in its proper place – both in actual experience and in writing. Under the influence of the drug De Quincey is enabled to locate himself in a world of objects from which he is not distinguished. Opium allows access to a state akin to the 'natural' state from which he has been removed. Alienation gives way under the power of opium to *fascination*:

> At that time I often fell into such reveries after taking opium; and many a time it has happened to me on a summer night – when I have been seated at an open window, from which I could overlook the sea at a mile below me, and could at the same time command a view of some great town standing on a different radius of my circular prospect, but at nearly the same distance – that from sunset to sunrise, all through the hours of night, I have continued motionless, as if frozen, without consciousness of myself as an object anywise distinct from the multiform scene which I contemplated from above (5: 211-12).

The drug is a figure of integration and painless presence, a state which recalls the pre-conscious state from which the Opium-Eater has strayed:

> But the expansion of the benigner feelings incident to opium is no febrile access, no fugitive paroxysm; it is a healthy restoration to that state which the mind would naturally recover upon the removal of any deep-seated irritation from pain that had disturbed and quarrelled with the impulses of a heart originally just and good (5: 198).

If the self is a state of bankruptcy, then opium is the compensation for this in which De Quincey invests. In an extraordinary passage De Quincey even characterises opium as being able to compensate for rising prices. When there is not enough to go round, opium allows for a semblance of sufficiency:

> If wages were a little higher, or were expected to be so – if the quartern loaf were a little lower, or it was reported that onions and butter were falling, I was glad; yet, if the contrary were true, I drew from opium some means of consolation (5: 209).

Locke's definition of Property (quoted above, p. 30) associates it with there being 'enough, and as good left in common for others'. De Quincey's investment in individualism – to the extent that feeding his sense of self is tantamount to curing social ills and solving economic problems – suggests that even where there is *not* 'enough', a source of 'fascinating power' may yet be tapped: opium is the saving grace for De Quincey. The Opium-Eater is a figure of the charismatic whose existence attests to a belief in a secret, mysterious reserve of energy, which opium releases. In his autobiographical writings, De Quincey consumes his past selves to achieve the semblance of a proper self. The consumption of opium, by which he achieves an approximation of self-possession, figures that of the past selves. De Quincey's interest in the drug may be readily understood as an articulation of his textual problems – problems concerned primarily with the 'flight and pursuit' of a definable autobiographical self.

CHAPTER TWO 36

Autobiographical Essays

The 'Autobiographic Sketches', which comprises the first volume and part of the second volume of De Quincey's *Selections*, consists of an amalgam of texts. De Quincey revises seven of the thirty-three essays published intermittently between February 1834 and February 1841 in *Tait's Edinburgh Magazine* as (generally) 'Sketches of Life and Manners; from the Autobiography of an English Opium Eater';[1] the apparently incomplete 'Suspiria de Profundis' (*Blackwood's*, 1845); and 'A Sketch from Childhood' (*Hogg's Instructor*, 1851-2). The 'Autobiographic Sketches' also includes a substantial amount of new material ('Laxton' and 'The Priory'). In the second volume of the *Selections* ('Autobiographic Sketches: with Recollections of the Lakes'), the autobiographical papers run into the biographical ones: 'Laxton' and 'The Priory' are followed by 'Early Memorials of Grasmere', then versions of De Quincey's papers on Coleridge, Wordsworth and Southey. It is unclear where one body of work begins and the other ends: the chapter numbers are sequential. Here I deal with aspects of the specifically autobiographical works, paying particular attention not to the individual works so much as to their relation to one another.

The 'Sketches of Life and Manners' are rather matter-of-fact in tone, rambling and with relatively little attention paid to the chronological sequence of events. In these 'Sketches' De Quincey mixes together reminiscences of childhood, of adulthood in the Lakes, portraits of literary contemporaries and a smattering of Irish history (curiously retained in the final version of the 'Autobiographic Sketches'). He had promised Tait 'a proper and a *full* finale' (NLS MS 1670 fos. 40-1: mid June 1838) to the sequence, but none can be gathered from the publication. Whereas the 'Sketches of Life and Manners' deal with experiences across forty-odd years, the 'Suspiria de Profundis', announced as a sequel to the *Confessions of an English Opium-Eater*, concentrates on a few years of De Quincey's childhood, in particular the events surrounding the death of his sister Elizabeth. The 'Suspiria' deals with dreams and the profound effect of death on the child De Quincey. 'A Sketch from Childhood' recounts more mundane events, centring on the antagonistic relationship of De Quincey with his brother William. 'A Sketch' deals with the forces opposed to dreaming mentioned in the 'Suspiria', the social pressures which limit the visionary introspection of the child. 'Suspiria de Profundis' and 'A Sketch from Childhood' represent contradictory experiences which are formally resolved in the 'Autobiographic Sketches'. This resolution, by which the various texts are used to form a single, fragmentary text, suggests that no absolute or totalising vision is possible for De Quincey. The 'Autobiographic Sketches' seemingly revises the message of (the versions of) the *Confessions* – that an irrevocable erroneous step was taken which led the writer away from an absolute and knowable self to an inadequate and 'bankrupt' self – though this revision is by no means a simple negation. De Quincey reiterates and reinforces the themes of the *Confessions* in a manner which suggests no final word is ever possible on the nature of experience. The 'Autobiographic Sketches' expresses a sense of the ultimate and essential contingency of the autobiographical intervention. It is a text which embraces the contradictions of self-definition with a certain violence: not the experiences recounted, but the violent juxtapositions, interruptions and revisions which comprise the finished text, produce the self – a fragmented, intermittent identity which consumes as well as produces itself. Production and consumption are one and the same process here: the process of revision, by which every text suggests a pretext and a sequel. The occluded pretext and sequel together form a sub-text which is alternately buried and revealed in the text of the 'Autobiographic Sketches'. The text is informed by the process of its being revised: it self-consciously suggests that self-consciousness *is* revision; that this revision has an ethical meaning; and that through it death may be transformed into something comprehensible and positive. Change – at a very basic level the change from quick to dead – is positively charged. The 'Autobiographic Sketches' is therefore an improvement on the source materials, since it formally valorises – and takes to an extreme – the process of change. The source materials still exist as separate texts, since revision does not entail a destruction of all previous publications. De Quincey makes this obvious in his revision by referring to these former works (for instance, he mentions the *Confessions* at the opening of the 'Autobiographic Sketches' [1: 13] and in 'The Priory' [2: 38]: and he comments in a footnote on the original versions of the chapters on Irish history [1: 287–8n]). The 'Autobiographic Sketches' functions as a mediating work: it points back to the original publications (as well as to the life of the autobiographer at various times) and points forward to an imaginary text, a *critical sequel* produced in reading. The finished text, which at first may appear a rag-bag of digressions and fragments, is deliberately and meaningfully incomplete: its form articulates the possibilities of doubt by which all absolutes, and above all the absolute of death, are (if not negated) called into question.

'Life is finished!'

The first chapter of the 'Autobiographic Sketches' is a revision of the first part of 'A Sketch from Childhood' (*Hogg's Instructor*, vol.VI, 1851). This 'Sketch' is a sequel to 'Suspiria de Profundis', itself a sequel to the *Confessions*. In the *Hogg's* 'Sketch' De Quincey (mis)quotes the 'Suspiria', diverging from the original work:

> I shall not here repeat any part of the narrative. But one extract from the closing sections of the paper I shall make [. . .] The point of time is during the months that immediately succeeded to my sister's funeral.
>
> The awful stillness of the summer noons, when no winds were abroad – the appealing silence of grey or misty afternoons – these were to me, in that state of mind, fascinations, as of witchcraft (*Hogg's Instructor*, vol.VI, p. 145; cf. *L* 111).

In turn, the 'Autobiographic Sketches' revises 'A Sketch from Childhood' and subtly alters its meaning. 'A Sketch' begins with a dramatic statement to the effect that a 'chapter' of life had come to a conscious ending after the death of Elizabeth, De Quincey's sister:

> About the close of my sixth year, suddenly the first chapter of my life came to a violent termination; that chapter which, and which only, in the hour of death, or even within the gates of recovered Paradise, could merit a remembrance. 'It is finished,' was the secret misgiving of my heart, for the heart even of infancy is as apprehensive as that of maturest wisdom, in relation to any capital wound inflicted on the happiness; 'it is finished, and life is exhausted' (*Hogg's Instructor*, vol.VI, p. 145).

In the 'Autobiographic Sketches' what is finished is not a 'chapter' (that chapter represented in 'Suspiria de Profundis') but, more far-reachingly, 'life' itself (recalling the last words of Christ: 'It is finished.' [John 19: 28]). The revised text begins with the announcement of death (1: 1). The end of life is the beginning of writing, which is always a revision: 'life' is the pre-textual state before writing.[2] The traumatic event which throws this state into relief is the death of Elizabeth. Elizabeth is a figure of pre-textuality, her death the occasion for De Quincey to speak of his so-called self, his childhood revelations. The disfigurement (her skull is cut open and as a result De Quincey's parting from her is anxious rather than calm) and burial of Elizabeth corresponds to the disfigurement (revision) and burial of the 'Suspiria de Profundis' and, moreover, of all De Quincey's previous writings, most emphatically the *Confessions*, on which the other autobiographical works draw.

Autobiographical Essays 39

The sequel to 'real events' is always contained within the text-as-it-is-written in the performative-present. That is, writing autobiography must necessarily always contain as part of the sub-text the realisation of *'And then I started writing'*. Each recounted episode or event will point to this occluded sense of being (*'and here I am'*) with all its implications: who is 'I', can I go on, *'What shall I say next?'* (11: 272). Problems of identity, an identity which seems grounded in the past, are also problems of coping with one's future state – the problem of what the sequel to 'being here' might be. Two sequels present themselves: first, being here still, going on living and writing; secondly, not being here, dying. As De Quincey's comments on 'Life is finished' indicate, in the text the two states are conflated: as he writes he is both dead to himself and still extant. De Quincey characterises his relationship with Elizabeth as being a life-before-writing, before he knows he exists as a self. The self is that which remembers its self, as an individual. Consciousness entails an awareness of a self, of a self which remembers its self – which is to say, of a self which has in a sense been forgotten already. Remembering entails the revivification of this forgotten state of selfhood, a state which De Quincey shares with his sister. Their relationship, which comprises the first chapter of his existence, is highly valued: it would be the only memory worth reviving in the hour of death. In the ultimate extremity, only recalling one's pre-self-consciousness is valuable. Yet there can be no possibility of reviving this state. The pre-text, the original and purely hypothesised consciousness without memory, may be only intermittently recalled; it may only be realised as a revision – never as the actual state. A sense of selfhood entails a kind of entrapment. Once one has a self, there is no escaping from it except through death. Death is at once inevitable – the self is grounded in the empirical fact of having to die – and optional – one can choose to kill oneself. In the latter case, the death-wish is something to be controlled: one exercises the death-wish, acclimatising oneself to death. Hence, in De Quincey's writings, the repeated experience of extremity, the flights into impassioned prose, into a highly stylised writing which effaces the self. Writing is in part an exploration of the writer's lack of self-control: the author is implicitly controlled by forces other than his self in the 'Autobiographic Sketches'. He has been produced by the pre-text of self-consciousness – his life with Elizabeth – and by the pre-text of his revised work – the *Confessions*, the 'Suspiria de Profundis' and so on. The self he comes to represent is already produced: his revision of the works is informed by a great deal of self-influence. His work produces the self, which is supposedly the same self which produced the work. A cyclical process emerges in which the possibilities of a stable identity, an individual self which 'belongs' to one, are severely limited. The stable identity exists as a potential state only, a state which may be suggested or inferred, but never fully articulated. A reversal of categories, by which the author is controlled by what he authorises, by which the writer is controlled by what he has written, and the self produced by the lack of self, asserts itself in the 'Autobiographic Sketches'.[3] The text comprises a series of deaths and rebirths, of reversible states. In the possibility of reversal, of refutation and change, De Quincey's self emerges as the inflection of a process of contradictions, a process which may be termed *cataphysical*.[4]

Authority

The burial and resurrection of the pre-text is accompanied by the death of authority in the 'Autobiographic Sketches'. De Quincey's writing articulates his severance from figures of authority, namely, his father and, more importantly, his brother William whose control over Thomas seems complete, but which terminates as violently as had the first chapter of De Quincey's life. In the *Tait's* 'Sketches of Life and Manners' De Quincey remarks as an important event the death of his father:

> My father's death occurred in 1792. His funeral, at which I and my elder brother were chief mourners, was the first I had attended. Then first it was that the solemn farewell of the English burial-service, 'Dust to dust, ashes to ashes,' and the great eloquence of St. Paul in that matchless chapter of his epistle to the Corinthians, fell upon my ear; and, concurring with my whole previous feelings, for ever fixed that vast subject upon my mind (*Tait's*, vol.I [February 1834], p. 23).

Both in terms of fact and style, this contrasts markedly with the 'Suspiria' and with the 'Autobiographic Sketches'. By making the funeral of Elizabeth significant, and by avoiding any special reference to his father, De Quincey alters the whole theme of the 'Sketches'. Authority figures in the later works seem less important than in the sketches of the 1830s and 1840s. De Quincey focuses rather on female saviours, figures suggestive of the inadequacy of the figures of authority, which, indeed, are characterised as essentially destructive. The importance of the figures of authority lies in the way they contrast to the female saviours: the two types of figure define one another. There is an element of ambiguity in De Quincey's relation to authority, for he too is directly implicated in the destruction of the female, involved in the wreck of the text.

The most significant of these authority figures is De Quincey's brother William, the presiding spirit of 'A Sketch from Childhood', a work which terminates with the report of his death. A figure of power and impulse, he oppresses his brother in a way which provides a profound contrast to the relationship of De Quincey to Elizabeth:

> Truest of all things it [his love for Elizabeth] seemed by the

Autobiographical Essays 41

> excess of that happiness which it had sustained: most fraudulent it seemed of all things, when looked back upon as some mysterious parenthesis in the current of life, 'self-withdrawn into a wondrous depth,' hurrying as if with headlong malice to extinction, and alienated by *every* feature from the new aspects of life that seemed to await me. Were it not in the bitter corrosion of heart that I was called upon to face, I should have carried over to the present no connecting link whatever from the past (1: 33–34).

> The next (which was the *second*) chapter of my childish experience, formed that sort of fierce and fantastic contradiction to the first, which might seem to move in obedience to some incarnate principle of malicious pantomime. A spirit of love, and a spirit of rest, as if breathing from St John the Evangelist, had seemed to mould the harmonies of that earliest stage in my childhood which had just vanished; but now, on the other hand, some wicked Harlequin Mephistopheles was apparently commissioned to vex my eyes and plague my heart, through the next succession of two or three years: a worm was at the roots of life (*Hogg's Instructor*, vol.VI, p. 146).

The 'Harlequin Mephistopheles', William, the personification of a patchwork authority, determines the course of De Quincey's childhood experience. He also determines the proportions of 'A Sketch from Childhood'. The actual events and the production of the text are part of the same process. De Quincey finishes the 'Sketch' with the death of William, which simultaneously marks also the decisive abandonment of his work. The exercise of authority entails its own cessation. William goes to an early grave, his talents as an artist leading him to a speedy death from typhus fever. De Quincey's (deliberately) almost clumsy ending of the 'Sketch' virtually refuses authority: William's dismissal is suggestive of the limitations of control. The paper formally articulates De Quincey's attitude towards the demands and responsibilities of authority. He relinquishes control, abruptly ending the sketch, as the figure of authority exits from his life.

Just as the beginning of 'A Sketch from Childhood' had revised 'Suspiria de Profundis', so too at its close the method of the earlier text is called into question. 'A Sketch from Childhood' verges on a parody of 'Suspiria de Profundis'. In the 'Suspiria' De Quincey had complained to the reader that he was unable to produce the work of art he had planned:

> Here pause, reader! Imagine yourself seated in some cloud-scaling swing, oscillating under the impulse of lunatic hands; for the strength of lunacy may belong to human dreams, the fearful caprice of lunacy, and the malice of lunacy, whilst

the *victim* of those dreams may be all the more certainly removed from lunacy; even as a bridge gathers cohesion and strength from the increasing resistance into which it is forced by increasing pressure. Seated in such a swing, fast as you reach the lowest point of depression, may you rely on racing up to a starry altitude of corresponding ascent. Ups and downs you will see, heights and depths, in our fiery course together, such as will sometimes tempt you to look shyly and suspiciously at me, your guide, and the ruler of the oscillations. Here, at the point where I have called a halt, the reader has reached the lowest depth in my nursery afflictions. From that point, according to the principles of *art* which govern the movement of these Confessions, I had meant to launch him upwards through the whole arch of ascending visions which seemed requisite to balance the sweep downwards, so recently described in his course. But accidents of the press have made it impossible to accomplish this purpose in the present month's journal. There is reason to regret that the advantages of position, which were essential to the full effect of passages planned for equipoise and mutual resistance, have thus been lost (*L* 136-7).

In 'A Sketch from Childhood' De Quincey suggests that William was such a 'lunatic', for it is he who controls a specific swing in which the young Thomas is obliged to sit. William may be understood as a figure of De Quincey's ambitious plans for 'Suspiria de Profundis' – and of the collapse of these plans. In 'A Sketch' the swing is in the hands of the lunatic brother, suggesting the conflation of William and the ambitious author of the 'Suspiria'. 'A Sketch' characterises the swing as essentially a sickening mechanism, the oscillations of which (representing the proposed methodology of the 'Suspiria') placed De Quincey in a terrifying and painful position:

It was a most ambitious swing, ascending to a height beyond any that I have since seen in fairs or public gardens. Horror was at my heart regularly as the swing reached its most aerial altitude; for the oily, swallow-like fluency of the swoop downwards threatened always to make me sick, in which case I fully believed that I must have relaxed my hold of the ropes, and have been projected, with probably fatal violence, to the ground (*Hogg's Instructor* vol.VIII, p. 177).

'Suspiria de Profundis', then, the text which De Quincey apparently never completed, but rather cannibalised for the 'Autobiographic Sketches', is criticised in 'A Sketch from Childhood'. The ambitions of the author, who wished to produce a balanced and artistically well-proportioned work, but was prevented by the inevitable 'accidents of the press', are called into question. Although 'A Sketch from Childhood' itself constitutes some form of complement to 'Suspiria de Profundis', it also throws into relief the assumptions made in

Autobiographical Essays

the production of the earlier text. De Quincey retreats from the sickening demands of 'equipoise' and balance, and instead proposes a more whimsical and perhaps more subversive methodology. In 'A Sketch from Childhood' the reader no longer receives an apology. Instead, with a studied sense of carelessness, De Quincey deliberately disavows responsibility for the form of his work:

> But the reader complains that I loiter. Now, then, he shall complain no longer; for I will hurry to the conclusion at a killing pace, that may perhaps anger him as much in the opposite direction. I fear there is no contenting this person called the reader. Strike high or strike low, move fast or not at all, finish the paper or leave it a *torso* – no course pleases him; and he writes letters against me to the editor of the gloomiest tendency: where, however, I have the advantage of him, for the editor kindly shows me the letters in all their naked wickedness. Naturally I criticise them with Rhadamanthian truculence; and, in the very worst case, I have the benefit of the last word. But now, whether it angers the reader or gratifies him, it really is my firm intention to conclude. And it is my intention, simply because it has come to be my necessity. Needs must, whom the fiend drives; and fiend there is not, one or other, so masterful as necessity. The necessity lies here. Take any drama you please, the best or the poorest, if in act the second all the characters should be seized with the craze of travelling to a dozen different points of the compass, that drama must clearly come into a condition of bankruptcy (*Hogg's Instructor*, vol. VIII, p. 338).

De Quincey replaces the demands of 'art' with the demands of 'necessity'. Intention and necessity become one and the same thing. De Quincey accepts the demands of the Press (as he does in 'Sir William Hamilton', also published in *Hogg's Instructor*: see Chapter 3) and proceeds to subvert his acceptance. What constitutes the disfigurement or ruin of one paper constitutes the satisfactory completion of the other. With 'A Sketch from Childhood' De Quincey begins a full-scale revision of the morbid and desperate striving after the absolute that characterises 'Suspiria de Profundis'. This revision is continued in the 'Autobiographic Sketches'.

'[. . .] absolute self-controul'

In the 'Suspiria' De Quincey concentrates on the traumas of rebirth, the pains of experience which form the individual adult. The work continues one of the themes of the *Confessions*. There the step into adulthood had proved crucially formative: it had led to De Quincey's trials in London, his nightmares, and his use of opium. In the 'Suspiria' the effect of opium on the dreaming faculty is again explored. So too, the sense of misgiving that accompanied the entrance into adulthood is amplified. The error of the *Confessions* is replaced by a generalised vision of a world of dread. Consciousness itself is characterised as suffering in 'Suspiria de Profundis'. De Quincey writes that the adult is obliged to act within an impossibly intricate set of relations. His fellow men hem him in and restrict his freedom on a scale that makes childhood sufferings seem simple by comparison:

> This truth is felt beforehand misgivingly and in troubled vision, by a young man who stands upon the threshold of manhood. One earliest instinct of fear and horror would darken his spirit if it could be revealed to itself and self-questioned at the moment of birth: a second instinct of the same nature would again pollute that tremulous mirror, if the moment were as punctually marked as physical birth is marked, which dismisses him finally upon the tides of absolute self-controul [*sic*]. A dark ocean would seem the total expanse of life from the first: but far darker and more appalling would seem that interior and second chamber of the ocean which called him away for ever from the direct accountability of others. Dreadful would be the morning which should say – 'Be thou a human child incarnate;' but more dreadful the morning which should say – 'Bear thou henceforth the sceptre of thy self-dominion through life, and the passion of life!' Yes, dreadful would be both: but without a basis of the dreadful there is no perfect rapture (*L* 161).

De Quincey's insistence upon the absolute in this passage of 'Suspiria de Profundis' is informed with irony. The set of relations he has to deal with as an adult are, as I argued in Chapter 2, those of the Press. He is not in control at all, but is rather controlled by this set of relations (and this is the case anyhow, the Press notwithstanding). Self-control, the condition of adulthood, entails abandonment, exclusion, and isolation. The alienated child, whose pariah wanderings already suggest this abandonment, becomes an alienated adult. Adulthood is a revision of childhood. Becoming a man is a revision of the experience of becoming a human being. Both are traumatic: the first because one is born, the second because one is thrown upon one's self. The conditions of childhood and adulthood are in fact similar. Self-dominion or self-control within the realm of adulthood corresponds to self-oblivion in the realm of childhood. De Quincey writes in the 'Autobiographic Sketches' of 'that self-oblivion in which only deep passion originates, or can find a genial home' (1: 3). Where the states differ in De Quincey's vision lies in the fact that the adult autobiographer makes *public* his *private* experiences. The *Confessions* and 'Suspiria de Profundis' are concerned with differentiating the public and private, thereby defining the two realms. In publishing details of his life, De Quincey privileges the individual. The comment above about self-dominion, which in the light of his relations with the Press is simply a deception, serves to reinforce the myth of his own individuality. Barthes has written of childhood as a mythical area and outlined the special investment of the bourgeoisie in it:

> Since the romantic era (i.e., since the triumph of the bourgeoisie), it has been a matter of remaining in childhood as long as possible; any adult action imputable to childhood (even to a belated childhood) participates in its intemporality, appears glamorous because produced *in advance*. The *displaced* overvaluation of this age presumes that we regard it as private, closed over itself, possessing a special status, a kind of ineffable and intransmissible essence.[5]

The similarity of childhood and adulthood for De Quincey lies in the traumatic nature of his entrance into the form of life entailed and in the fact that the privacy of the individual is maintained by the cordoning off of the complementary states. Entering adulthood, a source of regret and complaint in the *Confessions*, is also a necessity for the definition of De Quincey's individuality since it decisively finishes his childhood. The completion of childhood is further explored in the 'Autobiographic Sketches', in which De Quincey writes of his 'premature manhood' (a theme referred to in the *Tait's* 'Sketches of Life and Manners'). De Quincey implies that he was an adult ahead of his time: that childhood was special for him because it had ended before he had, strictly speaking, grown up. The labours of adulthood – for De Quincey principally the writing of his autobiography – are prefigured in the individual's self-consciousness which first distinguishes him from others. De Quincey's revisionary task reinforces his claims to individuality: his multiple labours express his separation not only from others but from himself. Self-definition eventually becomes self-destructive: the production of an identity is revealed as not simply traumatic, but at base violent. De Quincey positively valorises this violence under the guise of 'passion'.

'Suspiria de Profundis' constitutes the most extended of De Quincey's attempts at producing 'impassioned prose', writing which articulates at once the writer's lack of control (in that it simulates authority) and his individuality or uniqueness (the style is definitely his own).[6] Passion, in De Quincey's view, is localised, coincident to self-consciously recognised stages of the individual's development. Passion, then, expresses first the loss of control over what constitutes the self, and secondly the process by which what has been lost is recovered. The recovery of the lost selves that comprise the individual, which the 'impassioned prose' seeks to suggest, requires that the self be forever in the process of moving away from what it was – in the process of constantly changing. The dilemma lies in the fact that there will always be something extra to be recovered, since self-consciousness determines that the self is never complete. De Quincey's differentiation between the child and adult, between the private and public, is grounded in this sense of incompleteness. In the 'Autobiographic Sketches' he writes that the self is never fully unified, that the individual is a local manifestation of a process which conflates the lack of self with the assertion of self;

> Man is doubtless *one* by some subtle *nexus*, some system of links, that we cannot perceive, extending from the new-born infant to the superannuated dotard; but, as regards many affections and passions incident to his nature at different stages, he is *not* one, but an intermitting creature, ending and beginning anew; the unity of man, in this respect, is co-extensive only with the particular stage to which the passion belongs (1: 18).

The self is never proper, never present: a system 'we cannot perceive' and which is purely imaginary unifies the fragmented individual. Passion does not unify the individual (whose individuality is grounded in fragmentation), but rather invests the lack of unity with meaning. Passion 'belongs' to the fragmented stage, to a specific time and set of relations. This belonging is the individual's sense of isolation, of not belonging: it compensates for the lack of property of the self. In terms of De Quincey's writing, the 'impassioned prose' compensates for the absence of the author from his writing, transforming the 'impropriety' of revealing the private experience of the individual into the 'proper' – a 'proper' which conforms to the properness of art and beauty. In the 'Autobiographic Sketches' the sporadic impassioned flights punctuate the rambling unimpassioned prose. The difference is not (as some of De Quincey's critics would have it) between a superior and inferior writing style, but between differing expressions of a process of self-definition. Both styles are necessary and complementary.

The revised text of the 'Autobiographic Sketches' attempts to reconcile the violence of self-definition with the realisation that such violence is ultimately ineffectual: one is not a discrete entity, but is informed by others (including other manifestations of the self). In the *Tait's* 'Sketches of Life and Manners', De Quincey had underlined the impossibility of maintaining a 'proper' chronology, a singular set of relations between the self and others:

> The reader who may have accompanied me in these wandering memorials of my own life and casual experiences, will be aware that I have brought them forward with little regard to their exact order of succession. In reference to that particular object which governed me in bringing them forward at all – an object which I shall, perhaps, explain pointedly in my closing paper – it was of very little importance to consult the chronologies of the case, except in so far as sometimes it may have happened that the precise dates of a transaction

were of some negative value towards its verification. Consequently, I have wandered backwards and forwards, obeying any momentary impulse, as accident or sometimes even as purely verbal suggestions might arise to guide me. But, in many cases, this neglect of chronological order is not merely permitted – it is in fact to some degree inevitable; for there are cases which, as a whole, connect themselves with my own life, at so many different eras, that, upon any chronological principle of position, it would have been difficult to assign them a proper place – backwards or forwards they must have leaped, in whatever place they had been introduced; and in their entire compass, from first to last, never could have been represented as properly belonging to any one *present* time, whensoever that had been selected (*Tait's*, vol. V [March 1838], p. 152).

The leaps back and forwards made by the writer, which tend to disrupt the coherence of his text, are analogous to the obscuration and revelation of the pre-text in the 'Autobiographic Sketches'. What in the 'Sketches of Life and Manners' appears as random and accidental is formally deployed in conjunction with the methodologies employed in 'Suspiria de Profundis' and 'A Sketch from Childhood' to reinforce the theme of resurrection in the final text. The inevitable wanderings between one chronological time and another suggest a formal movement by which any remembered event participates in one which prefigures it and one which provides a sequel to it. The event no longer 'belongs' (least of all to the self): it shifts and ceases to be the property of the individual person, time, or text. De Quincey's 'Autobiographic Sketches' juxtaposes these articulations of un-belonging to the impassioned prose which articulates the desire for a 'genial home'. The impassioned prose exhibits signs of enormous labour, of ownership, of a striving towards a privacy and a precision which would be impenetrable if entirely realised.

'[. . .] the interests of truth'

The contradiction between the impassioned and rambling or digressive prose styles suggests an attempt on De Quincey's part to reconcile the social contradiction involved in the publication of an autobiographical narrative. Beyond the private and public he projects 'the truth', a hypothesised category in which reconciliation may be realised. From the vantage point of doubt, the truth is projected. The possibility of communicating it seems slim, given that for De Quincey all language tends to represent either too little or too much. The truth is not served by language: rather, it is damaged because of the effect of any language's 'doubtful expressions'. A footnote in the 'Autobiographic Sketches' suggests as much:

> But I [. . .] assert that there is not one page of prose that could be selected from the best writer in the English language (far less

> in the German), which, upon a sufficient interest arising, would
> not furnish matter, simply through its defects in precision, for a
> suit in Chancery. Chancery suits do not arise, it is true; because
> the doubtful expressions do not touch any interest of property;
> but what *does* arise is this – that something more valuable than
> a pecuniary interest is continually suffering, viz., the interests
> of truth (1: 61n).

This footnote echoes one in 'A Sketch from Childhood' where De Quincey complains that no writer is capable of properly managing language:

> Since those years, it is natural that mere culture of the subject, and long experience in the arts of composition, should have sharpened my vision, previously too morbidly acute, to defects in the construction of sentences, and generally in the management of language. The result is this; and perhaps it will shock the reader, certainly it will startle him, when I declare solemnly my conviction, that no two consecutive pages can be cited from any one of the very best English authors, which is not disfigured by some gross equivocation or imperfection of structure, such as leaves the meaning open, perhaps, to be inferred from the context, but also so little expressed with verbal rigour, or with conformity to the truth of logic, or to real purpose, that, supposing the passage to involve a legal interest, and in consequence to come under a judicial review, it would be set aside for want of internal coherency. Not in arrogance, but under a deep sense of the incalculable injuries done to truth, small and great, by false management of language, I declare my belief that hardly one entire paragraph exists in our language which is impregnable to criticism, even as regards the one capital interest of logical limitation to the main purpose concerned (*Hogg's Instructor*, vol. VI, p. 234n).

The imprecision of language is related to the fact that it does not touch upon any interest of property. Truth, like the individual self, is beyond property: De Quincey implies that the lack of property is something positive after all. Truth is disfigured by the mismanagement of language, a language which is open to contradiction, which can be penetrated and exploded. Literature is incoherent. It is invariably disfigured, invariably *revised*. Revision in this context entails a divergence from the truth, which necessarily cannot be communicated. This *impasse* would seem to negate De Quincey's entire intervention, rendering the revisionary process essentially empty. The irony of his objections to a language that is not 'impregnable' lies in the fact that De Quincey's various texts inform one another repeatedly, especially in the 'Autobiographic Sketches': not only are paragraphs not impregnable, entire volumes of texts, literature itself, culture in general, threaten to collapse under the demands for the truth. If to impart truth is the purpose of the De Quinceyan text, then the only truth it can impart is that the autobiographical intervention is a lie, a necessary fiction. The writing cannot be impregnable, since this would require that it be entirely private. The ideal of truth is allowed to stand, notwithstanding the possibility that it may not be realisable. Indeed, De Quincey's objections to the inadequacies of language can scarcely be taken too seriously, since his critical interpretation of the failed writings of others is largely productive. Quantitatively at least, he finds language produces more than is necessary. His search for precision leads him to a recognition that the further the search be conducted, the further he is led from his goal. The absolute is deceptive: to represent the truth to oneself produces an all-pervasive sense of doubt. In this schema, truth and doubt form complementary aspects of the same process; and it is doubt which, in representation of any sort, proves apposite:

> So far from seeking to 'pettifogulise' – *i.e.*, to find evasions for any purpose in a trickster's minute tortuosities of construction – exactly in the opposite direction, from mere excess of sincerity, most unwillingly I found, in almost everybody's words, an unintentional opening left for double interpretations (1: 61).

Communication involves the penetration of another's 'meaning'. There is always a gap between the representation and the interpretation; and between the intention and the effect of representation. De Quincey is the martyr to the demands of truth. Like self-definition, the attempt to represent the truth to oneself is a violent process. Language repeatedly tends towards the self-parodic in De Quincey's writings. In the 'Autobiographic Sketches' Bishop Wilkins's projected Universal Language (1: 46) contrasts with a real universal language of throwing stones (1: 51–2). The only universal language, De Quincey implies, is that of violence, a violence which mocks all efforts to order and grasp experience.

The real steadily contradicts the ideal, requiring that experience be interpreted in such a way as to counteract the negation of what is valued by the individual (including the valuation of individuality itself). All interpretation tends to diverge from what provides its source. Thus, while truth cannot be accurately represented, a representation may be so interpreted as to allow the interpreter to infer what the truth is. This requires some sort of shared code, inevitably. De Quincey characterises this code by delineating the temperament of the pariah or victim, the character to whom violence is done *inevitably*. He exaggerates his isolation, his individuality, his self-victimisation, lending to a potential state the status of the real. The victim engages in the reversal of the real and ideal: what should be *is* to the victim: nothing becomes something. Human activity is defined reductively as interpretation: activity is primarily psychological and is grounded in a passive acceptance of the violence which defines one's self. In 'A Sketch from Childhood' De Quincey touches upon the 'pariah mind' which is grounded in self-consciousness and has 'revealed itself *memorably*' (my italics):

> But my own feeling is, that no act, open to man or to the combined will of a whole people, could lay the foundation for a sorrow and sense of humiliation so deep and so enduring as that which characterised the Pelasgi of old, or for the recording badges of those deep impressions as they are found at this day amongst the lowest castes of the Hindoos. Not any *act* produced, or could produce, the melancholy temperament; but inversely the temperament must first have revealed itself memorably by some act which circumstances made abominable to other tribes or other races. Such a temperament lurks, probably, amongst all nations, smouldering through generations, until concurring accidents of bodily constitution, of disposition, of intellect, and of events from without, rouse it into open flames. Such a temperament must, in part, have been mine, though partially counteracted by a deep capacity of sympathy with joy in excess, and with Euphrosyne rapture. Ah, records of what to many would seem the lunatic darkness that belongs to the true pariah mind, what anguish of fear and sorrow are hidden in you! Fear of what? Sorrow for what? Simply *timor vagus*, fear that was objectless – *moeror vagus*, sorrow that was objectless; fear illimitable, sorrow illimitable, that alternately presided. But I must not enter upon a theme so large and so obscure as this (*Hogg's Instructor*, vol. VIII, p. 177).

The pariah mind is produced in the act of recognition, an interpretative act of self-definition. The pariah is remembered with a sense of abomination. In this, De Quincey figures the original remembrance in which the self is grounded as essentially painful, involving as it does the rejection by others of one's 'true' nature. One's temperament, what sets the individual apart from others, is in the case of the pariah excessively separate. The pariah represents the extreme of 'truth' and of the 'proper' and also of a passive acceptance of the violence of representation. By defining himself as a pariah De Quincey attempts to articulate the horrendous isolation of the individual while still retaining the value of the concept of individuality. The pariah is more virtuous than others, a 'natural' victim whose crime points him out and defines him. The form of the pariah mind is always prefigured. The pariah represents in part the prefiguration of selfhood, the forgotten moment of original self-consciousness which the individual repeatedly attempts to recover. He attests to the validity of the concept of prefiguration (an obsessive theme of the 'Autobiographic Sketches'). Not only the value of revision is emphasised in the figure of the pariah, but the solid reality of the revisionary process. The event which points out the pariah temperament, the symbolic act which revives in the process of self-consciousness, suggests that a principle of revivification already and always operates. The existence of the pariah mind gives a semblance of reality to the vagaries of self-consciousness, ordering the imaginary, the objectless and the visionary by providing them with a physical and psychological form.

'They are not dead, but sleeping'

The exclusion of the pariah type from the rest of humanity, and the oppression of this type, constitute a state analogous to that, first, of the individual in relation to the group; and, secondly and more importantly, of the remembering self in relation to the many disjointed memories that comprise its past selves. De Quincey's vain pursuit of a true presence and a proper identity concludes in the realisation that the self is always about to be pointed out – like the pariah – by an extant system. His self is always *about to be* realised, figured by the system of his memories. The identity of the living creature De Quincey is grounded in dead matter, in the past.

In the 'Autobiographic Sketches', De Quincey's brother William suggests that many of the living are in fact shams, dead men walking about in the world for obscure reasons (1: 42). The possible size of the army of the dead baffles De Quincey and testifies to his own insignificance – and to the insignificance of the living when compared with the dead. (The army of the dead walking among the living parallels the effect on the solitary individual of the crowds of his fellows: in 'Suspiria de Profundis' De Quincey remarks that modern life oppresses the solitary, whose 'brain is haunted as if by some jealousy of ghostly beings moving amongst us' [L 87].) De Quincey refers to dying in terms of *abiit ad plures*:

> The Roman Phrase for expressing that a man had died, viz., '*Abiit ad plures*' (He has gone over to the majority), my brother explained to us; and we easily comprehended that any one generation of the living human race, even if combined, and acting in concert, must be in a frightful minority, by comparison with all the incalculable generations that had trod this earth before us (1: 42).

To die is to join the majority, an *ad plures ire*. So too is being moved by beauty, as Walter Benjamin asserts:

> On the basis of its *historical* existence, beauty is an appeal to join those who admired it at an earlier time. Being moved by beauty is an *ad plures ire*, as the Romans called dying. According to this definition, the semblance of beauty means that the identical object which admiration is courting cannot be found in that work. This admiration harvests what earlier generations have admired in it. Words of Goethe express here the final conclusion

of wisdom: 'Everything that has had a great effect can really no longer be evaluated'.[7]

For De Quincey to remember is both beautiful and painful: the pain of memory is a constituent of its beauty, for memory attests to the absence of what is recalled. To remember is to join the beautiful dead (Elizabeth, De Quincey's former selves and so on). In De Quincey's view, to join the dead may be to be revived by them: the self receives life from the dead, from its remembrance of the past, so that while on the one hand to remember entails the death of the self, on the other hand, in counteraction, it entails the resurrection of the self: by going back to the past, the self dies to itself; by interpreting memory, the self revivifies the dead – including its dead self. De Quincey joins the dead only to separate himself from them: interpretation is the obverse of memory. It makes sense of one's future death by defining death as something grounded in the past. A straightforward reversal takes place here: the self realises that it does not exist as such, but as a resurrected being. Resurrection constitutes life for De Quincey, the way revision constitutes writing.

The relation of the living to the dead, which seems grounded in negativity (and in real terms entails a morbid fascination in the entire culture – the formation of *The Age of the Beautiful Death*, as Ariès calls it), is analysed at length in 'Suspiria de Profundis'.[8] De Quincey writes in this work of his experiences of hopelessness, and claims that grief need not be a state of despair:

> And howsoever a man may think that he is without hope, I, that have read the writing upon these great abysses of grief, and viewed their shadows under the correction of mightier shadows from deeper abysses since then, abysses of aboriginal fear and eldest darkness, in which yet I believe that all hope had not absolutely died, know that he is in a natural error. If, for a moment, I and so many others, wallowing in the dust of affliction, could yet rise up suddenly like the dry corpse which stood upright in the glory of life when touched by the bones of the prophet [. . .] then it was plain that despair, that the anguish of darkness, was not *essential* to such sorrow, but might come and go even as light comes and goes upon our troubled earth (L 119).

The bones of the prophet Elisha (2 Kings xiii, 20–1) revive the dead: the image suggests that the long-since dead may exert an influence on the recently dead; or, given that Elisha's bones are lower in the grave than the 'dry corpse', that the distant memories may have a powerful effect on the remembering self. The deeper one goes into one's experiences, the more of a sense of proportion one may gain. Revelation is sudden, unexpected, and takes place in extremity, under the influence of death. Death, then, is positively valorised by De Quincey: in 'Suspiria de Profundis' it even seems preferable to life.

Autobiographical Essays

There is an element of curiously extreme, even perverse, fascination in this work which is surely expressive of the times, and which represents a disconcerting articulation of social attitudes towards death in the nineteenth century. De Quincey's attitudes certainly change between 'Suspiria de Profundis' and the 'Autobiographic Sketches'. The earlier text moves from an exploration of the strength of the death-wish in childhood to a sketch or *tableau* which represents scenes of domestic affliction. In these scenes, various females are shown held motionless in disaster. This section of 'Suspiria de Profundis' in some ways represents an extreme in De Quincey's writings. Certainly, it articulates a strange and disturbing undercurrent which runs throughout his work. De Quincey introduces the tableau as an improvisation specially designed for 'the fair reader':

> Heavens! when I look back to the sufferings which I have witnessed or heard of even from this one brief London experience, I say if life could throw open its long suits of chambers to our eyes from some station *beforehand*, if from some secret stand we could look *by anticipation* along its vast corridors, and aside into the recesses opening upon them from either hand, halls of tragedy or chambers of retribution, simply in that small wing and no more of the great caravanserai which we ourselves shall haunt, simply in that narrow tract of time and no more where we ourselves shall range, and confining our gaze to those and no others for whom personally we shall be interested, what a recoil we should suffer of horror in our estimate of life! What if those sudden catastrophes, or those inexpiable afflictions, which have already descended upon the people within my own knowledge, and almost below my own eyes, all of them now gone past, and some long past, had been thrown open before me as a secret exhibition when first I and they stood within the vestibule of morning hopes; when the calamities themselves had hardly begun to gather in their elements of possibility, and when some of the parties to them were as yet no more than infants! The past viewed not *as* the past, but by a spectator who steps back ten years deeper into the rear, in order that he may regard it as a future; the calamity of 1840 contemplated from the station of 1830 – the doom that rang the knell of happiness viewed from a point of time when as yet it was neither feared nor would even have been intelligible – the name that killed in 1843, which in 1835 would have struck no vibration upon the heart – the portrait that on the day of her Majesty's coronation would have been admired by you with a pure disinterested admiration, but which if seen to-day would draw forth an involuntary groan – cases such as these are strangely moving for all who add deep thoughtfulness to deep sensibility. As the hastiest of improvisations, accept – fair reader (for you it is that

will chiefly feel such an invocation of the past) – three or four illustrations from my own experience (L 173–4).

De Quincey views the past sequence of events as if they were a future, an action which any contemplation of the future death of the self entails, in so far as death is familiar, is grounded in the past. De Quincey's point in 'Suspiria de Profundis' is that the complete reversal of fortune in life is shocking, and that only an inability, or unwillingness, to foresee the future prevents the general estimate of existence from being utterly altered. His task in the essay is to reverse the unthinking estimate of life: such a task is realised by a chronological reversal, which articulates a definition of life as inherently grounded in death. By representing the inevitable destruction of all that is valued in life, De Quincey purposes to provoke the kind of introspection that he has himself practised. The 'Suspiria de Profundis' scenes offer a minimal amount of hope. De Quincey presents them as a provocatively morbid 'mystery' which must be interpreted by the reader. He offers a psychological explanation, after a series of questions that build up an atmosphere of menace and depression:

> Who is this distinguished-looking young woman with her eyes drooping, and the shadow of a dreadful shock yet fresh upon every feature? Who is the elderly lady with her eyes flashing fire? Who is the downcast child of sixteen? What is that torn paper lying at their feet? Who is the writer? Whom does the paper concern? (L 174)

In this scene of fixed extremity the frozen gestures and silence of the women parallel De Quincey's own sense of complete ruin, which he expresses in an anecdote about an Abbess who, attempting to rescue a friend, arrives too late and finds a corpse instead:

> The sentiment which attends the sudden revelation that *all is lost!* silently is gathered up into the heart; it is too deep for gestures or for words; and no part of it passes to the outside. Were the ruin conditional, or were it in any point doubtful, it would be natural to utter ejaculations, and to seek sympathy. But where the ruin is understood to be absolute, where sympathy cannot be consolation, and counsel cannot be hope, this is otherwise. The voice perishes; the gestures are frozen; and the spirit of man flies back upon its own centre. I, at least, upon seeing those awful gates closed and hung with draperies of woe, as for a death already past, spoke not, nor started, nor groaned. One profound sigh ascended from my heart, and I was silent for days (L 91).

The design of 'Suspiria de Profundis' suggests that from the scenes of domestic affliction some positive lesson may be drawn, in a movement from despair to hope analogous to that recounted by De Quincey earlier in the text. However, the explanation that glosses the scenes leaves all parties dead: none of the women find happiness in life; none are able to interpret calamity in the De Quinceyan manner. The passages that conclude 'Suspiria de Profundis' are stark and horrific. The sense of finality is overwhelming and the former suggestions that the process by which death informs life may be transformed into a hopeful vision seem inadequate. Indeed, the revisionary method which might place death within a positively valorised context is called into question by the unchanging nature of the scenes: the passing of time merely reinforces a sense of hopelessness, repetitive events attest to a permanence that cannot be overcome. Thus, the chiming of a clock, signifying the passing of time (and perhaps therefore a change for the better), ironically indicates that the state of unease has been maintained over a course of years. The event seems an inflection of the mental state:

> Now again had come a summer evening memorable for unhappiness; now again the daughter thought of those dying lights of love which streamed at sunset from the closing eyes of her mother; again, and just as she went back in thought to this image, the same silvery voice of the dial sounded nine o'clock (L 177).

In keeping with this sense of meaningless repetition, the daughter becomes a wreck and dies. Time, which had seemed arrested in life, transforms her after she is dead. De Quincey depicts her death as a state to be desired. This seems distinctly unhealthy, the curious logic behind it notwithstanding:

> Suppose this time gone; suppose her now dressed for her grave, and placed in her coffin. The advantage of that is – that, though no change can restore the ravages of the past, yet (as often is found to happen with young persons) the expression has revived from her girlish years. The child-like aspect has revolved, and settled back upon her features (L 178).

The childlike aspect revolves and settles on the face of the daughter when she is dead. Death is a state identical to childhood: it resembles it precisely. Both states are analogous to that of adulthood. Where adulthood differs, however, lies in the fact that the adult is obliged to deal with other people. The child and the corpse are distant from the relations of the adult world. In privileging childhood and death, the desirable states which together serve to define adulthood, De Quincey seeks to control the set of relations which oppress him.

The fascination in 'Suspiria de Profundis' with death and childhood, of the experience of death in childhood, articulates a desire on De Quincey's part to produce a piece of writing on his own terms, outside of oppressive social relations. The experiences recounted are extremely private. The text expresses De Quincey's own ideas, a singular and idiosyncratic vision. Yet the paper is restricted by 'accidents of the press': De Quincey is obliged to compromise and destroy his work. The 'damaged' form of 'Suspiria de Profundis' attests to the control of the Press, of the adult world, over the writer in spite of all his efforts. The impassioned prose which expresses the incommunicable, the silence of ruin, is curtailed by the form of the journal, the demands of its proprietor and the market. The valuable experience of privacy can only be published *so far*: something unsaid, unwritten remains. The figures of childhood and death in 'Suspiria de Profundis' are at once figures of the production of the text within the context of *Blackwood's Edinburgh Magazine*; and of the desire of the writer to escape from this context. The disfigurement of the work (De Quincey claims he is obliged to improvise, that his art is restricted and so on) is figured in its publication. The form of the essay in the journal is significant, therefore. In the revision of De Quincey's writing at proof stage and publication stage, the image of the desired state of childhood or death is 'ravaged'. Private communication between individuals is interrupted by the Press: communication is made public. For De Quincey, publication prefigures all communication in writing. The text attempts to reverse the sequence of social relations in which it is published, to privilege the private. The occluded sub-text of 'Suspiria de Profundis' concerns the restoration of individuality (of the 'visionary'). The text cannot logically function as De Quincey would wish, the monadic nature of bourgeois society notwithstanding; at least, he fears that it cannot function. The fear of the loss of individuality and the fear of the destruction of the middle-classes (see Chapter 5) are united in this paper.

Death represents a desirable state – it is a figure for the complete realisation of the individual self. Its concomitant, resurrection, is not convincingly figured in 'Suspiria de Profundis', for reasons connected with its publication. In the 'Autobiographic Sketches' elements of 'Suspiria de Profundis' are repeated, here with the emphasis on resurrection. The entire work, which revises so many of De Quincey's papers, formally signifies the possibilities of resurrection. Just as the form of 'Suspiria de Profundis' had to some extent determined its 'message' (and left it ambiguously depressing in its effect), the form of the 'Autobiographic Sketches' produces a sense of its particular theme. The loose, disconnected form ironically suggests the very individuality that De Quincey had formerly sought in the highly wrought impassioned prose of 'Suspiria de Profundis'. The process of revising a number of contradictory texts generates the exploration of rebirth which unifies the chapters of the 'Autobiographic Sketches'. The form, then, to an extent generates the content: the means of production determine the substance of what can be written. De Quincey's work does not 'progress' as such, in the sense that means of production stay stable while he autonomously improves his ideas. Instead, the various working environments (by which I mean the different social relations) generate various possibilities which he then explores. (In a sense, this is quite obvious: his works for *Tait's* and *Blackwood's* differ considerably, even though his relationship to the proprietor and to the machinery of the Press in each case is similar. The political views and 'identity' of the journal demands a specific type of work). The revised text of the 'Autobiographic Sketches' draws on a variety of essays, each of which is significant of different working methods, and demands a new method by which the author rereads and rewrites his earlier works – works which prefigure his performative self in the present of composition. Hence the increased emphasis on the child De Quincey's 'pariah' character, an emphasis reinforced in the vastly expanded, meandering revision of the *Confessions*. Whereas in the *Tait's* 'Sketches' and 'A Sketch from Childhood' De Quincey had written of his father at some length, in the 'Autobiographic Sketches' references to him are minimal. Thus, in 'A Sketch from Childhood' he remarks that he knew his father 'through *a priori* ideas' (*Hogg's Instructor*, vol. VI, p. 147): he is aware of something which precedes him, a non-experiential authority. In the revised text, this comment is omitted: not his father but the acts which point out his character precede and form the De Quincey of the 'Autobiographic Sketches'. In a sense, his *other* texts are his 'father'. His revision of them entails a recognition of himself in them: they are symbolic acts which he interprets anew.

Revision, Christianity and 'the idea of woman'

The 'Autobiographic Sketches' overhauls numerous autobiographical papers, in all of which De Quincey characterises his task as one of gathering materials together for future interpretation. Thus, the pre-pubescent detective of 'Sketches of Life and Manners' collects evidence which allows him insight as an adult into otherwise 'mysterious' behaviour:

> My mother, agitated between the necessities of hospitality, on the one hand, and her horror, on the other hand, to meet a woman, for the first time in her life, openly professing infidelity, at length fell ill; and this hastened Mrs. L's departure; not, however, before I, a child of eight years old, had seen things which nobody else suspected (*Tait's*, vol. I, New Series, [February 1834], p. 23).

In the *Tait's* papers the Opium-Eater is a detective *par excellence*: in the main growing up is for De Quincey the accumulation of evidence for future analysis. In both 'Suspiria de Profundis' and 'A Sketch from Childhood' De Quincey writes of the 'involutes' of consciousness, again suggesting that the individual unconsciously accumulates impressions which only make sense later on:

> I [. . .] was quite unable to explain my own impressions from the passage in 'Aladdin;' but I did not the less obstinately

persist in believing a sublimity which I could not understand. It was, in fact, one of those many important cases which elsewhere I have called *involutes* of human sensibility; combinations in which the materials of future thought or feeling are carried as imperceptibly into the mind as vegetable seeds are carried in various states of combination through the atmosphere, or by means of rivers, into remote countries. One eternal babble we hear about Lord Bacon, and not theorising (by which all respectable blockheads mean *à priorising*, a far different thing), but relying only on experience: the truth being, that as soon as ever any the most positive experience does not quadrate with popular ideas, as in mesmeric phenomena, everybody treats the experience with laughter and scorn, showing thus the most obstinate hostility to Lord Bacon (*Hogg's Instructor*, vol. VIII, p. 277) (See also 1: 13.)

The major revision of these papers in the 'Autobiographic Sketches' constitutes an analogous interpretation of an extant body of ideas. The 'Autobiographic Sketches' emphasises the value of reinterpretation. In the revision De Quincey attempts to produce an entirely new text, one which formally does not rely on 'experience' – on the known methods of production. De Quincey does not sequentially repeat previous papers, but places diverse narratives in a context which alters their given meaning. The venture is decidedly risky. De Quincey's desire to articulate the 'truth' necessitates the creation of a radical, disturbing macaronic text which itself requires reinterpretation. Chronology is more or less abandoned: infant experience is followed by impressions of dreams some fifty years subsequent (the 'Dream Echoes' of the 'Autobiographic Sketches', placed so deliberately after 'The Affliction of Childhood', is the same text quickly rigged as a '*jury*-mast' in 'Suspiria de Profundis' [*L* 137]). Similarly, the autobiographical narrative breaks down: the text turns to Irish history.[9] The method seems quite random and incoherent. However, just as the form in part reinforces De Quincey's belief in the involuted production of consciousness, it also challenges the reader to accept, or at least consider, that apparent disorder is grounded in a 'hidden' ethical system. The text details a series of deaths and rebirths, all of which are informed by De Quincey's suggestion that the revision of experience (in memory, in writing) is a product of Christianity. The process of revision is itself revised: De Quincey places his work in a new register within which the 'truth' may be understood as a *method*. The writer's meandering autobiography is an imitation of Christ, not only in the journey he undertakes and the sufferings which it involves, but in the process by which he represents himself in the revisionary text. In the 'Autobiographic Sketches' De Quincey explains the significance of the term *metanoia*. His 'profoundly just' and 'undeniably novel' (2: 46) interpretation of what the term means reflects upon the entire enterprise of his writing:

> The *meta* carried with it an emphatic expression of its original idea – the idea of transfer, of translation, of transformation; or, if we prefer a Grecian to a Roman apparelling, the idea of a *metamorphosis*. And this idea, to what is it applied? Upon what object is this idea of spiritual transfiguration made to bear? Simply upon the *noetic* or intellectual faculty – the faculty of shaping and conceiving things under their true relations. [. . .] *Metanoeite* – contemplate moral truth as radiating from a new centre: apprehend it under transfigured relations. [. . .] Christ occupied another station. Not only was he the original Interpreter, but he was himself the Author – Founder, at once, and Finisher – of that great transfiguration applied to ethics, which he and the Baptist alike announced as forming the code for the new and revolutionary era now opening its endless career. The human race was summoned to bring a transfiguring sense and spirit of interpretation (*metanoia*) to a transfigured ethics – an altered organ to an altered object (2: 47).

Rebirth means establishing oneself at and as a new centre, re-centring the self. However, despite the fact that he defines the revisionary process as an articulation of a specific ethical outlook, De Quincey does not deal directly with orthodox religious matters, but rather approaches Christianity in an allegorical manner. Indeed, his religious beliefs are an inflexion of his method of writing, not the other way round: writing is primary. The tool by which Christianity is chiefly revealed to the individual in De Quincey's 'Autobiographic Sketches' is *woman*.[10] For De Quincey, women represent, on one hand, the continuation of humanity, biologically: posterity is dependent on people being born; and, on the other hand, the possibility of a revolutionary cycle, the inflexion of Christianity.

The 'Autobiographic Sketches' details the influence of a number of women on De Quincey and others. In the later sections of the work, the principal figure who attests to the beneficial effects of female company is Lord Massey. Massey is a figure of the transformed man with which De Quincey identifies (albeit with a sense of irony: Massey is reborn when he marries, but it is a bath and not a wife which makes the youthful De Quincey 'a new creature' [2: 4]). The identification is almost total, as De Quincey's description of the change in Massey's character emphasises:

> In passing through the park-gates of Laxton, on my departure northward, powerfully, and as if 'with the might of waters,' my mind turned round to contemplate that strange enlargement of my experience which had happened to me within the last three months. I had seen, and become familiarly acquainted with, a young man, who had in a manner died to every object around

him, had died an intellectual death, and suddenly had been called back to life and real happiness – had been, in effect, raised from the dead – by the accident of meeting a congenial female companion (2: 57).

Massey's wife, who revives his intellectual powers and calls him back to life, symbolises the positive powers of Christianity, a religious system which to De Quincey is valuable precisely in so far as it unifies experience. This equation between Christ and the woman is significant, for it provides the key to De Quincey's depiction of the various 'lost' females in his autobiographical writings.

De Quincey characterises Christ as Author, Interpreter, Writer and Reader (2: 47). The tasks that for De Quincey as an autobiographer necessitate mediate action – the use of language, the use of a journal to communicate his self to others – are for Christ a matter of immediacy. The analytical interpretation of memory is simultaneous with remembrance. Christ, like the redeeming females in De Quincey's autobiographical works, constitutes a unified pre-text. His practice of translation, of revising experiential reality by placing it within an immediately communicated code, prefigures the efforts of De Quincey. Christ provides a paradigm for De Quincey's literary methods. De Quincey's revised 'Autobiographic Sketches' boldly suggests that his otherwise fugitive efforts at providing 'entertainment' are in truth representative texts expressive of an essential and profound supernatural impulse.

Women represent to De Quincey the possibility of revivifying such an impulse: they signify 'the angelic ideal buried and imbruted in man's sordid race' (1: 353).[11] His own reaction to the ideal in the state of 'Premature Manhood' experienced in Laxton typically suggests the possibility of failure to achieve the ideal. It is ironic that De Quincey should wish to embrace the *brute depths* in the 'Eden' of Laxton (1: 368). He is obliged to attempt to overcome a special trial in order to reach the desired appreciation of 'true relations': faced with the spectacle of schoolboy society as one option and the company of women as the other, De Quincey remarks that he 'heard some irresistible voice saying:- Lay aside thy fleshly robes of humanity, and enter for a season into some brutal incarnation' (1: 365).

Women, or rather the singular De Quinceyan ideal of woman, reappear repeatedly in the 'Autobiographic Sketches'. The pattern of this reappearance constitutes a re-interpretation of the *Confessions* (just as 'Suspiria de Profundis' had been; the 'Autobiographic Sketches' formally parallels 'Suspiria de Profundis'). Read through the 'Autobiographic Sketches', the transformation of Ann in De Quincey's dreams in the *Confessions* alters in meaning. Whereas in the original *Confessions* Ann's resurrection was largely a delusion, an indication of the dreamer's unrealisable hopes, in the revised text (or in the *Confessions* read through the revision of the 'Autobiographic Sketches'), her transformation functions as an image of textual revision. The text of the *Confessions* is thus equated with a positive and wide-reaching principle of revision (which is not the case when it is read in isolation). This shift in meaning is, of course, reinforced in the revised *Confessions*: details such as the appendage of 'The Daughter of Lebanon' to the text bolster De Quincey's new investment in Christianity. A similar manifestation of De Quincey's optimism exists in the depiction of the orphan heiresses in the 'Autobiographic Sketches'. The lives of the heiresses provide a direct analogy to those of the women in the moribund scenes of 'Suspiria de Profundis':

> Strange, indeed, was the contrast between the silent past of their lives and that populous future to which their large fortunes would probably introduce them. Throw open a door in the rear that should lay bare the long vista of chambers through which their childhood might symbolically be represented as having travelled, – what silence! – what solemn solitude! Open a door in advance that should do the same figurative office for the future, – suddenly what a jubilation! what a tumult of festal greetings!
>
> But the succeeding stages of life did not, perhaps, in either case fully correspond to the early promise (1: 27-8).

The change of emphasis – the 'Autobiographic Sketches' is not nearly as grim as 'Suspiria de Profundis' – reflects De Quincey's characterisation of the woman as a figure of redemption, a characterisation reinforced in the revised *Confessions*. The woman saves the writer: he is dependent on her, as his revision is dependent on his earlier texts.

What De Quincey means by the 'ideal of woman' is a pre-textual principle which revives within the text, a principle which requires a continuation: not a ground of meaning as such, but the operation of a process which cannot be properly articulated.[12] Manhood is the recognition of the latent ideal of woman, the woman who points De Quincey out as a mature adult. Manhood consists of the manifestation of what he describes as 'the reverential feeling, sometimes suddenly developed, towards woman, and the idea of woman' (1: 353). Woman represents a state outside labour for De Quincey. In his writings, women are invariably confined to the domestic realm or to childhood (even the Ladies of Sorrow of the 'Suspiria' are 'of one mysterious household' [*L* 149]). Ann is a notable exception (one which proves the rule), a woman buried in the working environment of the capital. The loss of the prostitute who labours to support herself in the hostile city of London strengthens the links between the capital and the grave, two enclosing structures which De Quincey can penetrate imaginatively. The figure of Ann, a figure of the ideal text lost in the labour relations of the Press, complements that of Elizabeth, the child who need never enter the web of capitalist relations (see Chapter

6). Elizabeth figures an ideal text *outside the Press*: and in this sense, she is forever out of reach, necessarily.

Both Ann and Elizabeth are figures of imminent integration, which is to say, of positively valorised death. The woman signifies a state out of reach to the writer De Quincey. His investment in a conservative middle-class vision of life consists in part of a definition of writing as an inadequate and incomplete *version* of the pre-text which it can never fully reveal. So too the fascination with the death of the other, with the realisation of a self which the woman apparently is allowed, but which De Quincey can never obtain (since the death of the woman entails the loss of a part of himself), arises as the inflection of a process of writing.

The revisionary process suggests that life is not quantitatively enough: that there ought to be more. Further, it has a qualitative compensatory factor: the afterlife is the 'better' state that throws into relief the real. It suggests a set of values to which the real must aspire. The real, then, is always inadequate. There is an economy here: the afterlife is posited as the reward for what happens in life: one inputs so much effort here, but gets no reward. Payment is deferred, as the promise of proper communication, of a self, of a completed text is always deferred in the De Quinceyan text.

De Quincey is the master of deferred payment. His text expresses again and again that the payment is yet to come. But the contract is never fulfilled, nor will it be. His text articulates as an occluded agenda the possibility that the reward of an afterlife is nothing more and nothing less than a vain self-delusion. His writing attests to the possibility of the failure or collapse of his belief. The enterprise of writing does not necessarily entail 'payment': it may never be read as De Quincey intends – and in a sense, it *can* never be read in this way. De Quincey's text invariably functions in the absence of a 'confidante', an 'Elizabeth' whose remembered existence testifies to the possibility and lack of resolution. Having embarked on the infinite project of his autobiography he is trapped within the confines of a mediated discourse. Repeatedly his autobiographical text suggests an unresolved fear that resurrection, grounded in the delusive possibility of realising the ideal text, may be denied: that his writing is not read, that his self does not exist, that the ever-revolving fact of his own death cannot be positively charged. The form of experience for De Quincey remains essentially the same throughout his writings. It consists of a search after an ideal text – one which has yet to be written – and a chase after this text even as it is removed from the writer's control in the process of publication. De Quincey's actions consist of an attempt to retrieve, to repossess the already-lost:

> The search after the lost features of Ann, which I spoke of as pursued in the crowds of London, was in a more proper sense pursued through many a year in dreams. The general

> idea of a search and a chase reproduced itself in many shapes. The person, the rank, the age, the scenical position, all varied themselves for ever; but the same leading traits more or less faintly remained of a lost Pariah woman, and of some shadowy malice which withdrew her, or attempted to withdraw her, from restoration and from hope (5: xv. Prefatory Notice to the *Confessions*).

Ultimately, to suggest that he 'succeeds' or 'fails' in his task is inapposite, for the action of retrieval is paradoxical, reliant as it is on the *loss* of what he desires to *retrieve*. For De Quincey, the 'Pariah woman' – namely, the wandering, autonomous, rejected De Quinceyan autobiographical text – is always out of reach.

Biographical Interventions:
Sketches of Coleridge and Wordsworth;
and 'Sir William Hamilton'

> 'No man escapes the contagion from his contemporary bystanders' ('Alexander Pope', [9: 1]).

In this chapter I focus on some of De Quincey's biographical essays. I distinguish between 'autobiographical' and 'biographical' papers strategically, so as to allow for an exploration of these terms, which in many instances are arbitrary. Several of De Quincey's biographical papers appear within the body of his autobiographical essays; others again are in the main extended reviews; and a few are more or less straightforward sketches of his contemporaries. In the argument that follows I suggest that what purports to be biography is actually occluded self-representation. When De Quincey writes biography the self-in-writing, which always seems other than himself, becomes the subject of a series of substitutions: as other, it offers him the apparent security of negative self-definition – *I am not he* – only to become, in an endlessly repeated process, a doppelgänger – another who is also, appallingly, 'oneself repeated once too often' (12: 185). In his important biographical sketches of Coleridge and Wordsworth, this process is enriched by the conjunction of personal memory with literary influence. As a result, the problem of who De Quincey is – the autobiographer's anxiety – grows into the question of whether, as a writer, De Quincey can claim an identity secure from contamination by those who have influenced and formed him. Inevitably, these influences include the extant autobiographical text, which in revision (either at proof level in the case of the originally published sketches, or later for the collected works) tends to produce a radically new self. It would seem, then, that De Quincey's claims to be himself, which he makes in the autobiographical interventions, are always negated by those same interventions, while his biographical papers similarly offer little reassurance. Thus, in his curious papers on Sir William Hamilton, though De Quincey faces no threat from literary influences, the result, far from being 'pure' biography, is a kind of fantasia in and about the anxieties of memory, of writing, of publication. A series of wry textual jokes points to a fear that textuality itself – the accumulated mass of his own (and others') previous work, and the current paper with which he is concerned as it slides into previousness – constitutes a doppelgänger which threatens to negate the writer's claims to selfhood and which articulates, if not his non-existence, the sense of an identity constituted only within the restrictive confines of the Press.

The numerous allusions and references to, and quotations from, Wordsworth and Coleridge in De Quincey's writings (especially the overtly autobiographical papers) imply that a fundamental link exists between memory, writing and the relationship of the autobiographer to his influences. De Quincey cannot recall his past self (or selves) without also recalling the figures of influence whose existence 'contaminates' his own. The effect of these influences is to imply that self-definition, the autobiographer's purported task, is necessarily impossible: De Quincey does not possess that kind of independence. Conversely, his self-image informs his representation of others. The biographical papers tend towards autobiography.

This self-destructive tendency is perhaps most powerfully expressed in those of the *Tait's Edinburgh Magazine* 'Sketches' concerned with Wordsworth and Coleridge,[1] but the blurring of nominal subject and occult subject (De Quincey himself: or writing itself) is a feature of many of De Quincey's biographies.[2] De Quincey's own experiences, and the representations of these, tend to provide the basis for his representation of other people's lives.

Coleridge

This subjectivity is most obvious in his representations of Coleridge, the special butt of many of De Quincey's most merciless remarks. Coleridge's usefulness for De Quincey is extensive. He is by turns flawed genius, moral coward, intellectual giant, great poet, pathetic failure, clown and social misfit (among other things). De Quincey characterises Coleridge as a model of excess, an *extreme* figure placed at the end of a long line of substitutions – metaphorical substitutions for De Quincey's self or more particularly for his potential self. Coleridge can invariably be of use in De Quincey's writings because, more than referring to an extra-textual entity, 'Coleridge' implies the endless possibilities of substitution for De Quincey. He is a short-cut to meaningfulness, a figure of death or extremity which must continually be erased – only to be rewritten.

De Quincey's initial meeting with Coleridge as recounted in *Tait's* (September 1834) is of significance in this context. Having explained that his quest for Coleridge had been baffled more than once, De Quincey reports a conversation alleged to have taken place between himself and Thomas Poole, concerning Coleridge's supposed plagiarisms of certain ideas – or, more precisely, of certain tropes. De Quincey's Poole claims that Coleridge 'sometimes steals from other people [. . .] just as a poor creature like myself might do, that sometimes have not wherewithal to make a figure from my own exchequer' (*Tait's* vol. I, p. 510). Coleridge's compulsive and inexplicable consumption of other people's 'figures', arising from an inability or unwillingness to use his own 'figure', is a crucial part of De Quincey's characterisation of him. De Quincey first locates Coleridge psychologically, finding him out and establishing his chief mental traits. Next he reinforces this image of Coleridge in the description of how he physically locates him. Coleridge is sighted standing under 'a gateway corresponding to the description given me' (*Tait's*, vol. I, p. 513), De Quincey writes – and in this particular Coleridge corresponds to an apparition remarked in a fragment published posthumously. There De Quincey writes that every person has a year of crisis 'in which the light-hearted sense of the *irresponsible* ceases to gild the heavenly dawn. A year there is [. . .] within the gates of which, underneath the gloomy archway of which, sits a phantom of yourself' (*PW* 1: 25). Such a phantom is Coleridge: he is a figure of a gloomy, unavoidable future state. De Quincey recognises him from his eyes, 'from the peculiar appearance of haze or dreaminess, which mixed with their light,' into which De Quincey looks, though himself unseen 'for a minute or more' (*Tait's*, vol. I, p. 513). Physical characteristics notwithstanding, it is clear that a doppelgänger has been sighted. De Quincey, in announcing his own name, at once reconnects Coleridge to the waking reality from which he seems detached and takes control of the situation to the extent of implicitly claiming immediate insight into Coleridge's mind:

> The sound of my voice, announcing my own name, first awoke him: he started, and, for a moment, seemed at a loss to understand my purpose or his own situation: for he repeated rapidly a number of words which had no relation to either of us (*Tait's* vol. I [September 1834], p. 513).

This claim, that Coleridge's words (signifiers without referents which he *repeats*) meant nothing to *him*, is clearly only speculative. De Quincey has already absorbed (has stolen the figure of) Coleridge, who is unable in De Quincey's eyes to articulate the significance of this meeting. For De Quincey, Coleridge's existence is a spiritual and literary problem. In 'Modern Superstition' (1840), he writes of

> that universal faith which made it impossible for any man to survive a bodily commerce, by whatever sense, with a spiritual being. We find it in the Old Testament, where the expression, "I have seen God, and shall die," means simply a supernatural being: since no Hebrew believed it possible for

a nature purely human to sustain for a moment the sight of the Infinite Being. We find the same faith amongst ourselves, in the case of *doppelgänger* becoming apparent to the sight of those whom they counterfeit; and in many other varieties (3: 333–4).

That De Quincey deliberately searches out his doppelgänger Coleridge implies a death-wish, or at least a desire to experience extremity; or, conversely, the representation of Coleridge is another articulation of the extremity of writing, a way of dealing with self-annihilation. De Quincey's verbal self-identification which, in the sense that a doppelgänger anticipates or copies the 'original', should produce a similar response from Coleridge, instead causes the latter to articulate a meaningless series of words. 'De Quincey', the doppelgänger's expected response, is replaced with a garbled repetition which signifies the destruction of De Quincey's identity – and it is this that Coleridge suggests. Coleridge's disconnection from the world, demonstrated in his day-dreaming, is also a disconnection from what constitutes his identity. He has 'difficulty in recovering his position amongst day-light realities' (*Tait's*, vol. I, p. 513) and within language. Having relocated himself – at the centre of things, as a self-sufficient entity who is himself a centre – Coleridge embarks upon a three-hour long monologue (*Tait's*, vol. I, p. 515) which is interrupted only by the appearance of his wife (who, as 'the lady' of the passage given immediately below, seems herself to have a fragmented and uncertain identity). The result is again disconnection:

> In a frigid tone he said, whilst turning to me, "Mrs Coleridge:" in some slight way he then presented me to her: I bowed; and the lady almost immediately retired (*Tait's*, vol. I p. 515).

Here Coleridge's role as husband is virtually self-negating in that Mrs Coleridge is reduced to a cipher in the narrative. Her silent entrance and exit, marked only by Coleridge's anxious utterance, defines her as little more than a ghost. Implicitly, Coleridge and his wife, domestic doppelgängers, are mutually self-destructive entities. Mrs Coleridge's 'figure' has been stolen in marriage: she is existentially dead. De Quincey's narrative asserts that her personality has been eroded (and in doing so, one might add, De Quincey uses her as a figure in his autobiographical text, which makes his writing analogous to Coleridge's theft of others' figures). He reduces the Coleridges' marriage and asserts his control over a telling scene of domestic discord in this sketch. The brief vision of Mrs Coleridge acts as a warning of the possibility of annihilation that the existence of the doppelgänger entails. The meeting articulates Coleridge's destructive powers.

In the revised confessions De Quincey again crucially underlines

Coleridge's instability in domestic or social terms, indulging in a great deal of *schadenfreude*. Once again Mrs Coleridge is seen as a victim of her husband's destructive tendencies:

> It is notorious, that in Bristol (to *that* I can speak myself, but probably in many other places) he went so far as to hire men – porters, hackney-coachmen, and others – to oppose by force his entrance into any druggist's shop. But, as the authority for stopping him was derived simply from himself, naturally these poor men found themselves in a metaphysical fix, not provided for even by Thomas Aquinas or by the prince of Jesuitical casuists. And in this excrutiating dilemma would occur such scenes as the following:-
>
> "Oh, sir," would plead the suppliant porter – suppliant, yet semi-imperative (for equally if he *did*, and if he did *not*, show fight, the poor man's daily 5s. seemed endangered) – "really you must not; consider, sir, your wife and – "
>
> *Transcendental Philosopher.* – "Wife! what wife? I have no wife."*
>
> *Porter.* – But, really now, you must not, sir. Didn't you say no longer ago than yesterday –
>
> *Transcend. Philos.'* – Pooh, pooh! yesterday is a long time ago. Are you aware, my man, that people are known to have dropped down dead for timely want of opium?
>
> *Porter.* – Ay, but you tell't me not to hearken –
>
> *Transcend. Philos.* – Oh, nonsense. An emergency, a shocking emergency, has arisen – quite unlooked for. No matter what I told you in times long past. That, which I *now* tell you, is – that, if you don't remove that arm of yours from the doorway of this most respectable druggist, I shall have a good ground of action against you for assault and battery.
>
> Am I the man to reproach Coleridge with this vassalage to opium? Heaven forbid! Having groaned myself under that yoke, I pity, and blame him not.
>
> *Vide* "Othello" [De Quincey's footnote] (5: 9–10).

The dislocation of verbal authority here results in a dilemma. Coleridge claims that the verbal contract made with the porter is invalid, even though he has already insisted that this invalidation is invalid. His strategy amounts to a suicidal threat which attempts to shift the responsibility for self-destruction onto another. De Quincey explicitly condemns this action, though he still delights in the 'fix'. He characterises Coleridge as unable to maintain a consistent, logically coherent verbal motion. Coleridge denies the marital status of Mrs Coleridge and also her very existence. The quotation from *Othello* in this scene raises the question of the connection between Coleridge's use of opium and the apparent failure of his marriage. In the original *Tait's* sketch De Quincey observes that Coleridge was strangely unhappy and that 'the accursed drug poisoned all natural pleasure at its sources' (*Tait's* vol. I, p. 686). This explicit comment is modified in the revision of this sketch, where De Quincey instead asks, 'opium, was it, or what was it, that poisoned all natural pleasure at its sources?' (2: 209) – an open-ended question that allows for any amount of speculation.

De Quincey purposes in many of his later writings to differentiate between his own use and valorisation of opium and that of Coleridge. By characterising Coleridge as an irrational, excessive tyrant, De Quincey calls into question his condemnation of the *Confessions* and of 'the Opium-Eater', views made public in a letter published in James Gillman's *Life of Samuel Taylor Coleridge* in 1838. For Coleridge, the use of opium and De Quincey's writing are both 'sinful', a reading which the title of De Quincey's work prompts, but which contradicts his thesis. Coleridge questions the basis for De Quincey 'confessing' anything at all, both in the letter and in his own use of opium. His assertion that opium is sinful (he begs God to 'shew mercy on the author of the "Confessions of an Opium-Eater," if, as I have too strong reason to believe, his book has been the occasion of seducing others into the withering vice through wantonness'[3]) allows for a confession of its use; but Coleridge implies that the writing, far from being a confession is an articulation of De Quincey's 'morbid vanity' – that the *Confessions* is a series of boasts.

The adoption of the pseudonym of 'the Opium-Eater' involves De Quincey in an antagonistic struggle with Coleridge, the other opium-eater, whose claim to authority, if not exercised openly while he was alive, asserts itself after his death. Between the two versions of the *Confessions* lies a mass of commentary on Coleridge as an opium-user, a commentary which seeks to extend De Quincey's autobiographical persona. If De Quincey cannot forget the fact of Coleridge's habit, which threatens his adopted role, he can at least try to invalidate it, even though this is a risky business in the light of the laborious self-defence that must accompany such criticism.

Coleridge's life, apparently destroyed by opium, seems to negate all that makes De Quincey's experience coherent and valuable. Though Coleridge was prolific and astounding '*in spite of* opium', De Quincey states his belief that the drug had 'killed Coleridge as a poet' (*Blackwood's*, vol. LVII, p. 130). In contrast, De Quincey survives and transcends the negative effect of opium, placing his experience within the context of Christian belief, and strategically undermining Coleridge's objections. Perhaps the clearest expression of De Quincey's attitudes on this subject is found in 'Coleridge and Opium-Eating', first published in *Blackwood's* in January 1845. Here De Quincey draws a parallel between what he sees as the religious origin and rebirth of mankind (Adam and Christ respectively represent these states); and his own literary 'origin' in the first version of the *Confessions* and 'rebirth' in 'Suspiria de Profundis', announced at the end of this paper as 'a sequel or *finale*' to those Confessions' (*Blackwood's*, vol. LVII, p. 132) and published in March, April, June and July 1845. As an apt expression of the enlargement of the faculty of mental vision brought about by the use of opium, De Quincey cites some lines from Milton's *Paradise Lost*. In the poem Adam is enabled to penetrate 'Even to the inmost self of mental sight'. Opium's 'characteristic virtue', De Quincey argues, lies in the way it powers the introspective tendency of those with a 'higher sensibility'. He gives his own experience a broad social relevance and accounts for his writing as a worthy by-product necessitated by his use of the drug:

> Now, in the original higher sensibility is found some palliation for the *practice* of opium-eating; in the greater temptation is a greater excuse. And in this faculty of self-revelation is found some palliation for *reporting* the case to the world, which palliation both Coleridge and his biographer have overlooked (*Blackwood's*, vol. LVII, p. 132).

De Quincey's extenuatory gloss on the *Confessions* underlines the non-confessional status of the text. To circumlocute potential redundancy, De Quincey must so contextualise the *Confessions* as to allow the work to function as a valid, coherent text, in spite of its non-confessional status. (Indeed, it is possible to read many of De Quincey's writings as an extensive rewriting of the original *Confessions*.)

Coleridge's function as a figure of imminent catastrophe is important and the extra-textual entity whose actions and works are repeatedly referred to by De Quincey should not obscure the metaphorical use of 'Coleridge' throughout De Quincey's writings, especially as regards the theme of resurrection formally articulated in De Quincey's major autobiographies. Coleridge's failure to produce extenuatory text allows De Quincey to represent him as a pathetic failure (akin to Lawson and 'K' in the revised *Confessions*) whose life ends in, if not oblivion, irreparable disintegration.[4]

De Quincey, in contrast, represents his own life as a prelude to rebirth. He confesses his errors, but is astute enough to construct the means of redemption as well. However, his reliance on the figure of Coleridge (a disintegrated self-portrait) has the ironic effect of continually preserving the disintegrated Coleridge. His self-justification at Coleridge's expense has the destructive effect of realising the self-disintegration De Quincey wishes to avoid, in that his connection to Coleridge appears quite complete. De Quincey's malicious observations, the relish with which he depicts his rival's discomfort, turn him into a figure of destruction so that

Biographical Interventions

Coleridge tends to appear victimised by De Quincey as much as the other way round. In 'Coleridge and Opium-Eating' De Quincey deflects such connotations by referring to himself in the third person, defending 'ourselves and our friend the author of the *Opium Confessions*' (*Blackwood's*, vol. LVII, p. 131). Through the relocation of the self-disintegration embodied in the connection to Coleridge, De Quincey strengthens and preserves the persona of the Opium-Eater. Coleridge as doppelgänger is temporarily erased by the figure of the disinterested essayist who defends the Opium-Eater. The existential murder of Coleridge, though it is also De Quincey's 'suicide' (for he ceases to be the Opium-Eater here), dismisses the one while allowing for the resurrection of the other. At the close of the essay the success and survival of the Opium-Eater is emphasised by the announcement of the forthcoming 'Suspiria de Profundis'. The precedence of the Opium-Eater, of the written self, as a doppelgänger is underlined: Coleridge is emphatically reduced to the status of a useful tool. De Quincey eventually drops the fiction of being a disinterested third-party in the essay itself, a sign of the localised and variable demands of metaphor rather than of the writer's inability to sustain coherently a single metaphorical figure.

The argument in 'Coleridge and Opium-Eating' exercises De Quincey's fears of oblivion and the confrontation of his death-wish quite openly. The specular figure of Coleridge is an object of fascination for De Quincey, like death. Coleridge in many ways seems to embody extremity (as Adam and Christ incarnate origin and resurrection) and as such can be and is recalled again and again. The vast possibilities of the figure of extremity imply that Coleridge can be filled out (like the moments of catastrophe). De Quincey is led to return to him almost inevitably. The convergence of the two characters is bound up in the process of writing: as the present-time of composition is an instance of extremity, De Quincey is liable to use Coleridge for any purpose. The 'real' figure is not particularly important in this context. However, De Quincey, faced with a contradiction between the real (extra-textual, biological) and unreal (textual) figures of Coleridge is obliged to draw fine distinctions between the two. This action, as it takes place in writing, using the figurative Coleridge where it requires the extra-textual Coleridge (an impossibility), produces extreme anxiety. De Quincey reacts by denying any kinship with Coleridge, a patently false denial. A note to the revised version of the sketch originally published in *Tait's* asserts the 'fix' that De Quincey must face:

> But, *thirdly*, I must inform the reader, that I was not, nor ever had been, the 'friend' of Coleridge in any sense which could have a right to restrain my frankest opinions upon his merits.
>
> I never had lived in such intercourse with Coleridge as to give me an opportunity of becoming his friend. To *him* I owed

nothing at all; but to the public, to the body of his own readers, every writer owes the truth, and especially on a subject so important as that which was then before me (2: 347).[5]

De Quincey effectively denies that the metaphorical interdependence of the two characters in the autobiographical text had any basis in reality. Whereas his persona is grounded to a certain extent on his connection with Coleridge, here De Quincey transfers the validation of the text to a connection with 'the public'. De Quincey denies the existence of any social relationship with Coleridge such as might require consistent behaviour, though in doing so he also forges a new link with Coleridge, for the public is both De Quincey's and Coleridge's. The location of convergence is shifted, in a way which limits the implicit influence of Coleridge on De Quincey. Simultaneously, however, De Quincey's declared insight into Coleridge's mind and the 'truth' alleged in the writings he tries to defend are both rendered suspect. De Quincey clears new ground for himself only to fill it up as quickly as possible. The appeal to the metaphorical public produces more text, and De Quincey's apparently scrupulous attempt to clarify matters obscures the original error of making the delusive connection at all – between himself and Coleridge (locally), and between himself and the figure of the self on the page (generally).

At the moment of composition, De Quincey, in that he is alive, is faced with a problem. Unable to experience the oblivion represented by the figure of Coleridge (who at the time of De Quincey's writing of his 'Sketches' was dead), unable to ignore the demands of his writing, he is forced to react towards a signifier which threatens his own signified claim to uniqueness. 'The Opium-Eater' is not De Quincey, but a figure – one which is repeatedly rewritten. The writer's anxious attitude towards the figure of the self and of Coleridge, the doppelgänger, is also an articulation of his attitude towards the autobiographical text with which he is concerned. His anxiety is masked by a curiously morbid joke:

> Any of us would be jealous of his own duplicate; and, if I had a *doppel-ganger* who went about personating me, copying me, and pirating me, philosopher as I am, I might (if the Court of Chancery would not grant an injunction against him) be so far carried away by jealousy as to attempt the crime of murder upon his carcass; and no great matter as regards HIM. But it would be a sad thing for *me* to find myself hanged; and for what, I beseech you? for murdering a sham, that was either nobody at all, or oneself repeated once too often (12: 185).

Both Coleridge and De Quincey, as they are represented in the latter's writings, are 'shams' in the sense that both are figures for extra-textual entities. Coleridge is indeed 'nobody at all', merely a sign in the chain of substitution which De Quincey forges so that 'the Opium-Eater' or 'XYZ' (he rarely uses his own name) can keep

Biographical Interventions 73

one step ahead of oblivion. Both metaphor as emptiness (lack) and metaphor as an infinitely extendable series of substitutions – 'oneself repeated' for ever – require complex manoeuvring on the part of the autobiographer if he is to survive. The autobiographical text articulates and produces anxiety: it is a 'sad thing', a striving towards the impossible. De Quincey, especially in his later works, is obliged to react to the influential signified self embodied in his writing – 'his own duplicate'. That his revisions often distort and in some cases destroy the meaning apparently given by the 'original' papers can be interpreted as a sign of the lack of coherence of the self and also of the possibility of autobiographical definition. The problem as to whether it is the extra-textual writer or writing itself that is uttered finds its solution in the same destructive result: when De Quincey writes 'If I had a doppelgänger' &c. is the real self or the written self being referred to? The antagonistic struggle for authority can clearly never be resolved in these terms, which are nevertheless its limits. The equilibrium between antagonistic forces, which for De Quincey provide the form of reality, can be interpreted as the ideological projection of this problem with writing (rather than, as De Quincey implies, an extra-textual, observable form which itself requires representation in his prose).

This state of affairs, however, does not leave De Quincey in a completely intolerable position, since it offers the possibility of assuming a role by which the anticipated catastrophe can be temporarily circumlocuted, namely the role of victim. As such, the task of sighting the numberless doppelgängers that comprise the self, doppelgängers which must be simultaneously sighting *him*, can be handled. The collapse of meaning produced by the ironically destructive self-identification of the writer – involved as he is in a flight and pursuit with his other selves, aware that he is already 'dead', already 'resurrected', already 'dying' once more, that his identity is constantly shifting – can be overcome by locating what constitutes his identity within an oppressive structure of which he is the nameless victim. The threatening figure of the doppelgänger is translated into memory, whether this figure be Coleridge, De Quincey as Opium-Eater or the extant autobiographical text (that is, the body of writing De Quincey has already written at any point from which he prepares to write more). It is reconstituted so that the disintegration can be prefigured rather than acknowledged as the ever-present state of the autobiographer.

Such an activity is traumatic, for it results in an admission of being unable to know what constitutes or what limits the self. De Quincey's dependence on the figure of Coleridge is complemented by his reliance on Wordsworth, who functions as a figure of a hypothetically stable self (which, as such, is potentially about to collapse).⁶ Both Coleridge and Wordsworth indicate the impossibility of De Quincey's maintenance of a coherent self within his autobiography. It is a short step from this to a characterisation of De Quincey as failure and Coleridge/Wordsworth as success, a polarised relationship which is consistent with De Quincey's recourse to the role of victim (or, to enlarge upon this, his role as martyr in the *Confessions* and elsewhere). If the double influence of Coleridge and Wordsworth is accepted as constituting the most significant influence on De Quincey's writing (though the degree of influence of any one writer on another is indeterminate, it may be argued), then his characterisation of them – a biographical task – has important repercussions on the task of self-location necessary to De Quincey's autobiography. In writing about his relationship to Wordsworth, De Quincey risks a dislocation potentially ruinous to his attempts at autobiography.

Wordsworth

As a boy, De Quincey had written a letter to Wordsworth, seeking his friendship and stating that

> though you may find many minds more congenial with your own – and therefore proportionately more worthy of your regard, you will never find any one more zealously attached to you – more full of admiration for your mental excellence and of reverential love for your moral character – more ready (I speak from my heart!) to sacrifice even his life – whenever it could have a chance of promoting your interest and happiness – than he who now bends the knee before you. (Letter of 31 May, 1803).⁷

This offer of self-sacrifice had become a dark joke when De Quincey came to write those of the sketches for *Tait's* concerned with Wordsworth, some thirty years later. Reflecting on the fact that Wordsworth's financial needs seemed always to be met with the death of somebody who bequeathed him a tidy sum of money, De Quincey wrote that

> had I happened to know of any peculiar adaptation in an estate or office of mine, to an existing need of Wordsworth's – forthwith, and with the speed of a man running for his life, I would have laid it down at his feet. "Take it," I would have said – "take it – or in three weeks I shall be a dead man" (*Tait's* vol.VI, p. 250).

De Quincey represents his allegiance to Wordsworth as an interdependence necessary for his own survival. The hold over him that Wordsworth seems to exercise and which is given here as a part of the natural order, as an occult 'blind necessity', is also a threat which places De Quincey once again in extremity – as though the offer of his life were still under consideration. The motion De Quincey wishes to set up in his prose is precisely that of 'a man running for his life'. While he repeatedly praises Wordsworth's poetry, and quotes at length from much of his verse, De Quincey also represents the poet as a man whose personality is found to be ultimately stifling. This contradictory attitude (*Tait's*, vol.VII [October 1840], p. 635), both praising and damning, has a distinct effect upon the figure of the Opium-Eater, who is implicitly praised for his good taste and damned for the betrayal of his master. In this context, where the figure of the reader has a determining function, the *Tait's* 'Sketches' are especially interesting since many are specifically addressed to Wordsworth, the subject of the papers in which he is characterised as one who never reads anything. Given that De Quincey's own role as reader is interrupted (he claims that he is working too quickly to revise his sketches and correct any mistakes), the essays in *Tait's* concerned with Wordsworth may be understood as explicitly redundant as far as the inherent claims of the text are concerned. A reading of De Quincey's works in the light of those sketches addressed to Wordsworth suggests that the reader occupies a void where this absent figure should stand. The various conflated moments of extremity – the estrangement from Wordsworth, the death of De Quincey's wife Margaret (also touched upon in the sketches), the possibility of an evasion of these crises – have been passed, leaving De Quincey the survivor to attempt to reconstitute what has been lost, even though the impossibility of a such a task is declared in the very reading of his work. (The text is grounded precisely in the experience of loss for which it attempts to compensate.) The sketches are read as an unread piece of writing – completed as incomplete, as partial. The revision the sketches beg, undertaken for De Quincey's *Selections*, at once resolves this problem, by deleting all the passages that address the absent reader specified in the text (Wordsworth especially); and simultaneously extends the problem, since the deletions make the revisions even more incomplete than the originals they supersede.[8]

De Quincey represents Wordsworth as existing outside the narrative, impervious to his accusations, warnings and pleas. This figure implies, on the one hand, the possibility of a direct link between the textual and the extra-textual entity represented; and, on the other hand, the inevitable collapse of such a connection. Extremity is now expressed as excessively positive, a position to be envied: Wordsworth's worldly success prompts De Quincey to predict an apocalyptic change in fortune. This action, in consideration of the facts of the matter, is entirely futile since it rests on a hypothesis which is negated even as it originates:

> Yet, William Wordsworth, nevertheless, if you ever allowed yourself to forget the *human* tenure of these mighty blessings – if, though wearing your honours justly – most justly, as respects A. and B., this man and that man – you have forgotten

that *no* man can challenge such trophies by any absolute or meritorious title, as respects the dark powers which give and take away – if, in the blind spirit of presumption, you have insulted the less prosperous fortunes of a brother, frail, indeed, but not dishonourably frail, and in his very frailty – that is, in his failing exertions – and for the deficient measure of his energies, (doubtless too much below the standard of reasonable expectations,) able to plead that which you never cared to ask – then , if (instead of being 68 years old) you were $68\frac{1}{2}$, I should warn you to listen for the steps of Nemesis approaching from afar; and, were it only in relation to your own extremity of good fortune, I would say, in the case of your being a young man, lavish as she may have been hitherto, and for years to come may still be –

"Yet fear her, O thou minion of her pleasure!
Her audit, though delay'd, answered must be,
And her *quietus* is – to render thee."*
*(Shakspeare's Sonnets) [De Quincey's footnote]
(*Tait's* vol. VI, p. 250).

De Quincey wishes to establish a direct connection between Wordsworth and himself at the point of extremity, after the failure of any other connection. However, the necessary conditions for striking fear into the heart of Wordsworth are, at best, unlikely to be realised: he is not '$68\frac{1}{2}$' but 68; and there is no way of checking whether the various 'if's which De Quincey suggests are applicable will actually stick. De Quincey wishes to put Wordsworth at the point of death. His autobiographical essays are concerned with the articulation of moments of extreme experience, and here his concern is, at least in part, to communicate with the (lost) Wordsworth, to try to overcome the impossibility of penetrating Wordsworth's apparently coherent self (a self coherent in relation to De Quincey's self, in any case).

The return to extremity is also an articulation of having to return, a quotation of anxiety which is self-consuming, in the way that writing at length about death seems always liable to consume what might be the final precious moments of the writer's life. If Wordsworth is impenetrable, De Quincey can nevertheless formulate a quotation of Wordsworth's works, which may suffice instead. By becoming, as it were, the original quoter of Wordsworth, De Quincey finishes Wordsworth's work. His citations, many of them misquotations, revise Wordsworth's writings considerably. The *coup de grâce* of this limiting of Wordsworth is De Quincey's 'theft' of *The Prelude* before that poem's publication, a theft which places Wordsworth's autobiography within the context of De Quincey's, effectively reversing the authority of the former over the latter. Moreover, the quotation of the poem is also a theft from Coleridge, to whom *The Prelude* is addressed. De Quincey's revision of the sketch of Wordsworth (2: 227–314) goes even further, adding footnotes that refer to the then recently published poem (2: 290n) while retaining the introductory remarks from the original *Tait's* article:

And here I may mention appropriately, and I hope without any breach of confidence, that, in a great philosophic poem of Wordsworth's, which is still in M.S., and will remain in M.S. until after his death, there is, at the opening of one of the books, a dream, which reaches the very *ne plus ultra* of sublimity (*Tait's*, vol. VI, p.97; 2: 273).

De Quincey thus manages to indicate the existential death of Wordsworth by having published in *Tait's* what should remain in manuscript. Nemesis proves to be an unreliable editor whose motives are suspect. Wordsworth's own handwriting (MS) is erased by that of De Quincey, his autobiography reduced to part of De Quincey's biographical sketch, much of which reads like potted *Prelude*.

This action, though perhaps psychologically necessary, contradicts the characterisation of Wordsworth as a larger-than-life figure given elsewhere in De Quincey's writings. The threat he represents is, typically, concealed in humorous comments. In 'Protestantism' (1847), for example, Wordsworth is described as having 'a natural resemblance to Mrs Ratcliffe's Schedoni and other assassins roaming through prose and verse' (8: 142); whilst elsewhere he is compared to Lucifer: 'and perhaps it was I myself who once said in print of him – that it is not the correct way of speaking to say that Wordsworth is as proud as Lucifer, but, inversely, to say of Lucifer that some people have conceived him to be as proud as Wordsworth' (12: 184-5). Such comments on the poet's pride abound in De Quincey's essays.[9] A figure of destructive energy, Wordsworth is the prototype oppressor, different versions of which occur throughout De Quincey's writings. A tyrant whose self-knowledge is only partial, as if he had deliberately suppressed certain memories (De Quincey's own display of what he calls 'moral ulcers' [*L* 1] and his characterisation of Wordsworth as a boy [*Tait's*, vol. VI, p. 93] support such an interpretation), Wordsworth is judged as morally blind, '*einseitig* in extremity' and 'a *mixed* creature, made up of special infirmity and special strength' (*Tait's* vol. VII, p. 635). Wordsworth has over-reached himself, and the experience of extremity will not entail a rise to a godlike revelation but an ethical fall – and who will be there to save him? De Quincey, far from trying to redeem Wordsworth, predicts and colludes with a shattering change in Wordsworth's fortunes. The self-sufficient entity, static and proud, will experience not the *glory* of motion but the ignominy of a crab-like wobble, off-centre and awry. Though his face (the writing of which, his character, is deciphered as intellectually noble) makes 'amends for greater defects of figure' (*Tait's*, vol. VI, p. 8), the obliteration of that face in death will mark Wordsworth's collapse (to extend De Quincey's description of his 'wry or twisted' gait) 'from the middle to the side of the highroad' into the ditch (*Tait's*, vol. VI, pp. 7-8).

De Quincey's reading of Wordsworth's character, or more properly of his face, indicates that while De Quincey has survived, Wordsworth has deteriorated. 'No change in personal appearance ever can have been so unfortunate', he comments on the effect of Wordsworth's greying hair upon his features (*Tait's*, vol. VI, p. 7). Furthermore, the best portrait of Wordsworth De Quincey can think of is one of Milton – a sign of the difficulty encountered in reading the code of his character. De Quincey explains this difficulty in terms of Wordsworth's temperament:

> Some people, it is notorious, live faster than others; the oil is burned out sooner in one constitution than another – and the cause of this may be various; but, in the Wordsworths' one part of the cause is, no doubt, the secret fire of a temperament too fervid; the self-consuming energies of the brain, that gnaw at the heart and life-strings for ever (*Tait's*, vol. VI, p. 9).

De Quincey implies that Wordsworth, though able to maintain the motion by which the self can be continually rewritten, cannot read or contemplate this motion: he is burnt out, prematurely old. As with Coleridge, though not so forcibly, De Quincey's Wordsworth is a warning and a challenge. De Quincey's description of his initial meeting with Wordsworth is couched in much the same language as his sighting of Coleridge, a parallel he underlines:

> Coleridge was of opinion that, if a man were really and *consciously* to see an apparition [. . .] – in such circumstances death would be the inevitable result; [. . .] Judged by Coleridge's test, my situation could not have been so terrific as *his* who anticipates a ghost – for, certainly, I survived this meeting: but, at that instant, it seemed pretty much the same to my own feelings (*Tait's*, vol. VI, p. 4).

De Quincey's excitement is such, he adds, that he would have forgotten the presence of 'Death on his pale horse' had this been behind him. De Quincey desires exposure to the dangers he reads around him, desires to experience but also to survive intact. The text which records this tendency also signifies success, for the memory of events allows De Quincey to occupy that interface which reality implicitly did not. The *Tait's* sketches can be read as the confirmation that De Quincey is a unique survivor, one who, in direct contrast to Wordsworth, has somehow cheated time:

> I, wo [sic] is me! am the solitary survivor from scenes that now seem to me as fugitive as the flying lights from our lamps as they shot into the forest recesses. God forbid that on such a theme I should seem to affect sentimentalism. (*Tait's*, vol. VII, p. 807).

Yet to have survived is also to be stranded alone, tortured by a sense of loss. For De Quincey, the most poignant memory is when what is now lost had yet to come. He suffers most in recalling not 'those enjoyments themselves, and the days when they were within my power', but 'times anterior, when as yet they did not exist' (*Tait's*, vol. VI, p. 807). This memory of a prefigured delusive anticipation, which is itself a kind of inverted memory by means of which De Quincey represses the 'overmastering recollections' of the 'circumstances of happiness too radiant, that for me are burned out for ever', seeks to localise the effects of memory in spite of itself (*Tait's*, vol. VI, p. 807). De Quincey's control over time does not dispel his anxiety, as one might reasonably expect, but instead capriciously leads him to discover a lower depth of anxiety. Having survived, he finds that he is burdened with continually having to face new threats; and his life starts to resemble that anticipatory coach-ride which seems somehow to outrage the silent graves of the happy dead (*Tait's*, vol. VI, p. 807). De Quincey's recollections disturb the dead, exhuming them only to confirm that they are not alive.

Ironically, however, the dead exert their authority in his memory: there is no escaping the past. Even if he can formulate a 'death' of Wordsworth or Coleridge (their actual state is not important here), De Quincey is still influenced by them: they still exist. His sketches of them take, as their very foundation, the declaration that he has finished with them. This finishing, operating in a social context, is of course a beginning in the written context (or at least a continuation). If autobiography would seem to be in a state of perpetual auto-negation, a proclamation of one's approaching death rather than a document giving one's life, it also enables these threatening influences to be negated in the same manner, so that the complex relation of self-defining/self-destroying entities is at least brought to a state of equilibrium in which the difference between the written or writing self and the extra-textual self can be quietly ignored. De Quincey is enabled to concentrate on himself by writing about others.

The *Tait's* sketches mark an important step beyond the original *Confessions*. While in that narrative De Quincey occasionally claims to be in complete control (for example, in the final scene with the headmaster), his insistence on imbalance, on a polarity of good/bad, pleasure/pain, motion/rest and so forth inevitably tends to characterise him as a fluctuating, unstable creature – a whimsically Chattertonian survivalist whose confession ends with a grudgingly told lie:

> However, as some people, in spite of all laws to the contrary, will persist in asking what became of the opium-eater, and in what state he now is, I answer for him thus: [. . .] I triumphed' (*L* 78).

The Opium-Eater of the *Tait's* 'Sketches of Life and Manners from the Autobiography of an English Opium-Eater' is principally a detective, one who is able to penetrate the 'inner life' of others, analyse motives, and decipher apparently innocuous experiences. In the *Confessions* De Quincey had characterised himself as fundamentally 'a philosopher' (*L* 20), meaning one whose analytic and moral powers are put to use so as to allow him access to mysteries and therefore to hidden truth (*L* 4–5). His efforts at 'standing in equal relation' (*L* 20) to all human beings are, in the events described, limited: for instance, his distant observation of strangers in London reduces him to a distinctly detached voyeur; and his inability to trace Ann demonstrates that he is painfully deficient. It is only in writing, in the representation where his claims can be implicitly realised, that he can achieve anything like the state of an all-powerful seer. In the 'Sketches', De Quincey's sureness is as overwhelming as it is casual: Coleridge's plagiarisms are uncovered in an off-hand conversation with a virtual stranger; the failure of his marriage is gathered from a brief introduction to Mrs Coleridge; Wordsworth's verse is recognised years in advance of public acclaim; Wordsworth's character is minutely understood. The emotional and intellectual singularities of everyone encountered are so much code to the decipherer De Quincey.

The implications of this self-characterisation are considerable. That De Quincey is primarily a being whose major talent is his ability to read is of importance given the extensive labour of revision (the reading of the written self) which occupies him as an autobiographer, not only as regards the radical revisions prepared for his collected works, but in terms of proof-reading before the publication of all his papers. De Quincey, in reading people's characters, is immediately removed from what constitutes their 'inner selves'. He reads an already-written hieroglyphic. Access to the mysteries of life is never immediate and never complete. The philosopher, the detective, the seer – whatever we call him, his function remains the same. The inner life is defined by an outer text – a face, a character, an action, or, in De Quincey's own case, a printed essay which is itself the translation of a memory (the translation of a transcription of an exhumed writing). Since it is a mystery which is to be decoded, the reading can never be finished, for a mystery by definition confounds attempts at understanding it. In spite of this prefigured failure, De Quincey insists on trying to read and on the validity of his reading. Indeed, the very possibility of failure makes the text more interesting, for partial success confirms that the code *is* indeed mysterious.

De Quincey's fascination for pariah figures can be interpreted as precisely this desire to be validated by one's failures. His gloss on the relationship between Christ and Judas in the essay 'Judas Iscariot' (1853), is a bold attempt to strengthen such a stance. Here De Quincey expresses a wish to be enabled to recall Judas's death, which 'if once truly deciphered' might 'throw back some faint illustrative light, both upon the life and upon the offence' (7: 11), while he also implies that such a reading would be impossible: 'What search could be sufficient, where even the eye of Christ had failed to detect any germ of evil?' (7: 14). De Quincey's failure is thus analogous to that of Christ's paradigmatic failure; his errors are like those of the divine-man. De Quincey identifies with Christ-the-reader, the procrastinating saviour who is forced into action by Judas, whose reading of Christ De Quincey also identifies with:

> Indecision and doubt (such was the interpretation of Judas) crept over the faculties of the Divine Man as often as he was summoned away from his own natural Sabbath of heavenly contemplation to the gross necessities of action (7: 3–4).

Judas's misreading places Christ in extremity, forcing him to act. Christ's misreading has the complementary effect of creating the possibility for Judas's precipitation of the catastrophe. The apparent mistakes of these mutually dependent figures produce a positive result. This is not merely a case of two wrongs making a right: De Quincey's point is more subtle, in that it implies that *error* positively valorises the two antagonists. Judas is made more mysterious, stupendously ambiguous by his betrayal, Christ more inexplicable by his choice of disciple. In a similar vein, De Quincey's inability to define himself reinforces the 'mysteriousness' he wishes ostensibly to break down. Misreading is inevitable and necessary, and is implicitly the only 'true' reading in that it admits to its aberrance.

It is tempting to apply the elements of this drama of mutual dependence, destruction, and redemption by which De Quincey defines the relationship of Christ to Judas to the parallel master-disciple relationship of Wordsworth and Coleridge to De Quincey. Such an interpretation is quite pertinent. In his representations of Coleridge and Wordsworth, De Quincey can be seen to have betrayed not only their confidence (in the sense of social propriety) but, more significantly, some elements of their characters, of their private lives, that they would prefer suppressed. The 'Sketches' notoriously caused enormous offence, publishing 'truths' in the titillating way that has since become a journalistic commonplace. More interesting than the motives of speedy financial return which prompted De Quincey is the depiction of his standing in relation to Wordsworth and Coleridge as literary figures (producers and produced). De Quincey's persona, as well as being characterised by incredible powers of insight, comes across as jealous, malicious, arrogant, dismissive, pompous, pathetic and pitiful (to touch on just a few aspects). His character is not given merely by self-expression and insights into his emotional state (though there are many instances of this), but also by the analysis of his motives which the images of his 'friends' prompt. The reader is urged to interpret the play of motives, and by implication the desire to read is itself called into question. If the text really offends, is the fault the writer's? Or is the notion of fault applicable at all? The reader is the active and responsible agent in these sketches, a point underlined when De Quincey's text (as it is read) addresses the writer:

> You yourself, for example, who write these sketches, did it follow of necessity that the woman you loved should be equal (or seem equal in your own eyes) to yourself in intellect? No; far from it (*Tait's*, vol. VI, p. 247).

The writer is questioned by writing, and his answer confirms the authority of the text's claim to truth. The reader writes the question and erases the figure of the writer, then replaces it with a new figure which is in turn erased and replaced. 'De Quincey' is given as one among many, taken 'for example'; but is also the archetypal reader who functions as a quotation of the convergence of singulars. The written word becomes the sublime location of valid human activity. The reader is characterised as having already prefigured what is written, having already made an error in this prefiguration, just as De Quincey admits to having mistakenly prefigured a connection with Wordsworth which must eventually disintegrate. Influence for De Quincey means reading the figure of life as a figure of death, the figure of death having already been read as what constitutes the figure of life: a movement ostensibly towards an irrecoverable origin which draws an endless circle, or more properly (as more faithful to De Quincey's ideas) a sphere on which an infinity of circles may be drawn. The rediscovery or re-invention of influence is an attempt to form a base in which memory can be grounded, a substitution of forgetting for remembering, a kind of self-negation which serves the claims to self-continuity and identity of the influenced writer. The transcribed memory of influence articulates independence, but tends to unground itself. Yet both the remembered and he who remembers are revitalised by this bold forgery of binding together incompatible experiences, this compound of opposites. The admission of influence forces one into extremity, and procrastination (a matter of delaying substitution) gives way to action – an action which allows access to one's concealed powers. The 'crucifixion' of De Quincey between the two thieves of his identity, Wordsworth and Coleridge, or, to put it another way, his suicide coincident to the betrayal of his masters, is an extreme which must be faced and by which De Quincey may be redeemed.

The authority of the influential figures, however, calls into question the nature of extremity-as-redemption. The possibility exists for De Quincey that the antagonistic attempt to protect oneself from the humiliating oppression of others contains a latent form of damnation. How can he discover whether or not he has already gone too far? The revisions of his sketches provide an escape-route of sorts. Thus some of the darkest lines De Quincey wrote were obliterated in his overhaul of the text of 'Suspiria de Profundis';

> Too much, even in later life, I have perceived in men that pass for good men, a disposition to degrade (and if possible to degrade through self-degradation) those in whom unwillingly they feel any weight of oppression to themselves, by commanding qualities of intellect or character. They respect you; they are compelled to do so: and they hate to do so. Next, therefore, they seek to throw off the sense of this oppression and to take vengeance for it, by co-operating with any unhappy accidents in your life, to inflict a sense of humiliation upon you, and (if possible) to force you into becoming a consenting party to that humiliation. Oh, wherefore is it that those who presume to call themselves the "friends" of this man or that woman, are so often those above all others, whom in the hour of death that man or woman is most likely to salute with the valediction – Would God I had never seen your face? (*L* 162).[10]

Though it is possible to suggest a variety of faces which De Quincey would rather have never seen, it is Wordsworth's which comes inevitably to mind – the face that suggests to De Quincey the possibilities of self-definition and thus the symbol for the root of his problems as an autobiographer. There is a strong element of destructive self-loathing in this depressing passage, a nihilism that characterises the human race as fundamentally petty. The hour of death now offers only the expression of regret, a bitter comment on the understanding of the interdependence of innocence and experience formulated in the 'Suspiria'. Extremity is filled out here only with the realisation of one's parasitical dependency, even to the very end, on fraudulent connections with 'those who would have enslaved' one who would demand the freedom to choose his own form of slavery. At this point, De Quincey has effectively rewritten the conclusion of the *Confessions* where the choice of freedom leads ironically to the realisation that choice itself is a kind of oppression (something taken up in the revised *Confessions*). Entrapment is now given as the human condition. There is no waking up from the nightmare, merely the acknowledgment that life is like a nightmare in which the dreamer fancies himself awake.

'Sir William Hamilton'

What the passage from the 'Suspiria' implies, in its prefigurative quotation of De Quincey's 'dying words', is made more explicit in a later essay, 'Sir William Hamilton' (1852). In many ways the most extreme of De Quincey's essays, 'Sir William Hamilton' confronts the process of composition as a present actuality. Writing – representation rather than the supposedly represented experience – becomes the immediate source of anxiety, an anxiety that threatens to perpetuate itself *ad infinitum*. The expression of the inescapable interdependence of destructive complementaries – one's 'self' and 'influences', the 'individual' and 'others' – itself entails a painful but fascinating collision of past and present. De Quincey represents himself as occupying an unresolved and insoluble position in the extremity of suspense, of simultaneous stasis and motion. In this position, negatives become complementary and the status of the narrator, as both a figure in the text pointing to itself and one pointing to its doppelgänger, the extra-textual, real or imagined entity called De Quincey, is called into question. Resistance and acquiescence collide, the expressive and the oppressive form a fascinating laminate:

> Martyrdom it is, and no less, to revivify by effort of your own, or passively to see revivified, in defiance of your own fierce resistance, the gorgeous spectacles of your visionary morning life, or of your too rapturous noontide, relieved upon a background of funeral darkness. Such poisonous transfigurations, by which the paradise of youthful hours is forced into distilling demoniac misery for ruined nerves, exist for many a profound sensibility. And, as regards myself, touch but some particular key of laughter and of echoing music, sound but for a moment one bar of preparation, and immediately the pomps and glory of all that has composed for me the delirious vision of life re-awaken for torment; the orchestras of the earth open simultaneously to my inner ear; and in a moment I behold, forming themselves into solemn groups and processions, and passing over sad phantom stages, all that chiefly I have loved, or in whose behalf chiefly I have abhorred and cursed the grave – all that should *not* have died, yet died the soonest – the brilliant, the noble, the wise, the innocent, the brave, the beautiful (*Hogg's Instructor*, vol. VIII, p. 401).

The moment of extremity has already happened. De Quincey has died and will die again. Life only begins with the acceptance of the knowledge of death. The inability to sustain the motion which preserves life and the inability to control the involuntary motion of mnemonically resurrected phantoms results in the poisonous transfigurations by which the living appear dead and the dead appear living – a necessary perversion made all the more compelling by the fact that it seems somehow to define the nature of reality for De Quincey. He remembers that he will die. In his past an apparent death has already been announced. But he is still alive, and that he can remember at all constitutes his claim to being alive. Life consists of the reclaiming of dead experience, past selves forever out of reach, and with never enough present in which to know one's self. Knowledge of the self requires knowledge of the others whose part in forming the self cannot logically be denied. Influence is, in this context, not a historical result, not an extra-textual process, so much as a deliberated, consciously resumed fiction by which

Biographical Interventions

a dead connection is revived or which involuntarily asserts itself in the memory. De Quincey has been contaminated by Coleridge and Wordsworth – poisonously transfigured (just as, in his texts, he transforms them): and, similarly, his relation to his own text provokes unease. The doppelgänger autobiographical text, written, read, and revised by De Quincey is liable to assert its priority over the 'now dead' – suspended (hanging) – writer, much in the same way as De Quincey's memories affect his perception of the struggle for self-identification.

In 'Sir William Hamilton' De Quincey represents himself as tortured by the fraudulent resurrection of dead loved ones in his memory, seen 'forming themselves into solemn groups and processions', which produces a horrific vision of life:

> With these dreadful masks, and under the persecution of their malicious beauty, wakens up the worm that gnaws at the heart. Under that corrosion arises a hatred, blind, and vague, and incomprehensible even to one's self, as of some unknown snake-like enemy, in some unknown hostile world, brooding with secret power over the fountains of one's own vitality (*Hogg's Instructor*, vol. VIII, p. 401).[11]

The knowable doppelgänger figure has been replaced by the 'unknown' alien, the possibility of self-knowledge has led to the last resort of identifying oneself merely as one to whom something – again unknown, unknowable – is being done. This would seem to be the end of the line.[12]

At this limit, however, De Quincey can nevertheless still indulge in writing. Though the purported claim of the autobiographer is invalidated here, and a certain redundancy is at least partially recognised, the possibility of erasing the written self before rewriting (even if this appears futile) exists as an option for De Quincey – one he takes, because it allows endless scope and provides an infinity of localities for him to occupy. The disintegration of the self produces more text and allows the writer precisely that sense of motion which self-definition promises yet negates. Resurrection is again within his reach; extremity reproduces itself still further, without limits. In 'Sir William Hamilton' De Quincey flouts the demands of writing in terms of its function as coherent communication between a journalist and a paying public. The First Paper of the series of essays ('Sir William Hamilton, Bart.', *Hogg's Instructor*, vol. VIII) closes with a ludicrous lament over the restrictions of the magazine in which the piece was published. These restrictions demand that every volume be a coherent whole. De Quincey explains the magazine rules, but conceives of a way round them:

> This article, for instance, cannot prolong its life into another volume; but it may rise again – it may receive a separate birth *de novo* – in the future volume (*Hogg's Instructor*, vol. VIII, p. 404).

SIR WILLIAM HAMILTON,
WITH A GLANCE AT HIS LOGICAL REFORMS.
BY THOMAS DE QUINCEY.
FIRST PAPER.

HERE I am, viz., in vol. xv. Never ruffle your own temper, reader, or mine, by asking *how*, and with what right. I *am* here. So much is clear; and what you may call a *fait accompli*. As to saying that, though I am may-be here 'de facto,' nevertheless 'de jure' I am *not* so; that I have no *locus standi*; that I am a usurper; an intruder; and that any contraband process by which I can have smuggled myself from vol. xiv. to this present vol. xv., is not of a kind that will bear looking into. Too true, I answer: very few things *will* bear looking into. In particular, the revolution of 1688-9 will not bear looking into with eyes of philosophic purism. The object of the purist is to effect the devolution of the crown through a smooth lubricated channel known and conformable to old constitutional requisitions: and if the word '*abdicate*' could but be established, formally, were it, or even constructively, all would run as sweetly as the chronometers of Greenwich. As it is, I grieve to say that there is a deadly hiatus in the harness which should connect the pre-revolutionary and post-revolutionary commonwealths of England. It is not merely a screw that is loose, it is a link that is missing, and no use advertising for it now. But no matter: that is a grief which, being nearly two hundred years old, an extra glass of wine will do much to heal. And in reality I never heard of a man's meditating suicide, because he could not harmonise the facts of our revolution with its transcendental theory. Yet not the less the human mind does really yearn and sicken after intellectual modes of solution applied to any intellectual intricacy or nodus. Art must thaw the dilemma which art has frozen together: and never yet was there a reader of any sensibility that did not resent with clamorous indignation the removal by apoplexy from a novel or a drama of any impracticable character that ought to have been disposed of agreeably to the providential forecastings of the plot itself, and by the spontaneous evolution of the fable. My own personal embarrassment on this occasion, in effecting a transit or in evading a transit, was of a nature hardly paralleled in literature. I was to write a paper within certain assigned limits, which paper, by its very subject and the crying necessities of its nature, utterly rebelled against those limits. To transfer it (not in part but in mass) to a field of ampler limits, i. e., to another volume, was made impossible by certain arrangements which nailed the accompanying portrait to this punctual spot—to this instant *now*, and this momentary audience. The biographic record could not be disjoined from the portrait, and the portrait could not be removed from that particular place in that particular volume. But could I not, *secondly*, content myself with giving part, carrying forward the other parts by adjournment to another volume? No: because that would be establishing a dependency of one volume upon another, contrary to the plan and law of the whole work. But then, *thirdly*, at least I might have hyperbolically expanded on the spot the dimensions of that single paper which the fates allowed me to write? No: I could not do *that* even, for then I must have monopolised the entire train—first, second, and third class—and, in order to do *that*, I must have booked myself as the one sole passenger in this journal, at least three months beforehand.

It is strange to see what mountains of difficulty sometimes melt away before the suggestions of a child. *Accipe principium sursus*—solved the whole case. What is to hinder me from beginning afresh upon a new foundation in a new volume, and utterly ignoring all that has gone before? I now do so. And what follows is to be viewed as a totally new article, standing on its own basis.

Everybody, I believe, is young at some period of his life; at least one has an old physiological prejudice in that direction. Else, to hear people talk, one must really suppose that there are celebrated persons who are born to old age as to some separate constitutional inheritance. Nobody says 'Old Sophocles,' but very many people say 'Old Chaucer.' Yet Chaucer was a younger man at his death than Sophocles. But if not, why should men insist upon one transitory stage or phasis in a long series of changes, as if suddenly and lawfully arrested, to the exclusion of all the rest? *Old* Chaucer! why, he was also middle-aged Chaucer; he was young Chaucer; he was baby Chaucer. And the earlier distinctions of a man bear as much relation to posterity as his later distinctions. Above all, one is betrayed into such misconceptions when a man carries a false certificate of age in the very name which designates his relationship to one's-self. My great-great-grandmother naturally I figured to myself as having a patriarchal beard. Could I think otherwise of one so deeply merged in grandmotherhood? But a portrait of her taken immediately after death represented her as an attractive young woman not quite twenty-three, which it appeared that she really was. And I remember a similar case even still more striking, which occurred in Chester about the year 1803. Some overflowing of the Dee had exposed to view the secrets of the churchyard. Amongst the coffins in the lower tiers was one which contained the corpse of a woman, particularly blooming. According to my first precipitate computation, she might be rated as 120 years old; for she had died in Queen Anne's reign (about 1707, I think), and by the plate on the coffin lid had been 24 at the time of death. Yet her face was most blooming, her lips beautifully fresh, and her hair of the loveliest auburn. Ninety-and-three years of the eighteenth century, and two years of the nineteenth, had she spent in the grave; and adding these 95 years of rest to the 24 of her (doubtless unresting) life, for a moment I fell into the natural confusion of making her a very, very old woman; and proportionably I wondered at the vernal beauty which had not ceased to adorn her in the wintry grave. This special indulgence to a special beauty had been the gift of a soil preternaturally antiseptic. But inevitably the sudden collision of a youthfulness so apparent with an antiquity so historical, caused each idea reciprocally to illuminate the other; so that, for a minute or two, until I had distinguished the elements of this antiquity, and had separated the 95 years that did not belong to the young woman herself from the 24 that *did*, I struggled with the impossible and contradictory conception of crazy superannuation incarnated in perfect womanly loveliness. Some metaphysical perplexity of this same nature, I observe, besets those who contemplate us the tenants of a past generation through the inverted tube of the present. The Trophonian gloom which they ascribe to us, considered as present antiquities and relics, adheres to the image of the same poor *us* when traced upwards to our morning period. We that cannot attempt even to smile in this present stage of the world, is it credible that at *any* stage we can have laughed? Child of incredulity, if not credible, it is certain. 'Ginger* was hot in the mouth' in those long-past years; and 'because we were virtuous' at that era, not the less there were 'ale and cakes.' Though transcendental philosophers (αιροβατουντις) that walked the air, we condescended to sip at times from sublunary liquors; and at odd times it is possible that we even entered into the kingdom of 'civilation.'

'Civilation!† And what may *that* be?' Look below,

---
* I presume the reader to be familiar with the passage in Shakspere here referred to. But if not, let him look to 'Twelfth Night.'

† '*In a state of civilation:*'—And what state may that be? As the word is a valuable word, and in some danger of being lost, I beg to rehearse its history. The late Dr Maginn, with whom some of us may otherwise have had reason to quarrel, was, however, a man of varied accomplishments; a wit, with singular readiness for improvising, and with very extensive scholarship. Amongst the peculiar opinions which he professed was this—that no man, however much he might *tend* towards civilisation, was to be regarded as having absolutely reached its apex until he was drunk. Previously to which consummation, a man might be a promising subject for civilisation, but otherwise than in *posse* it must be premature, so he must be considered as more or less of a savage. This doctrine he naturally published more loudly than ever, as he was himself more and more removed from all suspicion of barbaric sobriety. He then became anxious with tears in his eyes to proclaim the deep sincerity of his conversion to civilisation. But as such an odiously long word must ever be distressing

reader, into the foot-note, which will explain it. Whilst you are studying *that*, I'll be moving on slowly overhead; and, when you come up from that mine to the upper air, you'll easily overtake me. Civilation, or (if you choose to call it so) civilisation, was not a state into which any of us made a regular habit of ascending: only at times we did so; and I presume that at such times Sir William Hamilton, being thoroughly social, would keep us company. From the circumstances given, I infer a probability. Else I protest against 'peaching,' and revealing secrets small or great, though forty years old. The range of time which is concerned in my present notice stretches over a dozen years; within which space intermittingly, as off and on I happened to be in Edinburgh, various persons, variously interesting, entered for a time, or quitted for a time, our fluctuating circle. The original nucleus had been John Wilson (i. e., *the* Wilson) and his brothers, amongst whom the naturalist (James Wilson) was known to me first, and subsequently Sir William Hamilton. Next, and after the war had finally reached its consummation in Waterloo—a *peripetteia* as perfect and dramatic as ever was exhibited on the stage of Athens—others at intervals gladdened our festal company; amongst whom, as the most memorable, I ought to mention Colonel Mitchell, the biographer of Wallenstein, so advantageously known by his bold and original views upon strategies, upon the efficacy of the bayonet, and upon the critical interpretation of some capital chapters in martial history; Captain Thomas Hamilton, the brother of Sir William, an accomplished man, latterly known amongst us by the name of Cyril Thornton, from the title of his novel; Sir William Allan, the distinguished artist, afterwards President of the Royal Scottish Academy; and, lastly, Mr R. P. Gillies, the advocate, whose name I repeat with a sigh of inexpressible sadness, such as belongs of right to some splendid Timon of Athens, so often as on the one hand I revivify to my mind his gay saloons, resonant with music and festal laughter—the abode for years of a munificent hospitality, which Wordsworth characterised as 'all but princely'—and, on the other hand, shudder at the mighty shadows of calamity, of sorrow, of malice, of detraction, that have for thirty years stalked after his retreating splendours, and long since have swallowed up the very memory of his pretensions from the children of this generation.

But, returning to the subject of civilisation, could it be said of Sir William Hamilton that he favoured it or promoted it? Hardly, I think. The age itself—that generation of Waterloo—sanctioned a certain degree of civilisation in young and old: and Sir William, in his fervid youth, was too social and too generous to retreat austerely within the circle of absolute barbarism. But it would have been difficult to civilise *him* effectually, such was the resistance opposed to civilation by his extraordinary muscular strength. Sir William's powers, in some directions, as an athlete, were indeed unusually great, and would have attracted much more notice, had he not, upon all his personal endowments, been so systematically shy, and even so disdainful of display. Nobody, therefore, fancied that he could gratify Sir William by recalling gymnastic feats of *his*. When he relaxed at all from his habitual mood of freezing contempt for all personal acts of ostentation whatever (no matter whether intellectual or physical), it was in pure overmastering sympathy with the spirit of genial fun—the *amabilis insania*—which some special gathering of youth and youthful gaiety had concurred to kindle. It was in mere deference to the expectations or wishes of others, that Sir William could be ever persuaded into a moment's display, and then not without an expression of scorn too palpable for his own complaisance. A person worse qualified than myself for recording the exact extent of his athletic powers cannot be imagined;

to a gentleman taking his case of an evening, unconsciously, perhaps, he abridged it always after 10 p.m. into *civilation*. Such was the genesis of the word. And I therefore, upon entering it into my neological dictionary of English, matriculated it thus: '*Civilation* by ellipsis, or more properly by syncope, or rigorously speaking by hiccup, from *civilisation*.'

and for the plain reason—that, having not the slightest pretensions in that way myself, I had not cultivated any interest in such powers, nor consequently any knowledge of their nature or limits. Ignorant I was of the human frame, and of its latent powers, as regarded speed, force, ambi-dexterity, in a degree that would have been inexcusable in an old woman. I was even proud of my own desperate ignorance to an extent that made penitence or amendment apparently hopeless. And the worst feature of my barbarism was, and *is* to this hour, that, instead of meditating occasionally on the possibility that *I* might be wrong, and the world might be right—on the contrary, with a stiff-neckedness (surely there *is* such a word) that is truly criminal, I then did, and I now do, exhaust myself in terms of bloody contempt for all the men, and all the races of men, that ever fell down in prose or verse to worship the idol of human physical excellence. 'The abject villains!' was the best term (how illiberal!) that I could afford to the ancient Greeks, when noticing their beastly admiration of good running, good wrestling, good cab-driving at Olympia. Oh heavens! that a fist, that a foot, that a hoof, should be viewed with a holy homage, such as belonged of right to a revelation of truth, or after a millennium of darkness that belonged to the first fruits of the rising dawn! The Romans, it is remarkable, had no reverence for individual physical prowess. They had no Olympic contests. On the contrary, they regarded all such animal exertions as mere gladiatorial glories, i. e., as the distinctions of slaves, and distinctions that were to be bought for copper and silver amongst the savages of earth. But the Greeks, who, with the tremulous and half-effeminate temperament of genius combined a hideous defect of dignity and moral stamina, figure as perfect lunatics in their admiration of animal excellence:—

> 'Metaque fervidis
> Evitata rotis, palmaque nobilis,
> Terrarum dominos evehit ad deos.'

Horace himself, *roué* as he was, is Roman enough to squint at his reader with a look half-aghast at this extravagance of descent into the superstition that glorifies the fleshly. Homer, the greatest master of traumatic surgery (i. e., the philosophy of wounds) that has ever existed, in fact (if it were not for his profound darkness on the subject of gun-shot wounds) the only poet on record that would, *sede vacante*, have been elected by acclamation, without needing any interest at all or any canvass, as house surgeon to St Thomas's Hospital, or the Hotel Dieu, has absolutely left nothing for posterity to do in what regards the description of wounds, ulcers, &c. That department of surgery has become a mere sinecure since the first edition of the Iliad. But in Milton, raised above Homer as heaven is raised above earth, who can tolerate the grovelling ambition of angels glorying in 'a *noble* stroke?' To have delivered a 'facer,' or a backhanded blow, or to have cut St George with a broadsword over the conk of an archangel—ah, faugh! who can blame me for being sick? Is it I, or is it Milton, that is in the wrong? At all events, reader, justifying these things, never dream yourself entitled to join the wretched and effeminate abusers of boxing, of the ring, of the fancy, as now languishing in England. How brutal, you pretend to say, is that savage practice in the London ring of thumping the human face divine into the semblance of a roasted apple dressed with a poultice! Doubtless. But, even as it is, you that laud the traumatic sagacities of Homer, and even of the heaven-born Milton, presume not to talk of brutality in that which carried glory and illustration amongst the heavenly host. To 'fib' a man, to 'punish' him, to 'draw his claret,' or to get his cocoa-nut into 'chancery,' cannot be so thoroughly unworthy of a bargeman, or the Tipton Slasher, if it's quite becoming to a Grecian Milo, or a Phrygian Entellus, or even—*horresco referens*—not beneath a Miltonic seraph.

Sir William Hamilton's prowess did not exhibit itself in that line. Professor Wilson had *thumped* his way to consideration; he had also *walked* and *run* into fame. But standing leaps it was—leaps upward without any advan-

The restriction is lifted, though De Quincey makes it clear that the artificiality of such limits is essentially an indication of meaninglessness (or, at least, of contradictoriness – of the power of meaninglessness in meaningfulness). The Second Paper begins with a flourish that rubs it all in:

> Here I am, viz., in vol. XV [sic]. Never ruffle your own temper, reader, or mine, by asking *how*, and with what right. I *am* here (*Hogg's Instructor*, vol. IX, p. 273).

The view that writing provides direct access to the writer has already been exploded by De Quincey in this essay and this insistence that, nevertheless, 'I *am* here' points to a fix at least as perplexing as Coleridge's contradictory instructions to his porter. 'Ah, what a chaos,' he writes (*Hogg's Instructor*, vol. VIII, p. 404). The incoherence of the writing process, the *'how'* De Quincey would prefer to ignore but cannot, prompts lengthy explanation and allows him to write more about the difficulty of writing – and so on *ad infinitum*:

> Art must thaw the dilemma which art has frozen together [. . .] My own personal embarrassment on this occasion, in effecting a transit or in evading a transit, was of a nature hardly paralleled in literature. I was to write a paper within certain assigned limits, which paper, by its very subject and the crying necessities of its nature, utterly rebelled against limits (*Hogg's Instructor*, vol. IX, p. 273).

The lack of control which, in the case of experiencing involuntary recollection (the translation of past events into the present), was a source of horrific pain, is, in the case of composing the essay (the translation of memory into writing and then into print) transformed into a nervous pleasure. The resultant text is extremely curious. The pleasure/pain polarity gives way to a compound, the formation of which calls into question the valorisation of any experience. Implicitly, not only 'Sir William Hamilton' but also all of De Quincey's works, and literature in its entirety, are invalidated. Representation of any kind might be aberrant.

This open-endedness, however, can be used to invalidate its own invalidation, and again promises an endless series of substitutive representations. Thus it can at once be acknowledged and dismissed as a paradox, an action which reduces it to a mere interruption. De Quincey's pointedly unfinished essays, with their footnotes, apologies, reiterations and so forth, indicate the author's ambiguous relation to this question of the degree of the validity of writing. Anything is possible for him, a realisation which leads him back to the search for some measure of stability:

> But stop. This will not do. I must alter the scale of this paper, or else – something will happen which would vex me. The artist who sketched the Vicar of Wakefield's family group, in his zeal for comprehensive fulness of details, enlarged his canvass until

> he forgot the narrow proportions of the good vicar's house; and the picture, when finished, was too big to enter the front-door of the vicarage. One side of the house must have been pulled down to allow of its introduction; and, as a natural consequence, the picture was consigned to a barn – which fate will be mine, unless an instant remedy can be applied to the desultory and expansive tendencies which besiege all personal sketches, and especially sketches of such men as, being largely philosophic, and controversially entangled in the questions of their own generation, stand in a possible relation to all things (*Hogg's Instructor*, vol. IX, p. 275).[13]

The only stability to be found, though, is in the process of searching. De Quincey's meandering style, with its innumerable digressions, implies that the sketch will never be proportionately adjusted. What is unsaid is possibly as important as what is said – as De Quincey's revisions indicate. In an unstable situation, where the experience represented and the experience repressed or omitted – or deferred, put off to the future – seem equally valid (yet, necessarily, implicitly invalidate one another), De Quincey seemingly opts for extempore tactics – the exercise of hidden powers under the pressure of demand or of a deadline. An examination of some of the strategies in 'Sir William Hamilton' is useful here, for this essay reads much like an improvisation.

The argument put forth is arranged in an apparently haphazard manner; the minimum of information about Hamilton himself is imparted; the writer admits that he is at a loss as to what he ought to be doing. The formal strategies which typify the De Quinceyan essay, however, belie the sense that this is a stream-of-consciousness effusion. De Quincey repeatedly signals the always-already-revised status of the text by his use of footnotes. There are several of these, including a massive comment on Mrs Coleridge and Leibnitz, a passage relegated to the outermost limits of a piece to which anything may apparently be admitted. That the text occupies two quite different time scales is most obviously signified when De Quincey directs the reader to the bottom of the page, thus:

> "Civilation! And what may *that* be?" Look below, reader, into the foot-note, which will explain it. Whilst you are studying *that*, I'll be moving on slowly overhead; and, when you come up from that mine to the upper air, you'll easily overtake me (*Hogg's Instructor*, vol. IX, pp. 273–4).

De Quincey indicates in this formal joke that his narrative is able to occupy two separate but apparently simultaneous times – that he can defy the limitations demanded by the movement of the present into the past by setting up two concurrent presents. Language apparently allows him perpetual motion. The essay's concern, which can be crudely said to be with the problems and pleasures of *translation*, is formally articulated in a way which reflects on all of De Quincey's autobiographical and biographical work. De Quincey identifies in 'Sir William Hamilton' the restrictions which pertain to his labour as a writer and then proceeds to flout them. Though it is clear De Quincey cannot arrive at any hypothetical 'outside' (this 'outside' would necessarily entail *not writing*), the essay is geared towards signifying the impossibility of ever articulating the promise held by its title. In 'Sir William Hamilton' the absence of the author is given as the absence of a stable point of departure on a particular subject. De Quincey implies that there is no basis for writing other than writing itself (i.e. other writings, previous writings); that, as he has already started (in that his local effort is always prefigured by writing), he can pick and choose limits at random; that the apparent beginning and ending of a specific piece of writing can occur anywhere; and that, given this, any piece of writing can have any number of beginnings and endings. As J. Hillis Miller has written: 'Since even a finite number of facts can be grouped in endlessly different ways, none of De Quincey's essays can be definitive or exhaustive'.[14]

De Quincey confesses early on to having 'no materials – not a scrap' (*Hogg's Instructor*, vol. VIII, p. 401) on which to base his sketch. As biography, its impact is certainly minimal. The nominal subject, Hamilton, and the potential or occult subject, De Quincey, are both circumlocuted. The maze of 'irrelevancies' erected by the writer has a special significance in that it allows the writer endlessly to defer embarking upon what is announced as a particularly difficult project. The essay opens with a judicious pre-emptive apology for what is (not) to come:

> I begin by entreating the reader, not so much in kindness (of which he may have none to spare) as in mere justice, to make allowance for this little sketch, as a sketch written under unfavourable circumstances. What circumstances? Why, written at a distance, in the first place, from the press; or, because in these days there is no such thing as distance, written under a difficulty almost incredible to myself of communicating with the press (*Hogg's Instructor*, vol. VIII, p. 401).

The translation of the handwritten word into print is De Quincey's principal source of difficulty. Though the sense of obvious irony this printed claim produces is not so pronounced in other cases, the claim of having difficulties with the Press is a feature of many of De Quincey's essays (as I have argued in Chapter 1). De Quincey's misgivings over technologically determined error reflect a fear of permanence and, by implication, of death. The published word takes on an aspect of definitive 'truth', a definitive but possibly mistaken representation which ties him down. The Press marks off time in an uncontrollable way (he cannot alter the text after publication) and at once decisively preserves and requires decisive action. In De Quincey's view, human error is barely allowed for by technology. Communication is dangerous, and, rather than directly face the danger, De Quincey procrastinates, repeatedly revising the moment before that of extremity (though of course this is a way of facing the danger). This procrastination, which in many instances also characterises his style, reflects a fear of a fluctuating present which apparently contains endless possibilities (looking towards the future) that immediately become past and permanent, erasing those possibilities (the process does the erasing). The composition of an essay demands some sort of decision, a decision De Quincey is careful to disclaim.

De Quincey's characterisation of the moment of decision in revising the *Confessions* as one of 'sickening misery' (5: xiii), which I discussed in Chapter 1 is complemented by his description of the miseries of involuntary recollection in 'Sir William Hamilton', where

> by recalling such vanished scenes too vividly, one obeys a summons to an active collusion and cooperation with one's own secret suffering, and becomes a fiery *heautontimoroumenos* (or self-tormentor) in the most afflicting sense (*Hogg's Instructor*, vol. VIII, p. 401).

Remembering is like revision, like reading and writing. For De Quincey, to remember is to become the victim of himself and of a process over which he has no control. In remembering, he is constantly revising and thus having to come to terms with an increasingly complex present (since the longer he lives to remember, the more there will be to revise: new combinations will arise and demand in turn to be collated and comprehended). The hypothetical moment at which De Quincey could remember everything as a totality would demand that he be on the point of dying: for, were he to live any longer, he would have to have that extra moment of life to remember as well. Given De Quincey's conviction that nothing can truly be forgotten (see 'The Palimpsest' section of 'Suspiria de Profundis' [*L* 139-46]), any memory implies the whole mass of memories and in turn implies his own mortality. In recalling the past, he finds himself placed in a position of extremity. De Quincey occupies an interface between total revelation (an intolerable concept) and total oblivion (which he desires when confronted by visions of the remembered dead) – an interface in which he is always about to die and always about to be reborn. Massive anxieties arise from such extremity. Thus, in the directions to the reader quoted above, De Quincey's playful manipulation of the page conceals a dark joke. The admission that the reader will 'easily overtake' the writer implies that the writer is essentially dead already; and that 'me' does not refer to any verifiable real entity outside the writing. The essay's concern with resurrection is artfully dramatised in terms of the two narrative locations (main essay and footnote): the reader's descent into the 'mine' is a descent into the grave; and by returning to the 'upper air' the reader resurrects De Quincey, reincarnates the writer. 'I' momentarily becomes the substitute for De Quincey.

De Quincey signals his extremity at this point. His position as author is more complex than that of the 'reader' he directs, for in the correction of his proofs he becomes his own reader, moving away from his status as author, but also reasserting his presence in the manner described (that is, in the specular connection forged between the dead writer and the reader: De Quincey the writer is revivified by De Quincey the reader). By writing, he becomes his own murderer; by revising, his own resurrectionist. In 'Sir William Hamilton' he is a literary Burke and Hare, involved in the evasion of (self) exhumation by resorting to (self) murder. Like the murderers, he suffers for his actions as much as any victim (see Chapter 4). He is further threatened by the fact that he must collude with the compositor and publisher, agents who can disrupt his activities, whose demands augment the series of limitations that determine the extent of his activities. De Quincey declares his own redundancy as regards the production of the expected biographical sketch, forcing his reader to 'make allowance' and accept a piece which is necessarily imperfect. Any concept of the writer's responsibility for his work (which lies behind such strategies) is shifted to a 'general circumstance' which can barely be explained. De Quincey is trapped in a chain of substitutions which print threatens to halt, exposing the absence of authority. His complaints about the Press are in a way an attempt to relocate authority. In 'Sir William Hamilton' a great deal of enjoyment is derived from this relocation, as De Quincey repeatedly lays claim to and denies the possibility of being 'given' by his labour.

Several pages into the essay, De Quincey resolves to begin afresh, a resolution that the reader's having read this far immediately negates. The new departure signalled by the sentence 'I am now going to begin' is modified by a formal joke that invalidates the promise of entering *in media res* and indeed, the supposition behind beginning afresh:

> I am now going to begin. You will see a full stop or period a very few inches farther on, lurking immediately under the word *earnest* on the off side; and, from and after that full stop, you are to consider me as having shaken off all troublesome companions, and as having once for all entered upon business in earnest (*Hogg's Instructor*, vol. VIII, p. 402).

Since the 'troublesome companions' comprise the whole of the essay, this resolution can scarcely be kept, unless De Quincey were to determine to finish once and for all rather than to begin. Every full stop now becomes a potential new beginning, every idea threatens to suggest new points of departure. The apparent purpose of beginning afresh, to avoid entrapment in the abominable sense that he is caught up in a never-ending process, is undercut by the realisation that every artificial start implies an infinite series of possible continuations, along any given line of thought. It is impossible to start or to finish: both concepts are invalidated by the realisation that in writing De Quincey is involved in continual flux. The limitations imposed by the journal, by the market, by the natural energies of the writer (he might perhaps fall asleep, die, &c.) or by the destruction of, say, the paper on which he writes, are all local. The immanence of writing provides a register akin to space or time which, for De Quincey, is constantly to be confronted and fiercely engaged with. Though representation seems aberrant, it cannot be bypassed. The confrontation (a desperate struggle with an oppressive doppelgänger) is eternal, infinite – even if its local manifestation is limited. The possibilities for resolution are nil. De Quincey must *continue* and yet this very continuation is potentially disastrous, involving contradictions and anxieties. Every expression of his situation reinforces the ultimate dilemma of what he calls 'our *aporia*, that is, our resourcelessness' (*Hogg's Instructor*, vol. IX, p. 277n).[15] Progress ceases to be meaningful, and De Quincey envisages a full scale revision of experiential reality – a reality which he depicts as a representation, a text written by Time that might somehow be repressed. This reversal of the actual state of affairs is highly ironic. De Quincey's wish that secular resurrection – the actual revivification of textual figures, the incarnation of the estranged entities representation should supposedly give – were possible is a wish which admits to the blatant artificiality of representation and thus undercuts all his efforts:

> Ah! that one might, if it were but for one day in a century, be indulged with the sight of Time forced into a personal incarnation, so as to be capable of a personal insult – a cudgelling, for instance, or a ducking in a horse-pond. Or, again, that once in a century, were it but for a single summer's day, his corrected proofs might be liable to supersession by *revises*, such as I would furnish, down the margin of which should run one perpetual iteration of *stet., stet.;*' [sic] everything that the hoary scoundrel had *deleted*, rosebuds or female bloom, beauty or power, grandeur or grace, being solemnly reinstated, and having the privilege of one day's secular resurrection, like the Arabian phoenix, or any other memento of power in things earthly and in sublunary births, to mock and to defy the scythe of this crowned thief! (*Hogg's Instructor*, vol. VIII, p. 401).

Time, De Quincey's enemy, a sort of anti-Christ he would have mocked and defied, is envisaged here as a writer whose eternal work denies the effectiveness of De Quincey's writing. De Quincey suggests himself as the one to do the work of revising Time's proofs, or preparing copy for a new edition of the past (an edition which would negate the past). De Quincey's own writing is a deliberate misreading of Time's copy, a defiant, hopeful, hopeless, marginal gloss which contradicts the 'truth' of his own oblivion. Secular resurrection he knows to be an impossibility, a privilege of metaphorical figures (the phoenix) and language. The desire for secular resurrection is akin to that for the recovery of the moment of anticipation. Both are variants of the wish for the extension of the procrastinatory moment which, for De Quincey, is always a prelude to the fascinating trauma of extremity. Extremity and procrastination, however, are interdependent. Thus De Quincey's awareness that his extension of the procrastinatory moment is both a pleasure and a form of self-deceit produces equal degrees of calm and agitation. Images of this compound state of mind abound in his works. The excessive deference of the 'true' start to the essay on Hamilton, coupled as it is with the sudden realisation that there is not enough time or space to enable the work to be produced, is merely an extreme example of what is a habitual practice with De Quincey, whose revisions are the complementary action to eluding entrapment in time.

CHAPTER FOUR 93

Fictions

My primary concern in this chapter is with demonstrating how De Quincey's fictions, which have been generally neglected, relate to his better known autobiographical writings. My approach is, on the one hand, to differentiate between fiction and autobiography; and, on the other hand, to suggest a possible reading of the fictions as complementary expressions or dramatisations of the same problems encountered elsewhere in De Quincey's writings – problems first and foremost of *writing*, of the production of the text.

Background

The first of De Quincey's known fictions was a novel, *The Stranger's Grave* (1823), an anonymous melodramatic tale of incest interspersed with moments of comic relief, rather cynical in tone. This was followed in 1825 by *Walladmor*, purportedly a translation of a German forgery of a *Waverley* novel. The German original had been produced in the absence of a new work by Sir Walter Scott for the 1824 Leipzig Book Fair. De Quincey's re-cast constitutes a new work, an 'original' fiction, since it does not attempt to follow the German text – rather, De Quincey specifically purposes to produce an altogether superior work. Again, the novel is a mixture of dramatic adventure and comedy. De Quincey contributed some shorter fictions to the numerous Annuals published in the 1820s. 'The Peasant of Portugal' (1827), a brief story of murder and revenge, is such a work. Far more ambitious is *Klosterheim* (1832), De Quincey's final novel, part Gothic tale, part political allegory. This was published by Blackwood, in whose magazine appeared two melancholy tales, written soon after the death of De Quincey's wife – 'The Household Wreck' (January 1838) and 'The Avenger' (August 1838). De Quincey wrote at least one other fiction after 'The Avenger', a tale called 'The Curse' (1839), the text of which remains undiscovered. It seems very likely that an earlier tale called 'The Caçadore' (1828) is also De Quincey's work: it is treated as such in this chapter. It is possible that other fictional works by De Quincey remain to be found.[1]

On the whole, where they have been mentioned at all, De Quincey's fictions have been dismissed by previous critics. Lyon's thoroughly pedestrian study comments that 'Few of De Quincey's works in pure fiction are of any interest today'.[2] De Luca, whose comments on this body of writings are generally sound and useful, remarks that they are unlikely to attract many readers. Eaton asserts that 'As literature, all his attempts at fiction are for us merely curiosities'.[3] Furthermore he goes on to suggest that the fictions are 'unoriginal' translations:

> So persistent was his habit of borrowing, that one may well suspect that even for *The Household Wreck*, *The Avenger*, and *Klosterheim*, which are generally accepted as of De Quincey's own invention, some obscure German originals may still be discovered.[4]

It need scarcely be affirmed that De Quincey was certainly influenced by German fiction. In 'Gillies's German Stories' (1826) he writes of his enthusiasm for it: 'Some years ago, we took lodgings at a German circulating library, and read "a matter" of three thousand tales, long and short' ('Gillies's German Stories', *Blackwood's*, vol.XX, p. 852). In the same paper he praises Hoffman's 'Meister Floh' and 'Phantasieen', saying that 'both tales, which turn upon the interest of secret murder, are powerfully attractive' (ibid., p. 854). However, there is no solid evidence to support Eaton's suspicions, nor those of Goldman, who argues that *Klosterheim* is probably 'a *rifacimento* of some obscure German original'.[5] This view cannot be substantiated, nor can Goldman's suggestion that 'The Avenger' is likewise a translation. This he asserts even though he quotes contradictory evidence from a letter of Emily De Quincey to Mrs James T. Fields (wife of the publisher of the American collected edition of De Quincey's works): 'He sends his kind regards to you and Mr Fields, and says that he did write *The Avenger*. It was written under circumstances forcing him to finish it very hurriedly'.[6] The suggestion is also contradicted by De Quincey's description of the story as 'A German Tale *(scene laid in Germ.* I mean, but entirely of my own invention), turning upon Secret murder' (NLS MS 3112, fo. 288, Friday 25 May 1838).

The notion of the fictions' unoriginality has recently been laid to rest by Lindop:

> In fact, this doubt need not trouble us too much, for all De Quincey's known works of fictional translation or *rifacimento* were first published explicitly as such, a feature which distinguishes them clearly from the 'original' stories.[7]

One may add that De Quincey's working methods, as revealed through his letters, indicate that the fictions (with the dubious exception of *Walladmor*) were his own work.[8] He was obliged to rewrite very rapidly sections of both 'The Household Wreck' and *Klosterheim*, under difficult circumstances. Having burned the manuscript of *Klosterheim* as soon as the proof was ready (NLS MS 4717 fo. 57), De Quincey could not refer back to his first draft; and when part of the novel went missing, he was obliged to recompose a chapter:

> Originally *Klost.* opened with a chapter describing the entrance of a body of Travellers &c after a battle. This arrangement was afterwards changed, and the opening chap. being very elaborately written was laid aside to be introduced wherever the [?composition] might prescribe. I fully believed that this had been done. However the Chapter is certainly not in the MS nor can it be found. I have therefore re-composed what is required, repaged, and reshaped, and revised the whole. – All is now *perfect* in any sense in which I can make it so (NLS MS 4717 fo. 52).

It seems unlikely, given this evidence, that De Quincey was working at a translation. With 'The Household Wreck', the proofs of the tale were found to be incomplete. De Quincey was unable to return to his lodgings to retrieve the MS and rewrote the missing section:

> I have sat up to re-write it and have developed it so much more, that I much fear it will prove too long. But it is better, and more effective – and I do not know how to shorten it. However, I can leave out (perhaps with advantage) nearly the whole of Proof 3, portion 2nd (NLS MS 4717 fo. 36, 19 December 1837).

Again, this provides a clear indication of De Quincey's working methods and contradicts the 'German original' notion, which thesis is presumably designed to excuse De Quincey's fictions. Such a misinterpretation is quite unnecessary. I can see no case for apologising for the fictions which, as Lindop writes, 'contain much that is of interest in adding to our understanding of the tensions that structure his work as a whole'.[9]

De Quincey's reasons for writing his half dozen fictions may be defined in various ways. First, the purely practical reason of earning some money must be taken into consideration; secondly, we may cautiously consider a psychological motive; thirdly, De Quincey's opinion that novels are little more than sources of 'pure amusement' notwithstanding (*Blackwood's*, vol. XX, p. 858), we may interpret the fictions as articulations of a specific literary problem. In this chapter I am concerned with the third approach.[10] I do not treat the fictions in chronological order, nor do I analyse all of them in depth. Rather, my approach here is to outline certain strategies which throw into relief those used elsewhere in De Quincey's writings, with particular reference to his autobiographical works.

In an essay analaysing the differences between autobiography and fiction, Barrett J. Mandel asserts that, while the two genres have much in common vis-à-vis techniques, the one 'borrowing' from the other, 'What defictionalises autobiography is both the readers' powers of cocreation and the author's animation in the present of his or her past'.[11] De Quincey's fictions may be distinguished from his autobiographical pieces by the absence of any vital relationship between the writer and his reader. The figure of the reader in autobiography is a figure of revivification. By reading the text, the reader makes a specular connection between his or her own identity and that given (produced) by the 'I' of the autobiography. Reading is a defiant continuation of a series of substitutions in this instance. In the fictions a similar action is *possible*, but it is not necessary, nor is it apposite. Instead, De Quincey incorporates into his fictions what could be called figures of terminal reading: as if the text of an autobiography had been appropriated and recast – finished by a misreading which, in negating this erased text's properties, had produced the fictional tale. The fiction thus has the properties of a translation, though it is a translation which now thwarts retranslation. Many of these terminal readers are witnesses to catastrophic events – victims of murder who can never voice the recognition of their assailants; oppressors who conceal their deeds even from themselves; and helpless bystanders who feel unable to act effectually. These figures imply the validity of objective reality. The text of the past is definitively read. The process by which the logically non-existent past is revitalised in the present of composition is artificially terminated. The terminal readers prevent the tales from being misread and provide an interpretation of events which pre-empts the efforts of the extra-textual reader. Whereas in his autobiographical writings the events recounted can be validated by neither the reader nor the writer, in his fictions De Quincey explores the meaning of permanent validity. His fictions are dramatisations of the death-wish which is often repressed in the autobiographical pieces.

'The Household Wreck'

The tale which most fully employs the techniques available to autobiographical narrative, and which clearly echoes episodes recounted in De Quincey's *Confessions*, the 'Suspiria' and 'The English Mail-Coach', is 'The Household Wreck' (1838), De Quincey's finest exercise in fiction. Like the Opium-Eater, the narrator of this tale is anonymous; his narrative tells of the destruction of his domestic bliss by a malicious, uncaring and unidentified society – a destruction which he has survived. Even in his happiest moments, catastrophe has been felt approaching. The narrator's sense of foreboding, expressed towards the beginning of the tale, is compounded when a fortune-teller – the Hungarian Prophetess – reads doom written in the palm of his wife, Agnes. One day Agnes, alone in the city, is falsely accused by the villainous Barratt, and is subsequently arrested. The efforts of her husband and her faithful maid Hannah to secure her release or defend her name prove futile. Agnes remains in prison, her obvious innocence provoking the sympathy of the public and the malice of the courts and a scheming minister. The narrator sinks into a stupor of apathy, from which he is roused by the attentions of Hannah. Later, however, at the courts he catches a fever, which he transmits to his son. After months of illness passed in a daze, he recovers to find his son dead and Agnes sentenced to ten years hard labour. With the aid of his brother-in-law Pierpoint, he attempts to rescue his wife by bribing the jailor. When this fails, they break in and out of the prison by force and escape to a a squalid quarter of the city. Agnes, however, is rapidly declining. The officers of the law pursue and surround the fugitives but, as they enter the hovel, Agnes expires. After her death the narrator determines to avenge his wife; but Barratt, caught trying to seduce another innocent, is torn to pieces by an angry mob. In his dying breath he confesses his crimes, and his testament is passed on to the hostile minister who had countenanced the unjust sentence imposed upon Agnes.

The time-structure of this bizarre tale is complex. The story proper is prefaced by a passage supposedly composed more than fifty years after the catastrophe described and over a decade after it had been set down by the narrator-protagonist. The narrator states that 38 years have elapsed between the catastrophe and the composition of his tale (*Blackwood's*, vol. XLIII [January 1838], p. 4), though elsewhere this is given as 28 years (*ibid.*, p. 23). A tonal discrepancy complements the temporal disparity. The remarks which preface the story are painfully melancholic, and while they allow for some measure of consolation even in the worst of disasters (*ibid.*, p. 2), in the main they alert the reader to hidden depths of experience (in this case, negative experience), and answer the question 'What is life?' by emphasising the meaninglessness of existence:

> Darkness and formless vacancy for a beginning, or something beyond all beginning – then next a dim lotos of human consciousness, finding itself afloat upon the bosom of waters without a shore – then a few sunny smiles and many tears; a little love and infinite strife – whisperings from paradise and fierce mockeries from the anarchy of chaos – dust and ashes – and once more darkness circling round, as if from the beginning, and in this way rounding or making an island of our fantastic existence, – *that* is human life; *that* the inevitable amount of man's laughter and his tears – of what he suffers and he does – of his motions this way and that way – to the right or to the left – backwards or forwards – of all his seeming realities and all his absolute negations – his shadowy pomps and his pompous shadows – of whatsoever he thinks, finds, makes or mars, creates or animates, loves, hates, or in dread hope anticipates; – so it is, so it has been, so it will be, for ever and ever (*Blackwood's*, vol. XLIII, p. 1)

Such a belief is at odds with the tale, which, though it deals at length with the narrator's apathy and despair, also recounts his apparent triumph over the destructive forces around him and ends with his assertion that 'my revenge was perfect' (*Blackwood's*, vol. XLIII, misnumbered p. 32). The introduction and the tale negate each other and thus stand in an ironic relation. The ambiguity which arises is reinforced when the narrator of the tale is considered as the author of the introduction as well; *or* whether they are taken as two different authors. In the first instance the conclusion drawn from the tale, namely that 'perfect' revenge has been achieved and equilibrium restored, is called into question by a reading which asserts that there are endless hidden depths to experience – that, in effect, the tale holds a series of hidden meanings, each of which may erase the others. In this case, the author, estranged from the narrative which defines him, posits through his introductory remarks an identity equipped with ethical values which negate those embodied in the tale. He fails to understand the nature of his experience; or, at least, of his representation of his experience.

In the second case, where the two possible authors are involved, the introduction's assertion that the tale is all 'strictly true' (*Blackwood's*, vol. XLIII, p. 3) is invalidated by the content of the tale, since only the protagonist can verify the material (which includes such wholly private experiences as dreams). The introduction misreads the tale, though in doing so it also colludes with the idealisation of the dead Agnes; and it implicitly instructs the extra-textual reader, reinterpreting and glossing the story in a way which renders it redundant. The introduction pre-empts the extra-textual reader's response to the tale of which it forms a necessary part. The time-scale discussed above implies that the identity of the narrator has changed drastically – that the two authors suggested by the discrepancy between introduction and tale are the same *entity*, but not therefore the same *identity*. The narrator of the quasi-autobiographical tale is essentially contained by the catastrophe he describes. As a (detached) commentator on his own narrative, he is himself the figure of Nemesis he claims to be awaiting. The crisis has happened – is past and complete – but it also continually recurs. To read the tale (as the introductory remarks imply) is to engage in a sort of mad rewriting of the figure of Nemesis, the 'I' of 'The Household Wreck'.[12]

The narrator rehearses every event surrounding the catastrophe in minute detail, 'recalling every circumstance the most trivial of this the final morning of what merits to be called my life' (*Blackwood's*, vol. XLIII, p. 9). By defining himself as the entity to whom the 'calamity' occurs, the narrator implicitly signals that the events are a self-fulfilling prophecy of his spiritual disintegration. His having to die (alternatively, his having been born) precipitates an obscene vision of life in which the self is pursued by incomprehensible forces, the 'mysteriousness' of which is informed by an apparently irrecoverable origin – the moment of birth – an origin displaced in the narrative to the present-time of composition. The narrator's acceptance (invention?) of the 'reading' provided by the Hungarian

Prophetess, and his compounding of her doom-laden message in a manner that admits of no alternatives, complements the prefiguration of his own death as an end to meaning. His despair, which arises out of a conviction that the catastrophe is inevitable (as indeed it must appear, since it has already happened), informs the creation of the narrative which purports to document the states of his mind. The events that have occurred are represented as having been definitively read before their unfolding, which makes the actual written narrative effectively redundant. The interpretation of the catastrophe as the fulfillment of the narrator's death-wish (even though he alone survives), as an analogy of the terminal reading of the formally necessary fiction of the disintegration with which the autobiographer must come to terms, dramatises De Quincey's realisation that writing is potentially meaningless.

The development of the narrative from despair to action hinges on the 'rebirth' of the narrator after several weeks of near-lunacy. Chronic anxiety, arising from the 'dim abiding feeling (that sometimes was and sometimes was not exalted into a conscious presentiment) of some great calamity travelling towards me' (*Blackwood's*, vol. XLIII, p. 7), gives way to the realisation of the possibility of a new beginning – and thus of a continuation of the anxiety:

> For some weeks I became a pitiable maniac, and in every sense the wreck of my former self; and seven entire weeks, together with the better half of an eighth week, had passed over my head whilst I lay unconscious of time and its dreadful freight of events, excepting in so far as my disordered brain, by its fantastic coinages, created endless mimicries and mockeries of these events – less substantial, but oftentimes less afflicting, or less agitating. It would have been well for me had my destiny decided that I was not to be recalled to this world of wo [*sic*]. But I had no such happiness in store. I recovered, and through twenty and eight years my groans have recorded the sorrow I feel that I did (*Blackwood's*, vol. XLIII, p. 23).

Madness is conceived of as the oppression of one's identity by fraudulent 'mimicries and mockeries' *ad infinitum*. The narrator's conviction that he is, initially, being pursued by a mysterious calamity; his subsequent efforts to visualise the return of his wife on the road from the town (*Blackwood's*, vol. XLIII, p. 11); and the dream-coinages by means of which he attempts to re-order experience, all dramatise a static position assumed by the self, in that the narrator's madness relates to his reading of his own character as a definite, determined and singular thing, rather than as the by-product of a process. The narrator's fixation – his various attempts to *produce* a reality of his own – provides evidence of a self which remains still, trapped in essentially repetitive activities. The fears, imaginings and dreams of the narrator of 'The

Household Wreck' all suggest immobility – apparent activity notwithstanding.

Images of madness and entrapment in a fixed position (a kind of displaced death) occur frequently in De Quincey's writings.[13] The narrator's sense of foreboding is couched in terms which reappear in De Quincey's superb sketch of Charles Lloyd (1840), who was evidently on the verge of madness and who was placed in a madhouse:

> Afterwards he told me that his situation internally was always this – it seemed to him as if on some distant road he heard a dull trampling sound, and that he knew it, by a misgiving, to be the sound of some man, or party of men, continually advancing slowly, continually threatening, or continually accusing him: that all the various artifices which he practised for cheating himself into comfort, or beguiling his sad forebodings, were, in fact, but like so many furious attempts, by drum and trumpets, or even by artillery, to drown the distant noise of his enemies; that, every now and then, mere curiosity, or rather breathless anxiety, caused him to hush the artificial din, and to put himself in the attitude of listening again; when, again and again, and so he was sure it would still be, he caught the sullen and accursed sound, trampling and voices of men, or whatever it were, still steadily advancing, though still, perhaps, at a great distance (*Tait's*, vol. VII [March 1840], p. 164).

Here Lloyd is obliged to fictionalise a state of repose, though this ironically entails that he drown out the approaching rumble with another, louder noise of his own. His 'artifices' reinforce that which they are supposed to muffle, as he is led to the conclusion that the prefigured disintegration of his identity cannot be altered in its essence. The reading of his fate is final, though he manages to delay the calamity by working on and publishing a translation of 'the whole of Alfieri's dramas' (*Tait's* vol.VII, p. 164) and by writing a novel – points De Quincey thinks worthy of mention. By engaging in the production of texts, Lloyd defers the moment of extremity. This action, however, is a treacherous ploy, a delusion that has the effect of compounding his derangement, in that the texts he produces (a procrastinatory task) separate him from the extreme situation, rather than allow him to cope with extremity in a De Quinceyan way (by prefiguring the crisis). Lloyd does not fill out the moment of extremity, but blots it out, attempting to render void the evidence of its continual imminence.

In the revision of the *Confessions*, De Quincey re-echoes this passage in the description of his approach to London:

> And at intervals I heard – in how different a key! – the raving, the everlasting uproar of that dreadful metropolis, which at every step was coming nearer, and beckoning (as it seemed)

to myself for purposes as dim, for issues as incalculable, as the path of cannon-shots fired at random and in darkness (5: 150).

De Quincey, however, is 'saved' by his inability to prefigure the precise signification of the uproar: the meaning of his life is hypothetical, as the very fact of revision indicates. Always coincident to the autobiographical tasks exists the possibility of reinterpretation; and the 'error' of going to London is also a crucially meaningful action. Similarly, the quasi-autobiographical narrative represented in 'The Household Wreck' is made up of a series of ambiguous images of catastrophe. Ambiguity is positively valorised in the tale, the introduction of which (itself standing in ambiguous relation to the narrative) is in part concerned with the threat on a social scale to the possibilty of reinterpretation. As society advances *en masse*, never pausing to think, it becomes a destructive force, analogous to death in that it makes the individual unimportant. The terminology employed here prefigures De Quincey's most comprehensive exploration of this (political) theme in 'The English Mail-Coach' (1849) (see Chapter 5):

> The mighty Juggernaut of social life, moving onwards with its everlasting thunders, pauses not for a moment to spare – to pity – to look aside, but rushes forward for ever, impassive as the marble in the quarry – caring not for whom it destroys, for the how many, or for the results, direct and indirect, whether many or few. The increasing grandeur and magnitude of the social system, the more it multiplies and extends its victims, the more it conceals them; and for the very same reason (*Blackwood's*, vol. XLIII, p. 2).

The narrator's mad sense of misgiving clearly responds to and complements the onrush of society. His acceptance of doom at once colludes with the social tendency; and, in that this connection is treacherously ironic but is also necessary for change to be accomplished (personally and socially), throws it into relief – thus emphasising the significance of the individual. This movement underlines the ambiguous relation of the individual, and more emphatically of the outsider or pariah, to the social system. The narrator registers distaste when Agnes is tried before 'the whole world of this vast metropolis – the idle, the curious, the brutal, the hardened amateur in spectacles of wo [sic]' (*Blackwood's*, vol. XLIII, p. 17); but later, craving 'Tumult [. . .] and distraction of thought' (*ibid.*, p. 23), he finds relief in the crowds assembled in the courts. After the trial, he wanders about, 'caring little for life or its affairs, and roused only at times to think of vengeance upon all who had contributed to lay waste my happiness' (*ibid.*, misnumbered p. 31). His revenge is made 'perfect' because the circumstances allow him to maintain a certain distance from society, a distance which arises from his sense of moral maturity and which has the curious effect of enabling him to indulge in the occupation of a station at one remove from the imminent catastrophe previously represented as entrapping him. His procrastination over whether or not to kill Barratt apparently concludes with Barratt's death at the hands of the enraged mob; but this resolution is significant of more than a simple exchange of one life (Barratt's) for another (Agnes's): the legal system and the society which condones it come under critical scrutiny. As the mob violence implies, all is not well with the system. So too, the narrator criticises the mob, whose actions are morally unacceptable for the individual. He can rejoice in the justice meted out, while still maintaining his pariah posture, as though his revenge were still a future thing, or a permanently revolving symbolic event. The movement towards this state of grace involves an apparent detachment from reality:

> I myself heard the uproar at a distance, and the shouts and yells of savage exultation; they were sounds I shall never forget, though I did not at that time know them for what they were, or understood [sic] their meaning. (*Blackwood's*, vol. XLIII, misnumbered p. 32).

The noisy destruction of his enemy registers as a hieroglyphic which must be reinterpreted after it has been read. The secret signal of the completion of the reading of events as projected by the narrator is invested with precise meaning only after the actual event: a reversal of the situation which, it is claimed, ensnares Agnes. Agnes is the victim of a real event which appears to be determined by a definitive text: not only the writing of her palm as read by the Prophetess, nor only her husband's unuttered prediction of catastrophe, but also the testament of Barratt, which at once compounds and completes the series of prefigurative readings, comprise this text. That Barratt's word is a lie which everyone takes for the truth underlines the process involved here. A fiction which relies on a terminal reading, a reading which admits of no revision, is constructed, and this self-sufficient text proves inherently destructive. Barratt's lie, taken at face-value by the Law (itself a self-sufficient text), produces Agnes's death. This text, which the narrator is obliged to rewrite in order to explain himself, and which, when written, must needs be invalidated (for otherwise he must conspire with the very process he criticises), is erased by the narrative which contains it. In terms of the plot, Barratt testifies to Agnes's innocence: the liar finally tells the truth. But just as this confession fails to bring Agnes back to life, so too the narrative of 'The Household Wreck' remains problematic in that, while it preserves Agnes as an ideal martyr, it also buries her beneath a mass of signifiers which succeed in obliterating her even before her death is announced. From the beginning, Agnes is dead – something inextricably linked to the quasi-autobiographical narrative form, as well as something which inevitably appears to be the paradigm of the terminal readings encountered in the story: the narrative, composed

Fictions

after her death, attempts to rewrite this fact which allows of no contradiction. The narrator expresses an awareness of the essential futility of reviving his dead wife, indicating that the tale is a form of therapy and of self-torture:

> But how escape from reviving, whether I give it utterance or not, that which is for ever vividly before me? What need to call into artificial light that which, whether sleeping or waking – by night or by day – for eight-and-thirty years has seemed by its miserable splendour to scorch my brain? Wherefore shrink from giving language, simple vocal utterance, to that burden of anguish which by so long an endurance has lost no atom of its weight, nor can gain any most surely by the loudest publication? (*Blackwood's*, vol. XLIII, p.4).

The story, then, can only lead him back to where he has started, and the intricacies of the plot are merely sophisticated images of his inability to tell the truth. The text of 'The Household Wreck' is itself the uncontrolled system of which the narrator complains, and his escape at the end is an indication of his ability to disconnect from the story rather than from 'society'. The tale asserts its own fictitiousness and dramatises the discrepancy between the 'I' of the narrative and the extra-textual entity this figure indicates.

Given that 'The Household Wreck' purportedly tells 'the truth', like De Quincey's autobiographical works, one may see indicated in this fiction a failure of De Quincey's belief in the redeeming features of autobiography. The types of truth to which access is claimed in the fiction and in his autobiographical pieces differ, however, in that the former case does not admit to inherent contingency, whereas the latter relies (as it must) on the possibility of being called into question. The fiction is read as if it were literally true (at face-value), the autobiography as if it were a hypothesis which requires validation. Thus, autobiography, though potentially readable as fiction, in its very realisation of this potential reinforces its claims to being (not non-fiction, but) itself: acceptance of self-doubt on the part of the entity given by 'I', while seemingly contradicting the apparent task of autobiography, is necessary to the autobiographer. This denial of the authority of 'I' provokes many of the strategies that comprise De Quincey's autobiography. The present-time of composition provides the location of the autobiographer. For De Quincey, the present can barely be verified. So too, by implication, what constitutes himself defies representation. In a note in the *Posthumous Works*, he writes:

> Death sinks to a mere collective term – a category – a word of convenience for the purposes of arrangement. You depress your hands, and, behold! the system disappears; you raise them, it reappears. This is nothing – a cipher, a shadow. [. . .] To and fro; it is and it is not – is not and is. Ah, mighty heaven, that such a mockery should cover the whole vision of life! It is and

it is not; and on to the day of your death you will still have to learn what is the truth.

The eternal now through the dreadful loom is the overflowing future poured back into the capacious reservoir of the past. All the active element lies in that infinitesimal *now*. The future is not except by relation; the past is not at all, and the present but a sign of a nexus between the two (*PW* 1: 229).

Despite his reliance on the past for his material and on memory to provide a semblance of narrative coherence, De Quincey's self exists in this 'infinitesimal *now*' of writing and only there. He is imminently present, so that even when his work has been read *in toto* his identity remains obscure. 'De Quincey' is always to-be-read rather than read. The reader of his autobiographical works must, in the act of reading, erase his or her own supposed 'existence' in relation to the text, as if he or she were absent, were about to read, or about to write the 'I' on the page – 'on to the day of your death'.

This inherent contingency differentiates De Quincey's autobiographical from his fictional writings. Although in many ways 'The Household Wreck' seems to be made up of (translated) autobiographical fragments, the coherence of the narrator-protagonist's identity never undergoes conscious scrutiny, though the intensity and ordering of experience in the tale promotes scepticism. The reader does not accept the tale as autobiographical 'truth' because the representation of events declares its pointed artificiality. Belief is not the issue here; rather, the estrangement of meaning from expression creates a complex response. Language takes on an uncanny feel, as if it were palpably delusive, but also as if this delusion were known to be all there is.[14] The lowest depth of experience is a hysterical sense of the futility of expressing a response to reality. Self-parody, self-ridicule is imminent. For De Quincey, creative composition, in that it is always a form of revision or self-conscious quotation (in the broadest sense), tends always towards the parodic. In 'The Household Wreck', the narrator's description of Agnes acknowledges the difficulties often encountered by De Quincey:

> Never yet did my eye light upon creature that was born of woman, nor could it enter my heart to conceive one, possessing a figure more matchless in its proportions, more statuesque, and more deliberately and advisedly to be characterized by no adequate word but the word *magnificent* (a word too often and lightly abused). In reality, speaking of women, I have seen many beautiful figures, but hardly one except Agnes that could without hyperbole be styled truly and memorably magnificent (*Blackwood's*, vol. XLIII, p. 5).

Exactitude leads to a realisation that, as much as it produces reality, language produces a sense of 'language'. De Quincey plays on the discrepancies of a highly structured narrative, underlining the ironic relation of representation and reality at several points in the tale. The narrator remarks how strange the words *'All's right'* seem to him as they flee from the prison (*Blackwood's*, vol. XLIII, misnumbered p. 28) and comments on Agnes's cell: 'her *"cell!"* what a word!' (*ibid.*, p. 21). Language seems inapposite to him. He tries 'to recover the lost connexion' of his thoughts (*ibid.*, p. 23) but is confounded.

The mania of the narrator of 'The Household Wreck', which implies that the narrative may be an unself-conscious 'fantastic coinage' like his dream visions, or a conscious but hideously ironic forgery (as his handling of language suggests), registers as a revision of De Quincey's experiences of intense ungrounding of the self in the *Confessions*. There is a marked similarity, for instance, between the two 'rebirths' in these texts: Hannah brings the narrator a reviving cup of tea: Ann procures a life-saving glass of port for the young De Quincey. A comparison of the episodes reveals obvious similarities:

> Suddenly, as we sate, I grew much worse: I had been leaning my head against her bosom; and all at once I sank from her arms and fell backwards on the steps. From the sensations I then had, I felt an inner conviction of the liveliest kind that without some powerful and reviving stimulus, I should either have died on the spot – or should at least have sunk to a point of exhaustion from which all reäscent under my friendless circumstances would soon have become hopeless. Then it was, at this crisis of my fate, that my poor orphan companion – who had herself met with little but injuries in this world – stretched out a saving hand to me. Uttering a cry of terror, but without a moment's delay, she ran off into Oxford-street, and in less time than could be imagined, returned to me with a glass of port wine and spices, that acted upon my empty stomach (which at that time would have rejected all solid food) with an instantaneous power of restoration (*L* 21-2).

> As the morning light began to break, somebody knocked at the door; it was Hannah; she took my hand – misery levels all feeble distinctions of station, sex, age – she noticed my excessive feverishness, and gravely remonstrated with me upon the necessity there was that I should maintain as much health as possible for the sake of "others," if not for myself. She then brought me some tea, which refreshed me greatly; for I had tasted nothing at all beyond a little water since the preceding morning's breakfast. This refreshment seemed to relax and thaw the stiff frozen state of cheerless, rayless despair in which I had passed the night (*Blackwood's* vol. XLIII, p. 19).

Like Ann, Hannah's role is that of saviour. The narrator is to some measure dependent upon her, and it is she who redeems the critical situation when Agnes is about to be shot. Whereas the narrator can only contemplate, Hannah is able to act. She indicates possibilities in the narrative which its author fails to acknowledge, and it is significant that her fate remains obscure: she is last mentioned when she informs the narrator that they are surrounded, before opening the door to admit the pursuers (*Blackwood's*, vol. XLIII, misnumbered p. 31). As a symbolic action in this story of confinement, infiltration and termination, Hannah's ambiguous 'exit' from the narrative (did she get out?) can be read as indicative of the redemptive potential inherent in a figure who thwarts expectations (*Blackwood's* vol. XLIII, p. 13) and contains hidden energy. So too, her palindromic name emphasises her role as one able to reverse and revise given texts. Hannah is an interpreter like the Hungarian Prophetess and like the narrator, but she has the advantage over both. While their readings of events admit of no continuation – of no action – Hannah can decode experience and change the 'inevitable'. When Agnes is about to be killed by the evil jailor Manasseh, she steps in where the narrator can only observe:

> I saw, I comprehended, the whole. I groped, as far as I could without letting my wife drop, for my pistols; but all that I could do would have been unavailing, and too late – she would have been murdered in my arms. But – and that was what none of us saw – neither I, nor Pierpoint, nor the hound Manasseh – one person stood back in the shade; one person had seen, but had not uttered a word on seeing Manasseh advancing through the shades; one person only had forecast the exact succession of all that was coming (*Blackwood's* vol. XLIII, misnumbered p. 27).

Hannah's action at the point of crisis (which contrasts with the narrator's lack of action when faced with a vision of approaching catastrophe: he does not utter a word, but neither does he act) reiterates the theme of 'The Household Wreck'. Simultaneously it exposes the failure of the narrator to realise fully this theme: Hannah is a redeemer and a witness to the narrator's lack of success in his attempt to 'resurrect' Agnes. He sees 'the whole', defining experience as a totality – a totality which is penetrated and burst open by Hannah's silent disruption of the apparently inevitable murder of Agnes. This invasion of a contained, closed space (in this instance a unit of time in which the fate of the narrator, Agnes *et alia* is effectually predetermined) is a recurrent theme in De Quincey's works, one closely linked to the idea of resurrection. 'The Household Wreck' records a failure of belief in the possibility of rebirth, with only Hannah hinting at its validity. The narrator, enclosed by the requirements of a coherent text, of a totality, enters trap after trap, and is continually led back to anxiety.

Thus, domestic bliss proves disconcerting and provokes unease: the narrator constructs a way out, which takes the form of a disaster (the penetration of his household by Barratt and by his ally, the third maid). Agnes is imprisoned and the narrator at first imagines her free, then perversely encloses her as surely as does the jail:

> Could it have been that in some moment of infirmity, when her better angel was away from her side, she had yielded to a sudden impulse of frailty, such as a second moment for consideration would have resisted, but which unhappily had been followed by no such opportunity of retrieval? I had heard of such things [. . .] Dreadful was the panic I underwent. God pardon the wrong I did; and even now I pray to him – as though the past thing were a future thing and capable of change – that he would forbid her for ever to know what was the derogatory thought I had admitted (*Blackwood's* vol. XLIII, p. 28).

The narrator's efforts to escape lead only to an increased sense of entrapment, which in turn fuels the urge to find a way out. He conceives of Agnes's crime in terms of his own psychological endeavour: she has 'yielded', has allowed herself to be infiltrated by an outside force (and thus, if one interprets the theme of infiltration as having sexual connotations, the story allows for lengthy speculation: Barratt's action constitutes a displaced rape). The crumbling jail which contains Agnes is broken into; and, once freed, Agnes is hidden away in a house in the middle of the city, a refuge reached by an extraordinarily complex escape route (*Blackwood's*, vol. XLIII, p. 29). Once again, Agnes is enclosed. The family, obliged to live in secrecy in decaying surroundings, are pursued by government agents and 'haunted by dreams' (*Blackwood's*, vol. XLIII, misnumbered p. 29), oppressed from without and within. Finally, the house is surrounded. Agnes dies as the officers enter – the ultimate exit. The narrator, however, is forced into a new trap: how to avenge his dead wife without becoming snared by moral and legal strictures? A chance encounter in a church fuels his procrastinatory unease, while the destruction of Barratt by hands other than his leads the narrator to shudder at what he describes as 'the narrow escape I had had from myself intercepting this remarkable retribution' (*Blackwood's*, vol. XLIII, misnumbered p. 31).

This exquisitely neat ending compounds the wish to escape from totalities with the need to enclose Barratt within the confines of the narrator's desire for vengeance. In narrative terms it brings to an abrupt conclusion the series of autobiographical strategies perpetrated by the egotistical protagonist, and the effect (as well as seeming somewhat improbable) is to throw into relief these strategies, questioning the 'truth' of the tale as a whole. The insistent, formally repetitive experiences which constitute the main body of the tale also create the autobiographical figure of the narrator: he seems in the process of avoiding definition in his avowed wish to escape determining events. When Barratt dies, this role is maintained in so far as the narrator represents himself as a wandering pariah who cannot interpret the noise of his enemy's destruction. However, once this *is* interpreted, and his revenge made 'perfect', the narrator becomes trapped once and for all. His role as 'autobiographer' has ceased, and this cessation indicates that, actually, he has been making it up; or that someone else has made it up. The repetitive form 'I', the content of which is given by the events of the story, is limited.

De Quincey's most 'autobiographical' fiction succeeds precisely in that it fails as autobiography. Its internal consistency demands a sequel, though it also denies the possibility of one in that the death of Agnes is balanced against that of Barratt. His death makes her resurrection impossible, while it nevertheless indicates her redemption. That is, her good name is cleared, so justifying the narrator's claims that she was angelic, perfect in fact. The narrative resolution places within a parenthesis the possibility of an 'untrue' or a 'guilty' Agnes, but also reasserts the impossibility of anything but a *dead* Agnes. Really and potentially the image of the 'dovelike woman' is absolute: the narrator involuntarily preserves her as a martyr in 'the fiery furnace' of her sufferings and of his memory. In doing so, he reaffirms that she is quite unobtainable, a lost object that cannot be recovered. This representation of Agnes, which purports to be a representation of a memory, implies that to create a memorial is to fictionalise. The sense of wholeness makes of the figure of Agnes a myth which does not require (indeed, cannot permit of) validation. Through the transformation of past experience into an ideal absolute, the narrative dehistoricises the memory of Agnes; the fiction is an object lesson in the failure of confining 'the past' within definite limits. The autobiographer must maintain the illusion of contingency or else become enclosed in a structure which denies the time continuum within (or during) which he claims to function. In an attempt to blur the import of the close of the fiction, the introductory gloss points to a 'moral' which can be drawn from the tale. This appeal to a universal value appertaining to the private memorial underlines its failure as such; and, indeed, the 'moral' is scarcely given by the tale, nor does the story clearly illustrate any other positive lesson.

'The Avenger' and other fictions

A similar claim to extenuating interest (as if, when all is said and done, a new and entirely separate meaning may be appended to the text) is also made at the opening of 'The Avenger' (1838). The first sentence of the tale claims that the 'events' described were 'too memorable' to be left without a 'separate record'; and, further, that the

> moral lesson, impressed by these event, is yet more memorable, and deserves the deep attention of coming generations in their struggle after human improvement, not merely in its

own limited field of interest directly awakened, but in all analogous fields of interest' (*Blackwood's*, vol. XLIV [August 1838], p. 208).

This broad-based claim is not obviously substantiated by the tale that follows. The narrator here is a Professor in a German university-town. He recounts how a series of murders, apparently quite random as regards the victims, but judged to be premeditated and connected, are committed in spite of every possible precaution. His story revolves around the handsome but melancholic Maximilian Wyndham, who vies with the noble Ferdinand von Harrelstein for the love of the beautiful Margaret, whom he secretly marries. Maximilian is responsible for the murders: the victims are those who were responsible for the death of his mother and sisters, persecuted as Jews by the townsfolk at a time when the Professor was abroad. Maximilian's final victim is Margaret's grandfather. This murder is accidentally seen by Margaret, who collapses and dies soon afterwards, torn between loyalties. Maximilian, having delivered to the Professor a testament justifying his crimes, dies also – his vengeance fulfilled but his happiness quite destroyed.

The lesson that would seem to derive from the narrative is that human life is insecure: the cosy domesticity of the torturers on whom Maximilian wreaks his vengeance, Maximilian's own connection with Margaret, the penetration of an entire town by a mysterious power – these, roughly, point to a moral: 'Beware!' But, if this is the case, suspicions are immediately raised as to the veracity of the Professor's history: on what does his story rest secure? His immediate claim to being in the best position to tell the tale derives from his knowledge of 'all the parties' in the tragedy, and the fact that he 'was present from first to last' while the murders terrified the town (*Blackwood's*, vol. XLIV, p. 208). Implicitly, the Professor's narrative is grounded on a connection with Maximilian, the murderer, whose testament is incorporated into and completes the tale. The Professor and Maximilian are mutually dependent. Their relationship is that of victim and oppressor. The Professor sees largely what he wants to see, and reads 'anxiety' rather than guilt in Maximilian's features, turning him into an object of sympathy:

> People felt it an intrusion upon the sanctity of his grief to look at him too narrowly, and the whole town sympathised with his situation (*Blackwood's*, vol. XLIV, p. 224).

This statement is enormously ironic. Clearly, the Professor, who prides himself on his 'faithful narrative' (*Blackwood's*, vol. XLIV, p. 209), is the dupe of the murderer. The narrative he constructs from his 'central station' (*ibid.*, vol. XLIV, p. 209) marks him out as Maximilian's posthumous victim, one willing to comply with the murderer's request not to publish anything immediately because it enhances and extends his own life. The Professor's ambiguous position as both victim and survivor has arisen from the demands of his narrative. In acting as the definitive witness whose text memorialises and purports to redeem Maximilian, the Professor fixes himself within a structure (in the 'central position') which negates his claims to being a free or independent agent.

The form of the fiction is reflected in its content: the series of deaths are indices of the writer's extremity, of the closure threatened by a terminal reading of an 'autobiographical' narrative. As in 'The Household Wreck', De Quincey experiments with the possibilities afforded by fiction to give some semblance of a self, and finds them delusive.

While De Quincey is able, in his autobiographical works, to step aside repeatedly from the central position he adopts, implying that the self is a sign at the moment of its potential identification (and thus that he can never be given by writing, but can only give writing instead), the quasi-autobiographer of the fiction is confined within the system he creates. As for the 'I' of 'The Household Wreck', the 'I' of 'The Avenger' (the Professor for the most part; his doppelgänger Maximilian at the close) cannot break free of the narrative. His identity is fully integrated into the past, and is read as realised, not as imminently realisable. De Quincey dramatises the enclosure of the narrator by his narrative in his depiction of the environment pertaining to the act of murder, an act which makes the murderer suffer as much as his victim. Thus, Maximilian recounts his wife's unexpected entrance upon the murder of her imbecile grandfather as *his* burden:

> I had relied upon her absence; and the misery of that moment, when her eye fell upon me in the very act of seizing her grandfather, far transcended all else that I have suffered in these terrific scenes (*Blackwood's*, vol. XLIV, p. 233).

The loss of Margaret, whose demise is coincident to the fulfilment of Maximilian's vow, emphasises Maximilian's isolation. He is controlled by his 'word', which admits of no qualification. The enactment of this word compounds the sense of the irrevocable. Just as Maximilian cannot resist avenging his dead family, so too the murder-victim apparently (or so the Professor asserts) cannot resist being killed, in spite of all precautions.

A figure of unbetrayed energy, the murderer can exercise his special authority over his victim without revealing its source. Maximilian's actions are 'mysterious' in that no reading of his irrevocable word is possible: no one can decipher the motive; the murders are read as unreadable. The murderer asserts finity, both in the action of depriving others of life, and in the secrecy which surrounds his motives. Attempts to penetrate the finite prove deceptive, and the Professor's justification of Maximilian finds its parallel in the admittance of the band of assassins to the secure house of their intended victim. Just as the Professor's narrative attempts to gloss Maximilian's otherwise inexplicable actions, and fills out his word with a mass of extenuatory details, the innocent stranger who admits the murderers is involved in an action of infiltration or expansive penetration. This occurs on two levels: first, the opening of the door destroys its function (to keep others out) and turns the enclosed space of the house into an extension of the dangerous town outside; secondly, this action is charged after the event with great significance – the moment is 'opened out', distorted in the narrative. The idle unlocking of the door is represented by the Professor as a nexus between meaninglessness and meaningfulness:

> Not one minute had he [the intended victim] been gone, when there came a gentle knock at the door. It was raining heavily, and being a stranger to the city, not dreaming that in any crowded town such a state of things could exist as really did in this, the young man, without hesitation, admitted the person knocking. He has declared since – but, perhaps, confounding the feelings gained from better knowledge with the feelings of the moment – that from the moment he drew the bolt he had a misgiving that he had done wrong (*Blackwood's*, vol. XLIV, p. 218).

The moment of decision here is analogous to the present-time moment of composition of the autobiographer. The Professor's quasi-autobiographical narrative attempts to recover the origin and substance of the past by feeding meaning into the moment of crisis or extremity. Similarly, De Quincey attempts in his autobiographical works to analyse his past life, elucidating the involuted points of heightened consciousness. In the fiction, the stranger acts out of a consciousness that he has no one to verify his statement of events: he attempts to gloss his action of unbolting the door, as does the Professor, whose narrative accepts (and compounds, by stressing the 'ordinariness' of the scene) this process of adding detail to a central assertion (that the door was opened) in an attempt to explain the 'inexplicable' (that the murderers entered the house after all precautions had been taken). De Quincey, in an attempt to analyse why he quit school, likewise details at great length in the revised *Confessions* the circumstances which surround the act of walking out the door. For the Opium-Eater, his exit into 'freedom' proves to be an entry into a different sort of trap. The events recounted (his trip to London, his later nightmares and so forth) attest to both a past life filled with unforeseen troubles and a present (that of composition) which threatens him with the imminent disintegration of what constitutes his self. The secret-murder story that is 'The Avenger' dramatically represents an autobiographical problem for De Quincey. Like the stranger at the door, his only witnesses are redundant (the dead host and the unknown assassins in

'The Avenger' cannot attest to the truth of what the stranger asserts; so too with the people with whom De Quincey once shared a specific experience, and, by extension, the person he then was himself). The stranger finds an accomplice in the Professor, who can verify his version of events, just as Maximilian and the Professor are mutually dependent. The autobiographer's awareness of the absence of the reader, of one who can verify the truth of what he says, allows for no such connection (thus De Quincey represents himself as a martyr to his memory, as the victim of his text). The autobiographical text is unverifiable, contingent where the fiction is a coherent unit, – 'A "sharable" proposition', as Louis A. Renza affirms.[15]

The action of the murderer, Maximilian, is also indicative of the autobiographer's dilemma. The only witnesses who could confirm his version of events (that his mother and sister were humiliated and killed by the townsfolk) are the victims whose deaths prevent their collusion with his testament. The Professor, however, by conspiring with Maximilian, resolves this problem. He adopts the position of a witness after the event, and implicitly becomes another of Maximilian's victims. This action nevertheless reaffirms the dilemma, for the Professor himself has no witness to the veracity of *his* narrative: hence his adoption of Maximilian's testament at the close of the tale. The Professor and Maximilian have both read the same events in the same way: the fiction is a confirmation of a shared experience. The resolution to the autobiographical dilemma is a certainty that destroys the specifically autobiographical nature of the writing. The extra-textual reader's function is dramatised within the fiction as a willing collaboration with a proposition that has already been verified. The 'problem' of the autobiographer (for De Quincey, his solitude, his errors in life, his sense of being the sole survivor, and so on) is insoluble: the lack of a reader leads to the enormous effort of autobiography, and curiously implies that, in that his claim to be his own reader is always invalidated of necessity, 'De Quincey' himself is entirely erased from the writing that is 'his'. Eventually he disappears, and his death fascinatingly extends his role as autobiographer.

In *The Stranger's Grave* (1823) De Quincey deals more directly with the destruction of a specifically autobiographical text placed within a fictional structure. The last testament of Edward Stanley (the Stranger of the title) is recast by the novel's supposed editor into a third-person narrative. An autobiographical work is openly translated into a fiction. In that the reading of the 'lost' text of Stanley's testament negates its purpose (as a confession designed to exculpate its author), there is something inherently futile, or at least destructive, in this recasting. An added complication lies in the fact that Stanley himself implicitly condones this misreading: his last wish is to be buried in a grave marked only as 'The Stranger's Grave' (an inscription which, having been placed on the grave of his dead wife, is itself a revision). His wish for anonymity bears with ironic force on his confession, while the translation of this confession turns him into a character in a novel, containing and obliterating his identity.

As with 'The Avenger' and 'The Household Wreck', *The Stranger's Grave* has a moral. Immediately after Wordsworth's 'A Slumber did my Spirit Seal' has been (incorrectly) cited, the reader is warned to 'guard well the first avenues which lead to sin; for if one false step be taken, thou canst not tell of how many evils it may prove the prelude' (*SG* 131).[16] In his autobiographical works, De Quincey is unable to put an end to the 'evils' of his narrative, reliant as it is on his being alive to write. Having begun to write, he is in a manner obliged to continue writing: all his efforts are at once the result of having begun and the prelude to more writing in the future. In the introductory remarks to the third part of 'A Sketch from Childhood' (*Hogg's Instructor*, vol. VIII, 1852) the means by which De Quincey may overcome this dilemma of autobiography is uncovered in a dark joke. Apologising for apparently having abandoned the second sketch, De Quincey comments that 'it is hard to see how any proper *end* could be devised for a paper of this nature [. . .] unless by putting the child to death; for which dénouement, unhappily, there was no solid historical foundation' (*Hogg's Intructor*, vol. VIII [1852], p. 1). Behind this suicidal comment lies another more subtle realisation: namely that, in the sense that the child no longer exists *as a child*, having become the (old) writer, the dénouement has in a sense already occurred.[17] The autobiographical writing announces the 'death' of the subject, which death repeatedly reaffirms the role of the autobiographer, who stands in a parasitical relation to his former selves.

For an entirely conclusive end to his autobiography, De Quincey's actual (i.e. biological) death does not suffice, since the intervention as a whole is dependent anyway on the formulation of his repeated death. Instead, the destruction of the *writing* of the autobiography would be necessary. In *The Stranger's Grave*, Stanley's autobiographical writing is absolutely and finally obliterated: the image of the novel (the grave of its hero) and the source of the novel (his testament) are erased entirely, and the suggestion is that, eventually, the novel itself will inevitably follow the same course:

> Time has swept them both into oblivion; – but what earthly thing is there which time will not sooner or later overwhelm in the same dark flood! (*SG* 41).

Yet oblivion is (obviously) only projected, not actual, in the text which suggests its own disintegration. To assert that everything will one day be forgotten, that writing will cease to function, ignores the fact that the assertion itself does and will function – whether it is correct in its prediction or not – even in the absence of a writer or reader. The oblivion which is projected has already happened, and is happening even now. Yet it happens not to the writing, but to human beings. The writer is already dead: this is problematic, but not as problematic as the apparently infinite 'life' of the writing, the written-life of autobiography, which even allows local readings of its own dissolution. There is no evidence in autobiography of this lack of authority (it is not necessarily a problem): there can only be the internal expression of the fact that the process of writing is in control, that the process cannot be terminated. It is endless, infinite; and, as the Professor of 'The Avenger' ironically observes, 'in anything which partakes of the infinite, the most unlimited expectations will find ample room for gratification' (*Blackwood's*, vol. XLIV, p. 210).

Images of infinity abound in De Quincey's fictions. In his autobiographical essays the labyrinthine prose acts as both a pleasure and a torment. Moments of extremity act as artificial pauses in, but also as preludes to, the continuation of the ever-extended narrative (as do, less pointedly, De Quincey's numerous apologies about lack of space and so forth). In his final novel, the quasi-gothic *Klosterheim* (1832), De Quincey deals with terminating a process which threatens to continue monotonously forever. The oppressive sense of infinite hopelessness and terror which informs the novel is at once increased and reversed by the action of its hero, Maximilian, 'the Masque'. His 'rule by night' subverts the gloomy mental state brought on by the rule of the Landgrave, his double in terms of station and simultaneously his opposite. The Landgrave sees only the negative aspect of infinity: he barricades the city, shuts himself inside the schloss and broods. To go on living is a hopeless struggle with forces that seem to entrap him. De Quincey neatly figures this psychological stasis in his depiction of the Landgrave's choice of environment:

> Vexed and confounded, fears for the future struggling with mortification for the past, the Landgrave was sitting, late at night, in the long gallery where he usually held his councils (*Klosterheim* 152).

The long gallery here represents a contained, definite but extended present-time; the dark of night which encloses the dark interior space suggests the Landgrave's state of mind. Wishing to preserve the present endlessly, and to obliterate the process which determines his self, the Landgrave desires the infinite finity of a perpetual *now*. His destruction in the novel, brought about by his wish to occupy all points of time and space, dramatises the problem facing the autobiographer, whose perpetual *now* of composition indicates his absence from writing – his existential disintegration. In the society of the novel (in which all the characters are defined by their social station: politician, aristocrat, nun, landlord, soldier, and so on), the Landgrave has forgotten his 'situation': an upstart, he becomes entangled in his own devices, the victim of his assumed position at the centre of the state. At the close of the novel, having accidentally killed his only daughter, the Landgrave dies repentant.

The Masque's triumph is to bring to an end the rule of the Landgrave. As the 'real' Landgrave of Klosterheim, the Masque also occupies a central position; but he is enabled to keep moving because of his understanding of the network of signs that threaten to enclose him. His knowledge of the system of underground labyrinths, by means of which he spirits away droves of the town's inhabitants without leaving any trace, underlines his immunity. He alone is unthreatened by the dimensions of the maze of signifiers which surround each individual. Working in darkness, the Masque becomes some 'mysterious agency', scarcely human (*Klosterheim* 148). His godlike powers are emphasised by the resurrection of the kidnapped townsfolk from the underground chambers. What functions as a grave or prison, as a maze, and as a device for re-ordering the state, finally becomes little more than a tourist attraction. The ordinariness of the labyrinths is made clear at the close of the novel, suggesting that the 'mysteriousness' of things is primarily a matter of perspective:

> Many changes took place in consequence, greatly affecting the architectural character of the town and its picturesque antiquities; but, amidst all revolutions of this nature, the secret passages still survive, and to this day are shown occasionally to strangers of rank and consideration, by which, more than by any other of the advantages at his disposal, The Masque Of Klosterheim was enabled to replace himself in his patrimonial rights, and at the same time to liberate from a growing oppression his own compatriots and subjects (*Klosterheim* 305).

The ambiguous aspect of the labyrinth (which remains even at the end: untouched by revolution, the labyrinths are yet the tools of change) is reflected in Maximilian's double-life – as the Masque, whose face cannot be read, and as Maximilian, whose features are mistaken for those of his murdered father; and is suggestive of the autobiographical figure in De Quincey's writings. The action of simultaneously writing and erasing the 'identity' of this figure on which the autobiography rests as a coherent body is dramatised in *Klosterheim*, where the struggle between the potential oblivion and the potential immortality embodied in the self-exploration of the autobiographer takes the form of a psychological duel between the Landgrave and the Masque.

De Quincey must opt for closure or infinity; or he can attempt to enter a state of ceaselessly mulling-over these options, an action which tends to equate them. Procrastination, De Quincey's forté, is a state of grace in which anxiety is transformed into fascination, a chronic luxury which allows him to occupy an interface between (within both, as if occupying the infinitesimal point where two perfect spheres touch) two extremes. Thus, in the *Confessions* De Quincey contemplates the sea from a closed room. In 'The Affliction of Childhood' ('Suspiria de Profundis') he stands between a corpse and an open window which frames infinite space. In *Klosterheim* the procrastination/extremity action of the autobiographical writing is not formally apposite to the fictional structure, but the considerations of autobiography thoroughly inform the novel. Klosterheim itself stands within an apparently endless forest, symbolic of the sense of loss and fear of oblivion that torments the town's inhabitants.[18] The refugees, for whom Klosterheim is a potential sanctuary, flee through an awesome environment that defies exploration:

> Every where they saw alleys, arched high overhead, and resembling the aisles of a cathedral, as much in form as in the perfect darkness which reigned in both at this solemn hour of midnight, stretching away apparently without end, but more and more obscure, until impenetrable blackness terminated the long vista (*Klosterheim* 41).

After a lengthy journey, the refugees reach the city, but far from being a haven it proves to be little more than a series of prisons. The forbidding expanse of forest is replaced by the claustrophobic atmosphere of Klosterheim: the two extremes have the same effect, preventing action, concealing foes. Closure and infinity seem to coincide in the city. Only the Masque can reverse the threat of monotonous oppression. By implication, the autobiographer must interpret the given meaning of experience (symbolised by the state of affairs in Klosterheim) and call into question the validity of this meaning: his task is to reread the apparently stable sign, a task which, in that it allows for an infinite series of readings, for any reinterpretation to be reinterpreted (as another sign), is always contingent.

Similar considerations are dwelt upon in *Walladmor* (1825), De Quincey's 'free translation' of a German forgery of a *Waverley* novel. Almost entirely recast, De Quincey's work bears little resemblance to its source (just as the German novel is not much like one of Scott's works).[19] In his dedication to the German pseudo-translator, De Quincey imagines *his* version being freely translated back into German, then retranslated back into English, and so on forever. The possibility that a fiction might, like autobiography, be open to contingent rather than terminal interpretation arises, and is briefly developed in a footnote concerned with the books provided for Bertram, the hero of the story, when he has been thrown into jail at the beginning of the second volume of *Walladmor*. Of these books De Quincey observes:

> Amongst which we are happy to say (on authority of a Welch friend) was the *first* volume of Walladmor, a novel, 2 vols. post 8vo.; the second being not then finished (*Walladmor* 2: 125n).

Another note, slightly later, hints at Bertram's interest in the books: 'Modesty forbids us to say *which*: but a truth is a truth: and his favorite volume, we understand, was "in post 8vo."' (*Walladmor* 2: 163n). Bertram's reading of the first volume of the novel in which he features provides part of the action for the second volume. This raises the possibility that he can (potentially) take control of the narrative; and that he may read the narrative representation of events rather than engage with the events themselves. The fictional reader who can hypothetically invalidate or change the course of the fiction which contains and defines him (though, for obvious reasons, De Quincey does not develop this further) threatens to destroy the narrative fabric by embarking on an 'autobiographical' process of infinite reinterpretation and repetition that is ultimately absurd – a sort of entropic self-consciousness of a character who reads in a book that he is reading in a book that he is reading ... and so on. This perplexing joke raises several questions, not least of which concerns De Quincey's disowning of *Walladmor*.[20] His claims that the absurdities of the plot are not his doing, that he is not really the responsible author, suggest that the written word, rather than the writer, is in control; and that the writer's task is principally one of translation of an extant text (even in the case of an original work, such as his autobiographical works: he 'translates' the text of the past).

Counterbalanced against the demands of the text, however, is the necessary act of volition that erases the already-written even as it is reinterpreted. In the review 'Gillies's German Stories', De Quincey insists upon a positive departure from source:

> For Heaven's sake, let every translator emancipate himself so far from thraldom to the book before him, and put forth so much activity of mind, as to think in English, and not passively to reproduce the phraseology of his German original (*Blackwood's*, vol. XX [December 1826], p. 857).

The translation, the '*rifacimento* or *remaniement*' (*ibid.*, p. 857) is an improved reinterpretation dependent on one's creative powers; and where, as in the case of *Walladmor*, the original is largely a 'disappointment' (5: 560), it stands as a new and original composition.[21] Goldman has discussed De Quincey's recasts of source material and has suggested that in many instances his essays may be considered as imaginative transformations of other works: not merely in the case of reviews and analects, but even in such autobiographical/biographical pieces as the story of Miss Smith (*Tait's*, June 1840) and the Greens (*Tait's*, September 1839), in which, having no first-hand knowledge, De Quincey works selected episodes into the framework of his own narrative, and reclaims (as it were) experiences through a sophisticated process of revision.[22] The implication of this process is that the original text of experience is already obliterated by memory, which in turn De Quincey translates into script (and then on through the various stages of printing: Goldman observes that there were several, involving on occasion other people who revised De Quincey's copy).[23] Authority would seem to reside always at one remove from a given piece of writing, as though human life were mostly a matter of reading and abstracting (but, in so far as this estrangement requires further 'activity of mind', these tasks are still vital): the process itself is the authority. A fictional work tends to deny this authority of process, in that a self-conscious awareness of the writer's radical estrangement from his writing, which in autobiography is always perceived as imminent, in its reliance upon a phenomenologically present reader, tends to be negated by the correspondence established between the text-as-written and the text-as-read. In that it stands for an authoritative reading of an actuality or series of actualities, the fiction declares its own status *as* fiction: its completeness is a deception.

This is crudely demonstrated in 'The Peasant of Portugal' (1827), a short story, the action of which consists of what may be defined as a series of authoritative readings. First, Juan, the peasant of the title, fulfils his vow to win Marguerita by proving himself the most accomplished man of the village. Then, after she is killed, he promises to do his utmost to destroy the members of the regiment responsible for her death. Just as his word (*as* a vow) admits of no qualification and cannot be interpreted other than as a decisive (non-contingent), controlling directive, so too Juan himself is later decisively misread by the regiment as a supernatural figure – 'some fiend possessed of supernatural powers, to whom human opposition was as utterly useless as the resistance of a feather to the winds' (*P* 214) – a misreading which contributes to their destruction. The obliteration of the entire regiment and of the peasant himself at the close of the story seems final enough. Absurdly, the desire to verify the details of the plot (since all the witnesses have apparently been destroyed) prompts De Quincey to explain that one of the regiment, 'hurled to an almost incredible distance by the force of the explosion, survived his companions a few hours to tell the dreadful tale' (*P* 223). This added complication pointedly insists upon the fictionality of 'The Peasant of Portugal'. The narrative emphatically breaks down at this point, and though the temporary escape of the murder-victim hints at the possibility of an exit from the short-circuit of the tale, his own inclusion within the text compounds the sense of entrapment and inevitability that informs the fiction.

In 'The Caçadore' (1828) De Quincey apparently attempts to rework 'The Peasant of Portugal' without having to rely on the earlier work's unconvincing ending.[24] However, the result is scarcely more satisfactory. Purportedly narrated by an army veteran, 'The Caçadore' tells of the murder at the hands of a French officer of the fiancée of Velasquez, the Caçadore of the title. This murder effects a change in the appearance and temperament of Velasquez, who neglects his duties and instead broods over the possibilities for revenge. When the Frenchman is eventually located, Velasquez determines to hunt him down, but his commander (the narrator) refuses to allow his troops to carry out such an attack. The regiment mutinies and sets forth to ambush the enemy, whose force considerably outnumbers them. The French officer, 'as if he bore a charmed life' (*TC* 13), for some time escapes injury, but is eventually killed. Velasquez, along with most of the regiment, dies in the battle and his body is later found lying across that of the Frenchman.

Whereas 'The Peasant of Portugal' concludes in a forced and self-baffling fashion, 'The Caçadore' embraces its own insufficiency and is structured in such a way as to indicate a conscious acceptance of failure on De Quincey's part. The narrative is framed so as to suggest that the purportedly true story is not suffficiently productive in itself. Both the opening, which promises access to a universal truth and hints at the 'horror and wretchedness' (*TC* 7) which the tale will bring to life; and the ending, with its self-critical admission of 'the impossibility of giving expression to any thing approaching the reality' (*TC* 15) of lived experience – both promise and excuse reflect on the failure of the fiction to function as De Quincey would wish. After detailing the events 'without amplification or colouring' (*TC* 15), the narrator admits to being quite dissatisfied with his efforts. The tale is left open-ended in a sense, not because the events recounted are open to question (though the story is peppered with apparently significant details left unelaborated), but because the representation of events cannot even approximate to experiential reality. The potentialities of the tale are effectively negated, emptied of meaning. All the tale can signal is its own structural limitations. 'The Caçadore' implies that to fix things in a predetermined order – to define experience in singular terms, as the narrator does – is ultimately to render them unproductive.

For the autobiographer, the sense of completeness that characterises these fictions entails a denial of experiential truth. De Quincey's dismissal of novels may be understood as the reaction of a highly self-conscious writer to the totalising effect of fictional representation;[25] while his own fictions deal to a great extent with such formal considerations by dramatically engaging with closure and termination as themes. In that these fictions can be grasped as being directly related to De Quincey's autobiographical efforts, they may be readily understood as expressions of a death-wish on his part fitfully articulated in his works. In Chapter 3, I touched upon this death-wish as it is presented in De Quincey's depiction of Coleridge as a figure of catastrophic disintegration. The fictional works deal more directly with disintegration: a violent death (or several) occurs in each, and the idea of a threat (often unknown) is central to the narrative of each. Though the narrative, in that it allows for the representation of a new version of events (that is, we accept that an actuality is being represented, though this is clearly only imaginary), would seem to offer something beyond experience, the potential resurrection hoped for in the autobiographical works (and which is formally implicit: 'the author' is always about to be given) is denied by De Quincey's fictions.

The finality which pertains to the fictional translation of experience is problematic for De Quincey. The termination of the authoritative process of writing denies the positive valorisation of experience as expressed in the autobiographical works. It is not simply that the author cannot be given as imminent, but further that De Quincey's thematic concern with resurrection is invalidated even as it is articulated (and hence the concern with dating the tales firmly in the past: this strategy tends to offset the death of writing and loss of resurrection faced in the fictions). The narrator in the fictions cannot be 'emancipated' from the events recounted, unless (as is the case in *Klosterheim* and 'The Peasant of Portugal') he does not feature at all, which is not so much emancipation as absence by default. Definition implies for De Quincey an end to meaning, the acceptance of prescribed limits to human activity.

CHAPTER FIVE

'The English Mail-Coach'
and De Quincey's political works

> It is the hackneyed artifice of political writers, either out of party violence, as a trick of rhetoric, or by way of stimulating attention, to speak of the country as on the brink of ruin; as though a mighty empire could so easily receive an impulse of that magnitude from the errors of some one individual, or of a single transitory cabinet. Extravagancies of that kind are disdained by men of sense. And we have little need of hyperbole, where the grave realities before us are more than sufficiently alarming ('French Revolution', *Blackwood's*, vol. XXVIII, [September 1830], p. 555).

De Quincey's politics have been characterised as 'a failure of imagination' by Tave, who, in *New Essays*, has usefully outlined the crucial events in the moulding of De Quincey's Tory beliefs (*Tave* 22). Central to his political vision is the battle of Waterloo, a catastrophic termination of the twenty-two years of war with France (1793-1815) which had united the country against a common enemy. The peace heralded by this decisive victory proves illusory in De Quincey's scheme of things: political problems within the country disturb the promised repose. Worse still is the resolution to these problems, namely the coalition with the Whigs formed by Canning in 1827, for this apostasy upsets the equilibrium of the Constitution. It irreparably obliterates the divide between the Tory and Whig factions, mutually dependent parties which 'are the two hemispheres of the total truth' (*Tave* 198), throwing society into turmoil. The catastrophe that will resolve the disorder, as victory at Waterloo had done, is projected but obscured 'in unfathomable darkness' (*Tave* 19). De Quincey does not alter these fundamental attitudes in the light of new events, but rather attempts to make political reality fit in with his preconceptions. The result is curious, for while the times are characterised as unsettled, De Quincey's observations remain mostly of the same uniform type. His are the politics of unease and disillusion, a rigidly insulated code which blots out the present and misinterprets the past. In this chapter I examine the form of De Quincey's political attitudes and pay comparatively little attention to the minutiae of the historical actualities that he claims to describe. My interest here is not in specific events as history, but in what De Quincey *says* is the case.

The false step: a pathological law of political power

An important example of De Quincey's attitudes is the paper entitled 'The Ministry' (*Edinburgh Evening Post*, 26 June 1828), in which he reflects on past governments and looks forward to the future. Castlereagh's last years, Canning's apostasy, Goedrich's ministry and the new government formed by Wellington all come under scrutiny. The first two figures are depicted by De Quincey as having made fatal errors which politically ruined them. As such, their actions are similar to those of De Quincey in the *Confessions of an English Opium-Eater* and, as will become apparent, to other figures in De Quincey's political writings. Castlereagh's failure is characterised in terms which echo Milton's description of Satan in *Paradise Lost*:

> Latterly, at least, he was led astray, and insensibly to himself, by the glozing tempters who beseiged his ear – to countenance a class of measures very alien from his own policy, and the principles on which it rested. His last three or four years (comparatively speaking) were imbecile and contradictory; and they paved the way for much of the confusions which followed (*Tave* 281).

This idea of wandering from the right path is crucial. Repeatedly in De Quincey's political commentaries, figures of power betray their principles and lapse into 'imbecile' behaviour. De Quincey's vocabulary suggests the existence of a pathological law in the exercise of political power: again and again 'imbecility', the disease of recurrent error, of a failure of judgment, overtakes the various Prime Ministers.[1] Thus, Castlereagh's mistake is echoed by Canning's decision to take office:

> A golden bribe was held forth, irresistible to *his* ambition, connected with *his* laxity of principle; and, at the price of fidelity to his party, and fidelity to his whole political creed, in an evil hour for himself, he became Prime Minister of Great Britain. From that moment there is no doubt that his peace of mind forsook him; and from the very day when he accomplished his utmost schemes of personal advancement, he bade adieu for ever to the luxury of an untroubled conscience (*Tave* 281–2).[2]

Goederich, like his predecessors, is plagued with doubts and burdened with responsibility, and is at odds with his ministers:

> Hence would arise frequent misgivings in the mind of the unhappy Minister; self-reproaches, self-conflicts, agitations,

distraction of purpose, and finally from over-excitement almost paralytic imbecility (*Tave* 285).

De Quincey depicts all three Ministers as psychologically troubled by the uneasy position of office. The exercise of political power proves destructive because the men cannot control the forces at work in society. Clearly, this characterisation is akin to that of the Opium-Eater whose *Confessions* tell of pariah wanderings in an unsympathetic environment: school, London, even his own body, seem to thwart his search for 'freedom' and peace. The calm experienced when he looks out over the sea, the sense of equilibrium and of infinite activity compounded with infinite repose, is only local. The Opium-Eater also suffers in the chaos of his nightmares. He experiences agitation and estrangement, falls into a state of apathy, is tortured and distressed before he finally 'triumphs'. In contrast, no triumph awaits the flawed Ministers, each of whom is damned by circumstances and personal failings. The conflict De Quincey sees existing within the country as a whole is reflected in the minds of the Prime Ministers. Each is divided against himself, in self-conflict and unable to act. The new untried cabinet under the leadership of the Duke of Wellington, the formation of which 'The Ministry' applauds, is characterised as bringing to an end the chaos and anarchy of the preceding years. It promises 'a system of light and order' (*Tave* 286), hope and coherence. De Quincey's optimism rests on his negative view of the previous administrations: several years of social unrest are depicted as giving way *necessarily* to repose. The reality fits into an already defined scheme. Even his (inevitable) doubts are dismissed as De Quincey states, with startling optimism, his trust in Wellington's powers. Having noticed the presence of the Canningite Huskisson in the new cabinet (number 7 in a list of its members), De Quincey nevertheless expresses no small measure of faith in the new Ministry. The following description of the Duke's powers is particularly interesting in that the terminology prefigures that of 'The English Mail-Coach', the important political content of which I shall discuss later in this chapter:

> In all cases, however, where the D. of Wellington sees his way clearly, he will act firmly; and, with regard to No. 7, in particular, his Grace knows him too well not to keep a tight hand over him. About three years ago, in an action brought against a mail-coachman for overturning the Liverpool mail, it was stated by Mr. Brougham for the defence, that this mail had been long used as a *break* for vicious horses, a coachman being always selected who realized in a more than usual degree the Homeric description of Hector Ἕκτορος Ἱπποδάμοιο: – Hector the tamer of horses; and all the unruly subjects on the road were regularly *civilized* in the Liverpool mail. Just such a break will be the present Cabinet under the firm hands of the D. of W. He

will keep a tight 'bearing-rein' upon any dangerous subject like No. 7; and, if No. 7 should 'jib', or plunge, or shew any vice, he will speedily be taught who it is that holds the 'ribbons', and will be brought into a beautiful state of civilisation (*Tave* 288).

De Quincey draws a parallel between Wellington, the figure of strength and authority who will bring order – 'civilisation' – to the state, and the driver of the mail-coach who can control unruly beasts and make them work for him. The recent 'drivers' of the state before Wellington were unfit to govern. They were flawed men who allowed themselves to be controlled by others and by self-interest. To maintain the metaphor, they did not drive so much as were driven: the position of driver was maintained, but without meaning, since other forces wielded the true power. They betrayed their principles, lost their grip and allowed the coach-journey to continue in spite of their own position.

De Quincey's main concern in his descriptions of the various flawed Cabinets is that the unity which, in his view, ought to prevail, and which is indeed a necessary prerequisite of effective government of whatever political persuasion, has been obscured and destroyed by selfish, misguided or hypocritical men. The joy expressed by De Quincey in 'The Ministry' at the choice of Wellington as Prime Minister is founded in the Duke's strength of character and determination. Wellington is a man who can exercise control over the 'unruly subjects'; he 'sees his way clearly' – and in this latter respect it is interesting to compare the driver of the coach in the 'The English Mail-Coach' (1849), a dozy Cyclops who allows the vehicle to go out of control and who leaves to the likes of such amateur drivers as De Quincey the responsibility of returning it to the correct side of the road. Over twenty odd years, Cyclops has replaced Hector, the monster has usurped the hero. The state has gone out of control.[3]

This upheaval is predicted in one of De Quincey's earliest published pieces, 'Philadelphus, on Mr Clarkson's Letter' (*Westmoreland Gazette*, 30 May 1818), where he warns that democratic forces will bring ruin to the country:

> That engine the mob, with which we begin in England, never fails in such cases to be brought at some period into action, and when the mad driver Democracy sits upon the dickey, an overturn must soon follow.[4]

The figure of the coach is used again in 'Political Anticipations' (1830), here applied to the Wellington cabinet, now gone astray. De Quincey predicts that the problems of dealing with a self-contradicting cabinet will pale into relative insignificance in the light of the threat from Ireland and Daniel O'Connell:

> Even a restive House of Commons, plunging and jibbing under every old rule of expert driving, will be a secondary concern.

> All anxieties, of ancient or modern growth, foreign or domestic, will be swallowed up in one overwhelming judgment – yes! we may call it a providential judgment – which is now gathering upon this apostate Cabinet from Ireland, the theatre of its apostasy ('Political Anticipations', *Blackwood's*, vol. XXVIII [November 1830], p. 734).

Ten years later the figure is taken up yet again in 'Hints for the Hustings', here applied to the Empire as a whole:

> In a set of horses under harness, it never happens that one begins to plunge or rear, but the rest are soon reached by the contagion of restiveness. The provinces and distant colonies of the empire, one after the other, according to the means of resistance which they found offered in their local administrations, began to "jib" and show signs of refractoriness ('Hints for the Hustings', *Blackwood's*, vol. XLVIII [September 1840], p. 296).

The coherence of De Quincey's political vision over the entire course of his career as a journalist need be stressed no further here. He repeatedly predicts ruin for England. Political events tend to be reduced to the same recurring event. Though the false step is not inevitably necessary, in that it always involves a moral choice, it yet constitutes a formal law which the inadequate leaders obey. In 'The Duke of Wellington and Mr Peel', De Quincey affirms that betrayal is the order of the times:

> Every month summons us to the afflicting spectacle of a fresh perfidy in some conspicuous public servant: apostacy has now run the circle of all the political leaders: or, if there be one who is notorious for opinions which menace the national welfare, he only has *not* apostatized. Fidelity is to be found nowhere, except to principles of ruin (*Blackwood's*, vol. XXV [March 1829], p. 294).

The betrayal of the nation may be linked to the betrayal of the self, which De Quincey fully explores in 'The English Mail-Coach' and which is indeed a feature of many of his autobiographical writings. In both the personal and the political spheres the difficulty of maintaining a sense of unity is encountered. In the autobiographical works this is reflected even in the form of the text, in which attempts to draw disparate elements together, even where the connections are obscure and the relations of one idea to another seem illogical or random, result in macaronic narrative structures such as the final version of 'Autobiographic Sketches'. In this context, 'The English Mail-Coach' may be readily understood as a political statement of a singular kind. The unity of the essay is grounded in a belief in a political imperative. As a statement of belief, it admits to its lack of correlative in the real world. That is, the belief is expressed in spite of the reality, not because of it. The essay, though set firmly in memory, in the past, in specific lost events, voices the aspirations of one who has been stranded by political history. The result is curious, because it means that hope and hopelessness occupy the same mental space. As with the *fascination* De Quincey exhibits for extremity and death, the divergence of apparently opposite states of mind (hope, despair) is a complex reaction to confusing, destructive forces. This needs to be understood, otherwise De Quincey is likely to be too easily dismissed as a hypocrite, extremist, or just a naïf. All these descriptions do come to mind as one reads his political papers; and, indeed, in some instances the application is apposite. However, to comprehend precisely what is involved in his political pronouncements requires holding judgment in suspense, for otherwise a full and proper understanding of the meaning of his autobiographical works cannot be arrived at. Like Maniquis, Tave and De Luca before me, I find De Quincey's politics distasteful.[5] My task here is not to apologise for De Quincey, but to analyse his vision and to suggest the ways in which the political essays may be seen to form an integral part of his work.

Unity

For De Quincey the self cannot be defined except negatively, as something which is betrayed or which betrays; and, as his comments on the traits of the flawed Ministers suggest, the state will similarly be repeatedly betrayed. De Quincey's party political beliefs involve a special effort. He must make a conscious connection with a potentially deceitful representative figure, the Prime Minister. In this, he remains true to his predetermined political identity (a Tory to the end, with the possibility of being dug up as 'a specimen of the fossil Tory' [9: 294]), but so severely limits the role of this persona as to render his participation in social reality negligible. That is to say, his fugitive political papers attempt to articulate an ideological position, but fail to come to terms with the possibility that the feared betrayal has already happened in his fervent connection to the Tory cause. This possibility is analogous to the central mistake in the *Confessions* and again suggests that writing is the true area of extremity. In his political papers, De Quincey's task is always to interpret reality, to reduce it to a master code, never to engage with it. That is, he is employed as a propagandist.

The main organ for De Quincey's party political commentaries is the pre-eminently Tory *Blackwood's Edinburgh Magazine*. In De Quincey's view, the British Press has a generally anti-social function, is lacking in principles and (where it does not create) adds to an air of unrest and agitation. He criticises the tactics of the Press in general for misrepresenting the meaning and function of the state:

> Never yet was any nation in the condition of England; her whole constitution of political power, as it exists both in church and state, being the object of profound hatred from

all the classes below the gentry, and of long – earnest – and systematic hostility from the press ('France and England', *Blackwood's*, vol. XXVIII, [October 1830] p. 717).

The Press, then, has an overtly political role. It publishes news and in doing so is engaged in the production of the political climate. (This, again, is one of the themes of 'The English Mail-Coach'.) The role of *Blackwood's*, is, in De Quincey's view, to represent the 'truth' about the state and the constitution to the public.

In terms of party politics, De Quincey's identity has already been determined. He has aligned himself with the Tory, aristocratic cause, instead of the Whig – the two being, in his view, the constituent, interdependent halves of the state. In this, De Quincey has allowed himself to be controlled by past events (in particular, by the forging of the post-Civil War Constitution). He is trapped, as in the *Confessions* and elsewhere, only here he apparently has no positive desire for 'freedom'. Or, at least, he creates the facade of a true supporter of his part of society – often, it seems, the only true supporter – even if this is only locally maintained.[6] The incongruous compound of being a 'free agent' which his autobiographical works suggest (as does the fact that he was published simultaneously by the Radical Tait and the Tory Blackwood in the 1830s), and of being a party-man, even a hired hack, as his fugitive political papers suggest, is disturbing. It suggests that De Quincey's self, that barely existent localised convergence of disparate influences, is composed of uncomplementary, even auto-destructive constituents. Like the apostate Cabinet, it is the reflection of a deeply fragmented society, and is itself split up, atomised, a collection of 'unruly subjects' under the leadership of his memory (the 'conductor' of the 'Dream-Fugue''s musical prose) For De Quincey, his political identity and his personal identity are at odds. 'The English Mail-Coach' does, I think, attempt to create an interspace in which this problem of the writer's identity may be resolved.

Before dealing more directly with that essay, however, it is necessary to analyse some other manifestations of the possibility of self-betrayal expressed in De Quincey's overtly political papers, as well as those which, though less ideologically loaded, are yet crucially important. To begin with I wish to turn to De Quincey's depiction of the East. Maniquis has prefigured some of this commentary in his useful monograph 'Lonely Empires'.

Elements of the East

De Quincey's 'opium-eater' is a new term which makes him the type by which all other users of the drug are to be defined. The specifically 'English' gloss signifies a wish to distinguish himself from other nationalities and cultures. De Quincey's method of dissociation necessitates two things. First, he must reveal something of the hidden 'other world' of the opium-user, and attempt to delineate its constituents. Secondly, he must justify apparent self-indulgence by demonstrating the value of opium to the Christian, while simultaneously throwing into relief the pagan use of the drug. This action does not entail a complete severance, in that De Quincey relies largely on already existing myths, which he adapts for his own purposes. He 'confesses' his self-indulgence and defines opium as a spiritual rather than a material thing, investing it with specific properties which in turn inform the character of the Opium-Eater. Implicitly, De Quincey reinforces the mythological status of the East and fuels a racist characterisation of the oriental opium-user – an action of broad political significance. The East of De Quincey's dreams is a fictional area, an antagonistic land of madness:

> I know not whether others share in my feelings on this point; but I have often thought that if I were compelled to forego England, and to live in China, and among Chinese manners and modes of life and scenery, I should go mad (*L* 72; 5: 266).

China is another interface in which De Quincey confronts a death-wish. He stands 'loathing and fascinated' (*L* 74; 5: 269) between oblivion and immortality (antagonistic forces which, like Whig and Tory in his party political scheme, define 'the total truth'), 'kissed, with cancerous kisses' by the crocodile (*L* 73; 5: 268). This creature is an important component of De Quincey's visualisation of the East. The crocodile symbolises finity, and its unchanging nature seems to mock the infinite and to mock any sense of progression. It remains static, ageless, and 'does not live fast' (*L* 198; 4: 309). In this final respect, it signifies the inability of the individual to step aside from, and thus to evaluate and delineate, the self. Living fast, the passionate firing of 'the self-consuming energies of the brain' (*Tait's*, vol. VI [January 1839], p. 9) entails the repeated occupation of a space aside from the past self, a continual progression which rewrites the self and invests it with meaning. The possibility of 'burning out' always exists as an adjunct to this process (as De Quincey observes in his comments on the Wordsworths, who are characterised as being constitutionally impassioned in this way: they 'live faster than others' (*ibid.*).[7] The autobiographer risks madness, death, or loss of identity; and he strives to extend the autobiographical text *ad infinitum*, continually rewriting the past and thus asserting presence. The metaphor which binds the past selves together also deconstructs, however. As rewriting equals erasure, the inscription on the 'palimpsest of the human brain' (*L* 144) obliterates what has gone before. The collapse of metaphorical substitution and the oblivion entailed by the halting of self-conscious motion, is engaged with in De Quincey's representation of the East. The progression from past self to present self involves the autobiographer in the circumscription of the infinite, as though he were travelling towards a point in the distance, known to be unreachable but made 'less unreachable' by sustained motion. (That is, presence can never be established.) Motion allows a semblance of finity to the infinite, a conscious approximation of which oppresses the dreamer in the *Confessions* as an abomination if, as happens in the nightmares in which he is incarcerated in stone coffins (images of closure), he is held still, prevented from sustaining motion. The crocodile is a manifestation of actual time felt to be 'of a duration far beyond the limits of any human experience' (*L* 68; 5: 259), suggestive of the futility of maintaining the series of substitutions in the autobiographical text as well as the danger of *not* doing so. When De Quincey wakes from the dream, the crocodiles beneath the 'vertical sunlights' of the dreamed world are replaced by children under the 'broad noon' of a familiar sky. The juxtaposition of opposing natures suggests that the two are mutually dependent, inseparable, and define one another. The children will die, they have to in order to be born again, resurrected according to Christian beliefs. So too, the dream crocodile, while it is dismissed by reality, will rise again in subsequent dreams.

In a passage deleted from the 1854 revision of 'The English Mail-Coach', De Quincey returns to the idea of an essential but destructive interdependence of apparently conflicting natures (basically, the human and the non-human or sub-human) and analyses further the 'horrid inoculation' (*L* 200) that had been tentatively uncovered in the transitional moment between sleeping and waking in the dreams of the *Confessions*. The horror of a self-destructive, but self-defining, tendency which cannot be denied, only repressed by deleting the representation of it, he now understands to be the result of the displacement of the self. Motion leads him to revulsion and confusion, and reveals an innate treachery:

> The dreamer finds housed within himself – occupying, as it were, some separate chamber in his brain – holding, perhaps, from that station a secret and detestable commerce with his own heart – some horrid alien nature. What if it were his own nature repeated, – still, if the duality were distinctly perceptible, even *that* – even this mere numerical double of his own consciousness – might be a curse too mighty to be sustained. But how, if the alien nature contradicts his own, fights with it, perplexes, and confounds it? How, again, if not one alien nature, but two, but three, but four, but five, are introduced within what once he thought the inviolable sanctuary of himself? (*L* 201).

This antagonistic doppelgänger (a figure of termination, like Coleridge), this crocodile-within which refuses exposition (*L* 201), represents a part of De Quincey's self which he cannot or will not read and which he cannot replace. The problematic relationship between the self and the alien infiltrator calls into question the nature of the connection between the autobiographer, the autobiographical text, and the revision or reading of this text; and reveals the extremity of absence. De Quincey pre-empts the disintegration which his writings inevitably suggest by placing this relationship within the context of the dream. As in the *Confessions* before and 'Sir William Hamilton' afterwards, in 'The English Mail-Coach' De Quincey has recourse to the representation of his self as a victim in order to reclaim his identity. So too, his imaginative infiltration of the East involves a form of martyrdom akin to that produced by the action of his memory. Thus, in his dream of Ann in Judea on Easter Sunday in the *Confessions*, De Quincey sees Ann resurrected; but he is separated from her as well. Similarly, he is separated from himself in the dreams, annihilated amid 'monsters and abortions', barricaded, hemmed in and buried. The 'barrier of utter abhorrence, and want of sympathy, placed between us by feelings deeper than I can analyse' (*L* 73; 5: 267), which De Quincey sees separating himself from the Orientals, is strategically erected, so that what encloses *him* also acts as a means of keeping *them* out.

If resurrection originates in death, the vision of death in a godless world will be shocking. For De Quincey the East is the container of both paganism and Christianity. On the one hand he depicts an Asia where antiquity 'overpowers the sense of youth in the individual' (*L* 73; 5: 267), a land which is the product of 'ancient, monumental, cruel, and elaborate religions' (*L* 72; 5: 267), sublimely crowded, peopled by creatures with impenetrable, unreadable faces which De Quincey thinks are like the faces of 'antediluvian man renewed' (*L* 73; 5: 267). The Chinaman's origin has been miraculously erased in this mythological land which has escaped God's revision, the Flood. The Chinese face betrays nothing, his past is 'untraceable to any European eye' (4: 65). The coded script of the Chinese face signifies a lost origin to De Quincey; but it refuses to be deciphered. Implicitly, the Chinaman cannot read the faces around him: he has no mirror, no means of contemplating his fellows or himself. Unable to stand aside from the crowd (or the crowds of selves) of which he is a part, he dies in ignorance, absorbed and able only to recognise the image of his own mortality.

On the other hand De Quincey directly sets against this aspect of the East his visualisation of Judea, which he conceives of as a land of rebirth. Here Christianity has miraculously revealed man's (revised) origin to him, and has erased mortality by writing its script on the palimpsest of the face. Ann is read as a revised, contingent text: 'Her face was the same as when I saw it last, and yet again how different!' (*L* 76; 5: 271).

In the political context, De Quincey's role as martyr and his characterisation of the Chinese is translated so as to justify the subjugation of foreigners by the British imperial power. The reality of China, India, Ceylon and Judea does not disrupt the vision of the world posited throughout his essays. In 'Toilette of the Hebrew Lady' (1828, 1859), De Quincey states that he would 'be grieved if anything were to unsettle in our feelings the mysterious sanctities of Jerusalem, or to disturb that awful twilight which will for ever brood over Judea, by letting in upon it the "common light of day"' (12: 115–16); and he insists, in a later article concerned with the British Empire, that the relationship between Britain and Asia can be quite abstract: 'It was, Mr Mill argued, desirable – it was a splendid advantage – not to have seen India' (*UW* 1: 318). As he imaged himself as a victim in the dreams of the *Confessions*, so too De Quincey figures the reader as one in danger from the Orientals.[8] He warns the potential victim not to allow himself to become the dupe of the Chinese in a foot-note (concerned with the reputed size of cities) in 'The Caesars' (1832, 1859):

> And, universally, with regard to Asiatic cities (above all, with regard to Chinese cities), the reader must carry with him these cautions: –
>
> 1st, That Asiatics, with rare exceptions, have little regard for truth: by habit and policy they are even more mendacious than they are perfidious. Fidelity to engagements, sincerity, and disinterested veracity, rank, in Oriental estimates, as the perfection of idiocy.
>
> 2d, That, having no *liberal* curiosity, the Chinese man never troubles his head about the statistical circumstances of his own city, province, or natal territory. Such researches he would regard as ploughing the sands of the sea-shore, or counting the waves (10: 2n).[9]

Because all Chinese are untrustworthy, the Chinese text must be interpreted *cum grano salis*. De Quincey attempts to depict Asia as a sort of realisation of the Crete of the 'liar paradox', in which the Cretan Epimenides asserts 'All Cretans are liars.' Also, by representing Asian thought and language as perverse, he attempts to force the Orientals into an impasse in which they are forever trapped.[10] Ironically, as De Quincey begins to read meaning into the 'unreadable' character of his Orientals, making a connection as he denies any common ground, judging that they cannot be judged by Christian standards and so on, he runs aground, scuppered by his own devices. In 'The Opium Question with China in 1840' (1840), he objects that

> the present Ministry are not so much opposed to the Tories, as to a fantastic party of moral sentimentalists, who, by force of investing the Chinese with feelings unintelligible to Pagans, (substituting at the same time a romance for the facts of the case,) have terminated in forcing upon the public eye a false position of the whole interest at stake' ('Postscript on the China

and the Opium Question,' *Blackwood's*, vol. XLVII [June 1840], p. 850).

This objection effectually negates his own propositions. The 'wrong' meaning has been read into the cipher: a 'false position' has been produced because the Chinese have been allowed into that dynamic interface which their non-presence had previously helped define. De Quincey must thus either admit that they are human beings like himself, with some reality to them, or else insist that 'a fantastic party' has invented a pseudo-Chinese race, has misread the text and used the wrong master code. The latter option calls his own fantasy into question, but also allows him to extend (perversely enough) his role as martyr – here as *political* martyr. As in others of his political papers De Quincey had interpreted political reality as a series of failures, betrayals and missed opportunites, so too he here stands outside that which he purports to observe accurately. Once again, as with Canning *et alia*, the Tories have betrayed him (or, the Tories, with himself as their only true representative, the man of principles untainted by actual involvement, have been betrayed). De Quincey is the martyr of his beliefs and of the steadfastness with which he maintains them. The Whigs, his enemy in principle, and the Tories, his enemy in practice, oblige him to adopt the position of one crucified between them. Doomed and right at the same time, De Quincey's position seems politically nonsensical in that it has no correspondent in the actual world; or, rather, in that the connection between the remembered dream-world of the East and the historical actuality cannot logically be maintained. Obviously there is a difference between the two. De Quincey's insistence upon abstraction as a basis for political action renders him inadequate as a political observer, and his commentaries look inwards to his autobiographical concerns, to his writing.

'Ceylon' and 'The English Mail-Coach'

De Quincey's later political papers repeatedly sound a note of warning, and the possibility that a false step has been taken on the political as well as the personal plane informs the revised *Confessions* of 1856 along with the commentaries on India and China of 1857, the last footnotes to his career as a journalist. In 'Ceylon' (1843), a review of Bennett's *Ceylon and its Capabilities*, parts of which De Quincey wrote *'expressly with a view* to effect and [sic] rhetorical impression' (NLS MS 4065 fo. 196: letter of 12 October 1843) for *Blackwood's Edinburgh Magazine*, the political concerns manifested elsewhere are voiced in a hysterical, though gloomy, key.

The connections made in this paper compare significantly with those forged in 'The English Mail-Coach', in that in both the flow of language gives the paper its coherence. Logical clarity of thought, indeed, gives way in 'Ceylon' to a kind of musical charade as the 'secret philosophy' behind the 'science' of colonisation, the 'blessing' and 'gifts' of which hint at a 'regeneration' arising from the 'natural advantages' of the winners of the 'competition' of human progress (the British), are discussed while the writer attempts, with the aid of every available prop (God, nation, nature, law, duty, science and so on) to justify the colony in Ceylon. One's initial temptation is perhaps to imitate De Quincey's example whenever he met Charles Lamb unaccompanied by Mary: ' you sighed [. . .] and asked no questions' (*Tait's*, vol. v [April 1838], p. 246). With the notable exception of Maniquis, critics have tended generally to avoid De Quincey's political works. However, 'Ceylon' contains several quintessential De Quinceyan motifs and as such demands some analysis. The fear of Orientals first expressed in the 'Confessions' of 1821 is extended. De Quincey now delineates the Oriental, the representative figure of forgotten origin, in terms of his (the Oriental's) inability to progress much beyond this origin. While the British are represented as an 'advanced' people, their antagonists, the Ceylonese, are seen as virtually retarded. De Quincey's conception of an eternal push forward (which gives the struggle some meaning) allows him to explain away apparent oppression with a bland chauvinism:

> Britain *has* advantages at this stage of the race, which makes the competition no longer equal – henceforwards it has became gloriously 'unfair' – but at starting we were all equal (12: 3).

That the 'race' may entail a few casualties is of minor importance to De Quincey at this juncture. The actual occupation of physical space in Ceylon by the imperialist force is not considered as such. Rather, De Quincey's interest lies in Ceylon as the realisation of that imaginative interface, posited in the *Confessions*, in which fascination can be maintained. A psychological colonisation takes place here:

> Too subtly she will lay her fascinations upon man; and it will need all the anguish of disease, and the stings of death, to unloose the ties which, in coming ages, must bind the hearts of her children to this Eden of the terraqueous globe (12: 9).

The 'unloose/bind' metaphor suggests a wholesale revisionary action; and the thrust of the argument towards the end of the paper is that a new connection between this 'Eden' and its inhabitants must be forged. Furthermore, the colonisation of Ceylon, in that it incorporates the introduction of Christianity into a virtual 'Eden', is a divinely inspired revision. De Quincey indulges in a lengthy rumination over this idea, though he admits that such characterisations are 'bravuras of rhetoric' (12: 9). The defiance of death which the fascinations of Ceylon will stimulate is nevertheless clearly embodied in the rhetorical movement of this essay, which strategically defies the logical thought necessary for such proselytism to appear convincing. This suggests that language is out of De Quincey's control and that the writer moves randomly, even whimsically, from one suggestive or stimulating image to another. The question of intent arises. If this action has any validity, as it must if writing has any validity, what purpose does it serve? 'Ceylon' strives to work as propaganda, but the sense of irony that inevitably accompanies the process of recasting other works, of critically examining and revivifying others' ideas and propositions, is clearly signalled when De Quincey, far from confining himself to the limitations of his source (or his title), has recourse to personally-significant images which expand the argument to a point where the 'original' is entirely obliterated – as it always must be, given that writing is (mis)quotation, is rewriting. This latent irony invests De Quincey's assertions with, on the one hand, a certain air of detachment, often humorous, as when he suggests Lapland and Wapping as alternative sites for Paradise (12: 8); and, on the other hand, with a sense of anxiety which arises out of choice. In the latter respect, the possibility that writing involves an error which publication compounds informs the political dogma which De Quincey attempts to expound, so that although 'Ceylon' ends on a high note, even here an element of ambiguity, of doubt, is evident:

> Ceylon will be born again: in our hands she will first answer to the great summons of nature; and will become, in fact, what by providential destiny she is, – the queen lotus of the Indian seas, and the Pandora of islands (12: 38).

The dangers of Pandora's Box, of the Kandyan threat and the reaction to it of Major Davie, a man 'encrusted with the leprosy of cowardice' (12: 21) have not been eliminated by De Quincey's writing. Davie is yet another flawed leader who goes astray, a man whose existence subsequent to the fatal moment of cowardice which costs his men their lives is passed as if 'there flowed a river of separation – there were stretched lines of interdict heavier than ever Pope ordained – there brooded a schism like that of death' between him and his fellows (12: 22). Davie's error produces a narrative closure which leaves him in a state of limbo reminiscent of the fate of Stanley in *The Stranger's Grave*. Whereas De Quincey can extend into a vast autobiographical text the 'irrevocable word' (5: 154) uttered as he enters adulthood and can come to terms with the prospect of death, for Davie the moment of extremity gives way to oblivion. Unlike De Quincey, he cannot transform his mistake into a glorious error. The Major's social role, determined by action and therefore by a definitive 'reading', relegates him to the status of a redundant tool, in that it admits of no procrastinatory potential. Davie is denied the resurrection available to the autobiographer since the remembered moment of decision cannot be filled out. De Quincey underlines this point, criticising Bennett's characterisation of Davie as 'gallant' in spite of his collusion with the Kandyans in the massacre of his men. Yet this characterisation suggests that De Quincey's version of events is similarly suspect: what is the basis for his (or, alternatively, for Bennett's) representation? Davie is a useful figure in De Quincey's polemic in that he is both a victim and a murderer. As the dupe of the Kandyans (12: 17) he satisfactorily fills the former role, upon which De Quincey's characterisation of Orientals rests. As the betrayer of his own men (who are the victims of the Kandyans, of Davie, and of their own superior knowledge: 12: 17), Davie fills the latter role as well and conforms to the political 'flawed leader' type already discussed in this chapter.[11] The connection, in these terms, between Davie and the autobiographer is clear. Davie is the death-wish personified in a political context, a figure of total negation for De Quincey.

Such a figure makes De Quincey's position intolerably uncomfortable – although to represent Davie at all suggests that some advantage arises from this discomfort. De Quincey's efforts at extracting himself from an impasse of his own making are interesting. Obliged to argue that the control of the army might be in the wrong hands, that the soldiers were able to 'judge more truly of the crisis' (12: 17-18) than their officers, De Quincey comes dangerously close to throwing into relief his allegiance to the aristocracy and his entire argument in support of colonisation, which rests upon the assumption that some men are 'naturally' superior to others. De Quincey's political beliefs are, however, tempered by his sense of betrayal. Davie's conduct is exactly what is to be expected, for De Quincey's first allegiance is not to policy, nor again to historical actuality, but to a psychological system in which the disciple is forever let down – to the vision of a fragmented world, the concrete reality of which figures such as Davie assert exists. The clear-headed soldiers whom Davie sends to their death are primarily figures of imbalance. That is, they are sacrificial victims whose betrayal is not justified, not revised by atonement or revenge. Similarly, the puppet-prince given up by Davie to the Kandyans is yielded 'for nothing in return' (12: 21). In 'The English Mail-Coach' De Quincey pauses to comment on the acceptance of death without a struggle. A moral test is examined in the later essay, as it is indirectly in 'Ceylon'. Davie has failed the test: extremity has been faced but the responsible protector has proved a coward. In 'The English Mail-Coach' De Quincey examines further the meaning of such a failure:

> But if he makes no effort, shrinking without a struggle, from his duty, he himself will not the less certainly perish for this baseness of poltroonery. He will die no less: and why not? Wherefore should we grieve that there is one craven less in the world? No; *let* him perish, without a pitying thought of ours wasted upon him (L 222; 4: 340).

The case of the coward who fails in his duty is prefigured in 'Ceylon':

Davie is Adam, the betrayal of his men is an example of how 'as in aboriginal Paradise, the man falls by his own choice' (4: 327; *L* 212) – and is Ceylon not Paradise?

De Quincey's political misgivings are directly connected to the problems he encounters as an autobiographer, so that his perception of the world (as represented in his writings) is always formulated in accordance with his self-image and with the writing that substantiates that image (both, like the world, are atomised, fragmentary yet coherent). His search for actualities that will fit a particular form leads to a repetitiveness which severely undercuts any notion that his fugitive political papers are concerned with history. The recurring crisis has an ahistorical significance. History is reduced to a few reflex actions by which experience can be easily explained. It is always a matter of an ideologically loaded 'principle' for De Quincey, rarely a matter of conflicting human needs and aspirations. His political papers seek to reinforce a singular set of social relations grounded in a hierarchical, property-based, bourgeois individualism. De Quincey wishes to articulate the validity of such a position, to keep in constant, vital motion the workings of a principled, self-conscious society. That De Quincey's papers on China in the 1850s could be brought out as a book, *China*, as well as appearing in Hogg's *Titan* demonstrates that the vision De Quincey represents of the Orient satisfied a demand and articulated a commonly accepted, racist viewpoint. In the introduction to *China* he explains that the purpose of the publication is 'to diffuse amongst those of the middle classes, whose daily occupations leave them small leisure for direct personal inquiries, some sufficient materials for appreciating the *justice* of our British pretensions and attitude in our coming war with China' (*China*, p. i: Preliminary Note).[12] He comments further that he wishes to address the question 'What is it that our brutal enemy wants from us?' (*ibid.*, p. ii).[13] The perverse phrasing of this question – as if the Chinese had invaded Britain – now strike a perhaps ludicrous note. However, it must be appreciated that such perversity was surely acceptable and even constituted 'the truth'.

As late as 1857 De Quincey reiterates the ideas contained in the 'Ceylon' paper of 1843, albeit with a slightly different focus of attention. He again defines Asia as a land which will be reborn: 'Asia will begin to rise from her ancient prostration, and, without exaggeration, the beginnings of a new earth and new heavens will dawn' (*UW* 2: 36); the colonial administration is still represented as a dynamic result of 'a natural and spontaneous evolution of consequences, most of which would have followed us as if by some magnetic attraction' (*UW* 1: 306). But the betrayal of sacrificial victims for no good reason (for no *profit*) worries De Quincey:

> I that write these words am not superstitious; but this one

superstition has ever haunted me – that the foundations laid in the blood, of innocent men are not likely to prosper (*China*, 148–9).

The victimisation of the colonist by the colonised, like the oppression of the autobiographer by his recollections, establishes a dynamic relationship between complementary opposites. The antagonism at once produces equilibrium and projects, as its ultimate result, complete harmony. The equilibrium consists of the permanent struggle between forces which define one another, which I have represented as victim and victimiser (or murderer) and which revolve around the imminent collapse (death) which their inter-action continually erases and rewrites. Equilibrium has a procrastinatory function, but, like the death with which it is connected, it is defined by its absence, by the lack of harmony. For De Quincey, the political world has gone haywire: he maintains an interest in affairs, but this is primarily an interest in abstractions. De Quincey's professed belief that the human race is progressing, that a 'new era' (*PW* 1: 165) is in the offing, similarly involves an entry into an imaginative realm (akin to the East). The future, like the past, is absent; and, perhaps not surprisingly, the two tend to coalesce so as to become the axis of a metaphorical globe across which De Quincey has been condemned to wander.[14] Reality is subordinated to the representation of the motion from loss to recovery:

> Ah, reader, scorn not that which – whether you refuse it or not as the reality of realities – is assuredly the reality of dreams, linking us to a far vaster cycle, in which the love and the languishing, the ruin and the horror, of this world are but moments – but elements in an eternal circle. The cycle stretches from an East that is forgotten to a West that is but conjectured (*PW* 1: 26).

De Quincey desires to bring the political turmoil of the world, the fragmentation of society, under the control of his memory – to restore harmony, the lost 'equilibrium', by translating struggle into a memorial, something implicitly better than the decaying real world. In 'The English Mail-Coach' (1849, 1854) the death of this projected/remembered equilibrium is recorded:

> Ah, reader! when I look back upon those days, it seems to me that all things change – all things perish. 'Perish the roses and the palms of kings': perish even the crowns and trophies of Waterloo: thunder and lightning are not the thunder and lightning which I remember (4: 309; *L* 197).

In 'The English Mail-Coach' De Quincey's highly artificial language renders his commentary suspect, in that he consciously acknowledges and embraces artifice and declares that this is entirely apt. What he confronts is the ever-absent – the exquisite forgery is all there is. His *redundancy* in the political papers is also, therefore, his *function*: he provides an image of failure, of triumph in failure. The 'Dream-Fugue', in which he represents himself as the dramatic space in which a life-and-death struggle is enacted night after night for forty years, expresses the triumphant consolidation of the writer's self-justificatory strategies; decomposition and reconstruction occur in the same imaginative interstice. Along with collapse, potential renewal exists as an imminent possibility in the midst of the disastrously fragmented social world.

Motion

De Quincey forges in 'The English Mail-Coach' (1849, 1854) a direct equation between the autobiographer, the mail-coach, and the text. All three are united by the idea of 'motion'. The autobiographer's ability to maintain a state of continual precipitation, a state in which the imminent destruction of the self is transcended through writing, is complemented by the acceleration of the mail-coach (most obviously) in the 'Sudden Death' sequence. The coach itself is an image of a lost past; of a political and mythical state; and of writing – it is literally the 'vehicle' which carries the physical and remembered/imagined self. De Quincey's memory binds him to the coach (a bold connection, all the more extraordinary because it actually works) and, as ever, to writing – to the point where 'De Quincey' is almost entirely a mnemonic residue, pure process. A typical joke underlines the complexity of the connections forged in the essay, while also hinting, again typically, at the possibility of an exit, a hidden interface within which De Quincey may survive the erasure of identity:

> Meantime, what are we stopping for? Surely we have now waited long enough. Oh, this procrastinating mail, and this procrastinating post-office! Can't they take a lesson upon that subject from *me*? Some people have called *me* procrastinating. Yet you are witness, reader, that I was here kept waiting for the post-office. Will the post-office lay its hand on its heart, in its moments of sobriety, and assert that ever it waited for me? What are they about? The guard tells me that there is a large extra accumulation of foreign mails this night, owing to irregularities caused by war, by wind, by weather, in the packet service, which as yet does not benefit at all by steam (4: 331; *L* 215).

Here De Quincey calls into question the relationship between the 'real' time represented in the narrative and the actual time of the narrative as it is read. That is, he explodes the connection forged between the times as being just that – a forgery. The waiting on top of the coach in 1816 or 1817 (when the events recounted are said to have occurred) is co-existent with the waiting for something to happen – to be written, remembered, or read – in 1849, 1854, or now. For a moment, De Quincey checks the motion of the narrative (of the coach, and of the connections between figures) – an action which has an element of bravado about it. In demonstrating this temporal co-existence, De Quincey implies that the past may be recovered and even altered. One reads 'De Quincey' (the figure of the writer) as occupying two interdependent but quite separate times simultaneously: yet this apparent claim to a continuous self is invested with a powerful sense of irony. The representation of the present of composition, of authorial procrastination, attests to the non-existence of the past; while the present-self of 'The English Mail-Coach' is, as memory, always becoming past, always fading from the present. The dynamics of the essay in part rely on this occupation of complementary opposites. De Quincey consciously exploits coincidence and formally reinforces the theme of sudden death by prefiguring in this joke the elision of singular, past experiences within the 'Dream-Fugue' which forms the climax of the essay. Sudden death, 'the fiercest of translations' (4: 340: L 222), is approached here with a disarming coolness, as a less solid and perhaps more unnerving series of translations becomes apparent. The issues raised by this apparently whimsical delay are far from trivial. The journey that now follows cements the connection formed between self, coach and text. The reason for 'stopping' lies in the fact that this moment immediately before the commencement of the flight towards the vision of death is one of crucial decision for De Quincey. Motion, the heightened self-conscious occupation of a variety of different vantage points, by means of which a 'true', total, appreciation of any given or projected state may be gathered – and by which a vision of society from the position of the individual may be realised – is both glorious and painful. By examining the disparity created by representation, he extricates himself from the too definitive link about to be forged. Just as he is to survive the collision, to live to tell the nightmares, to revise the essay, so too De Quincey here steps aside for a moment to demonstrate his singularity in spite of language. Yet this strategy exists also within language, as a punning translation which is inevitably undone even as it is created. Extremity exists at this moment too, the 'death' to come happens even here. 'Great wits jump' (4: 294; L 187). So too, the figure of Death leaps up from the road (4: 344; L 224). De Quincey stays put on the coach. He maintains the substitutive movement, but the dangers inherent in attempting the impossible are acknowledged and he accepts the termination coincident to having begun. The checking of motion, a reversal which is to be examined more fully in the 'Dream-Fugue''s freezing of frenzied life (4: 353; L 230), is at this juncture an artful reinforcement of motion. Not merely is a state of suspense created, but more significantly the denial of the connection between autobiographer and mail-coach embodied in the question 'Can't they take a lesson [. . .] from me?' also strengthens the connection. As De Quincey gets on with his narrative, the coach, inevitably, starts to roll. The procrastination of the post-office which has allowed him to catch the coach, though too late to do so under ordinary circumstances, arises from a surfeit of letters; the foreign mails mentioned are an image of the surfeit of letters in the words of the narrative. De Quincey accounts for the 'extra accumulation' as resulting from forces beyond his control – war, weather and wind – as well as the absence of technologically-augmented communication (no steam) which might overcome these obstacles, but which might also prevent him from catching the coach. The text, then, is partially controlled by random, unexpected accidents; by things outside the author's control (involuntary memories, association); and is at least not helped by the technology of the Press.

De Quincey calls the reader as a witness to the fact that he has lost control. This appeal to the phenomenologically absent figure (the reader was not there to see the event; nor is the reader present in the sense of being able to validate the autobiographical narrative) to substantiate a state of affairs which his appeal itself negates, is clearly absurd. Yet the apostrophe also signals the contingency of the narrative, the impossibility of substantiating what it asserts. Were the reader 'a witness' to the actual scene, it would be as a redundant witness only, a consideration which throws into relief the relative positions of the writer, the reader, and the figures in the text with which they are connected (that is, the extra-textual to the textual figures). De Quincey figures himself in 'The Vision of Sudden Death' as the witness to a catastrophe in which he cannot effectually intervene. The projection of the self into the crisis is transformed into the projection of the crisis into the self, in the form of the dream vision. The crisis is contextualised both before and after the fact. It is given a loose historical context in the first section of the essay, 'The Glory of Motion/Going Down with Victory', wherein De Quincey recalls the mail coach system in the early decades of the nineteenth century, chiefly in terms of the political and psychological meaning with which he invested it. The following section, 'The Vision of Sudden Death', represents the crisis itself which, in the third section, the 'Dream-Fugue', is translated in the writer's brain as a recurring dream. This movement, in that it represents the memory of a dream, posits an origin forever erased but which, as translated memory (both psychologically and actually: the dream and the text are coincident to one another), constitutes a re-origin, a recursion to the originating faculty of De Quincey's brain; so that the 'fact' of the crisis (death) resides both in itself and before/after itself. Contextualisation indicates that death is ever-imminent and that intervention is only valid if it takes the form of a continuation. De Quincey's lack of action at the moment of extremity is undercut by his ability to set up substitutive metaphors – continually to do so, thus validating an apparently passive and therefore useless position.

The contingency of the autobiographical text figuratively frees De Quincey, and the act of reading (which he performs on the coach in extremity and also in revision; and which the reader of the autobiography also performs) realises a 'divine' potential inherent in the text and in the estranged individual. God in 'The English Mail-Coach' is, like the reader of the autobiography, phenomenologically absent. So too, God's task is to continue the efforts of, specifically, the man in the gig in collision with the coach; and, implicitly, of the human race – including the autobiographer. God and the reader share a similar task, as De Quincey's imagined prayer, delivered by the potential victim of disaster, seems to assert:

> Already in resignation he had rested from his struggle; and perhaps in his heart he was whispering, 'Father, which art in heaven, do thou finish above what I on earth have attempted' (4: 342; L 223).

The potential victim must rely upon an absent agent to make valuable his efforts through continuation, just as must the autobiographer. De Quincey juxtaposes 'finish' not with 'begin' but 'attempt': the potential victim is also involved in a task of *continuation*, one which God as origin ('Father') has begun. The reader's activity exists in the thick of multiple extremity. The text that is being read is a return to a now-erased original reading, a resurrection. The flight towards an unknown death is transformed into a recursion to a secret origin. This reiteration of the value of extremity also expands the role of the reader of the (autobiographical) moment of crisis, so that reading becomes as horrific and as glorious as writing. The apostrophe to the reader discussed above is also a self-apostrophising act by De Quincey. His revisionary task makes him his own reader, which suggests the existence of a certain redundancy inherent in representation. Indeed, the basis of the autobiographical task would seem, in its reliance upon death as a pivotal factor, to be inherently futile. De Quincey faces this futility by implying that the autobiography is out of his hands, that the post-office, the weather and so on are in charge. Writing alone 'continues', and continues to allow him to pretend otherwise. The coach journey begins in the narrative when, De Quincey aboard and unable to jump except *wittily*, textual motion is resumed. The transition of the self, of any identity, is complete: death has been faced already even though it has yet to be faced (again) in the future/past of the collision.

Life contains death, which is contextualised as a procrastinatory pause in an unending sequence (the individual's death is offset against the survival of the society or race of which he is a part: his identity is absorbed in the past). But, if the motion set up, or continued, by De Quincey is to carry on perpetually, the quality of this continuation is still impossible to control. That this consideration runs as an undercurrent through 'The English Mail-Coach' can be gleaned from the material which De Quincey incorporates in the work. The range of references is extraordinary, both as regards the literary models formally alluded to and the idiosyncratic images, in the dreams and elsewhere, that are brought to play in this *tour de force*. So too the flow of the narrative is impressive; the connections forged are reliant upon the 'musical' prose, a point hinted at near the opening of the essay:

> For my own feeling, this post-office service spoke as by some mighty orchestra, where a thousand instruments, all disregarding each other, and so far in danger of discord, yet all obedient as slaves to the supreme *baton* of some great leader, terminate in a perfection of harmony like that of heart, brain, and lungs in a healthy animal organisation (4: 290; L 183).

The 'mighty leader' in this work is, first, De Quincey's memory which 'composes' both the essay and, by implication, the life of the autobiographer. In the *Confessions* De Quincey had written that certain pieces of music would provoke a recollection of the whole of his past life, 'as if present and incarnated in the music; no longer painful to dwell upon; but the detail of its incidents removed, or blended in some hazy abstraction' (5: 207; L 46). An abstracted identity without self-consciousness is apparently contained in the notes of a specific piece of music. If we accept Barrett's assertion that 'A piece of music, heard as whole, is much more than the real present of experience than the single notes that occur within its structuring presence',[15] the present-time of a hypothetical life-long piece of music (coincident, that is, with De Quincey's life) would be constantly reasserting itself and would be defined not by reduction to a specific unit or phrase but by its totality. De Quincey's efforts to construct a 'musical' prose can be taken in part as an attempt to speak accurately of the self in the on-going present.[16] Such a style implies the possibility of immortality, in that it involves a death-defying effort to realise presence at all times, obliterating the past/present/future schema. De Quincey also transcends in this way the demands of memory in its apparent ties to the past and, without denying its validity, overcomes the logical impossibility of self-identification through introspection (in that it takes time to point to happenings in time and therefore he cannot state 'I am now x or y without entering upon a series of self-conscious acts). Rather, De Quincey tends towards an erasure of self, leaving only process: 'being' rather than 'I am'. The autobiography functions without a subject and it is by severing the connection between himself and the 'I' on the page that De Quincey paradoxically asserts his 'authority' – an authority complementary to that of writing, an occult power of a doppelgänger gone missing in action. This absence is reliant nevertheless on the self-assertion which it strives to erase. Hence, it is in the dream-visions that De Quincey's prose is most musical, for it is in the realm of dreams, of unconscious experience over which he has no control, that the 'painful' sense of having lived is transformed into a terrifying fascination.

The de-historicising process by which past and future become one in the shifting present produces a pointedly mythical autobiographical narrative. 'The English Mail-Coach' dramatises the appropriation of language, of writing, of process by the self (which is itself an appropriation: the self is revised and revivified by the autobiographer: an identity is assumed as soon as the autobiographical venture commences). The essay also contains its own disintegration in the form of the 'repayment' or 'handing back' of the process in the dream-vision, the appropriation of the self by writing. The return to Eden and an aboriginal paradise before a knowledge of death is also a return to death, so that even as it progresses the essay alerts us to the fact that what is represented here is a recursion to the only available origin of realising that humanity is stuck – that it is 'TOO LATE' (*L* 199). The 'Music too passionate' (4: 346; *L* 225) is 'heard once, and heard no more,' and its translation in the 'Dream-Fugue' is a sign of both its continued 'presence' and its certain 'absence'. The music, contrasted to 'aboriginal silence' (4: 353; *L* 230), signifies the interdependent complementary opposites of life and death. Resurrection is grounded in death, and it is this – a return to a death that has yet to be but has always been – that De Quincey proposes.

The individual identity cannot act effectually to prevent the inevitable. Death, by definition necessary, can only be observed, reinterpreted or predicted from the position of immunity afforded by De Quincey's seat on the mail-coach.[17] De Quincey represents himself as one unable to act save as a reader who might redeem the victims of catastrophe:

> I pretend to no presence of mind. On the contrary, my fear is, that I am miserably and shamefully deficient in that quality as regards action. The palsy of doubt and distraction hangs like some guilty weight of dark unfathomed remembrances upon my energies, when the signal is flying for *action*. But, on the other hand, this accursed gift I have, as regards *thought*, that in the first step towards the possibility of a misfortune, I see its total evolution; in the radix of the series I see too certainly and too instantly its entire expansion; in the first syllable of the dreadful sentence, I read already the last (4: 336; *L* 219).

The ability to fuel the motion that might transform disaster and which in its incarnation as musical prose harmonises disturbing forces, is set against the autobiographer's inability to alter through decisive action the apparently inevitable experience of extremity. The redemptive possibilities of reinterpretation are, however, characterised as inherently oppressive. The maintenance of a substitutive process arises as the product of an 'accursed gift'. The ability to translate seems at all stages to victimise De Quincey. He is a martyr not only to his lack of energy in action, which he represents as akin to repressed guilt, but also to his prophetic and interpretative faculties. Doubt is unpleasant, certainty a sophisticated torture. As Spector has observed, 'The glory of motion is always the horror of motion'.[18] Translation leads to confusion, the knowledge that he too, 'De Quincey', is involuntarily changed by the process of change he has started or, more correctly, appropriated. As a strategy in reaction to this perplexing state of affairs, De Quincey is led to emphasise his role as victim and to represent motion as partially accidental, as reflex.

Accident goes some way towards exculpating De Quincey from an anxious sense of guilt – guilt connected locally (as in the passage above) with the failure of the self to intervene in a positive way; and guilt as a universal state, a mythical expansion of the problems coincident to writing, connected with a possible collusion with a latent tendency towards an acceptance of death – a wallowing in the 'luxury of ruin' (4: 327; L 212) which is perhaps a rehearsal of 'the original temptation in Eden'. Yet accident does not alter the belief that 'the man falls by his own choice' in De Quincey's view. In 'The English Mail-Coach' the balance between the accidental and the deliberate is closely examined. De Quincey writes that the mail was delayed 'By some rare accident' (4: 329); that 'it so happened' that there were no other outside passengers (no accomplices or witnesses) (4: 329; L 213): that taking laudanum 'by accident' drew his attention to the driver, who 'by accident' was known to him (4: 330; L 214); and that the coach was observed to be on the wrong side of the road immediately before the crisis – an 'ominous accident' (4: 337; L 219). This accumulation of uncontrollable forces tends, on the one hand, to substantiate De Quincey's role as that of passive martyr to inexplicable and irrevocable disaster; but, on the other hand, this tendency is tempered by his vaunted abilities to forsee potential outcomes to all situations Thus, he reasons that his cloak might have been stolen by a fellow-passenger, but that as in actuality there was no one to do the stealing, 'the crime, which else was but too probable, missed fire for want of a criminal' (4: 329; L 213). Such extravagant jests are suggestive of a luxurious anxiety which arises from an awareness of too many choices: the lack of control is also a blessing in disguise.

The notion of what *might be* is re-emphasised when the gig is sighted on the road ahead. De Quincey cannot immediately 'decipher the character of the motion' (4: 338), while, having done all he could do and having decisively assumed the role of observer, he ruminates over the moral character of the man driving the gig: is he 'a brave man' or a 'craven' (4: 340; L 221–2) – a complication already touched upon in this essay. Sudden death, De Quincey explains in his introductory remarks to 'The Vision of Sudden Death', is most hideous when a chance of evasion occurs; and this, 'the sickening necessity for hurrying in extremity where all hurry seems destined to be vain', is exasperated when one is obliged to preserve the life of another, 'accidentally thrown upon *your* protection' (4: 326). The quality of death is chosen, even if death is not a matter of choice. To fail to sustain the motion by which others might be preserved is to accept death as and for itself (nothing). In the fictional works De Quincey's attempt to preserve the dead had led only to a partial understanding or articulation of this death-wish. In 'The English Mail-Coach' he confronts the problem directly. The introverted hopelessness of the stories of 1838 is replaced by a remarkable expansion of the personal problem into one of broad social significance. Here the potential collapse of substitution which the fictions had embraced is so contextualised as to be admitted as a necessary, even acceptable, evil. A fearful, anxious sense of uncertainty replaces the certainty of despair.

The journey towards death is transformed in the 'Dream-Fugue' into a complex drama of antagonistic forces finally harmonised in a general celebration of victory and resurrection, heralded by the blast of the Dying Trumpeter which brings to life the static bas-reliefs in the necropolis. In the dream, disaster is averted and the motion of the mail-coach is checked at a moment of extremity signalled by the trumpet blast, a sound significant of publication and of warning (as De Quincey announces in his prefatory remarks to the revision [4: xii-xiv]). The stasis of the coach transformed to stone 'by horror' signifies the extremity of fascination, a rewriting of the dreams in the *Confessions* in which the autobiographer's death-wish is contextualised in the landscape of a mythical Orient. There the crocodile had oppressed the dreamer – the finite had become infinite, the hope of rebirth had apparently been destroyed:

> All the feet of the tables, sophas, &c. soon became instinct with life: the abominable head of the crocodile, and his leering eyes, looked out at me, multiplied into a thousand repetitions; and I stood loathing and fascinated (*L* 74; 5: 269).

In 'The English Mail-Coach' dead matter is once more invested with life, and its relation with the death of the living is more clearly stated. Motion is halted in a horrific interchange between flesh and stone, between the *vital* and the *memorial*, a reversal of roles that becomes a coincidence of roles as the narrator rises and freezes while the Dying Trumpeter simultaneously rises from a frozen state – both under the influence of 'horror' at the thought of the female infant's imminent destruction. The interchange is followed by the triumph of life: infinite motion in resumed and the finity of the *Confessions* gives way to 'endless resurrections' (4: 355; *L* 233). Stasis is here given as the prelude to victory. The physical realisation of suspense is represented in the apocalyptic dream scenario:

> Immediately deep shadows fell between us, and aboriginal silence. The choir had ceased to sing. The hoofs of our horses, the dreadful rattle of our harness, the groaning of our wheels, alarmed the graves no more. By horror the bas-relief had been unlocked into life. By horror we, that were so full of life, we men and our horses, with their fiery fore-legs rising in mid air to their everlasting gallop, were frozen to a bas-relief. Then a third time the trumpet sounded; the seals were taken off all pulses; life, and the frenzy of life, tore into their channels again; again the choir burst forth in sunny grandeur, as from the muffling of storms and darkness; again the thunderings of our horses carried temptation into the graves (4: 353; L 230).

Stasis is invested with potential motion as the 'everlasting gallop' of the horses suggests; while fascination is now a challenge, not to prevent the fulfilment of the death-wish, as the dreams of crocodiles and of 'lying down before the lion' (4: 327) would have it, but to tempt the dead from their graves.

Under the influence of memory De Quincey envisages the impossible as a higher reality – 'the reality of dreams', as he puts it. Ultimately the music of the 'Dream-Fugue' is understood to be a prelude to the universal clamour of humanity:

> All the hosts of jubilation, like armies, that ride in pursuit, moved with one step. Us, that, with laurelled heads, were passing from the cathedral, they overtook, and, as with a garment, they wrapped us round with thunders greater than our own (4: 354–5).

The burial shroud becomes a flag of rejoicing in which the riders of the coach are wrapped. The passive witness (De Quincey; the Trumpeter) serves a purpose – to warn and to publicise. The redundant observer of personal and political disaster has become a seer.

The 'Dream-Fugue'

De Quincey's gloss on 'The English Mail-Coach' denies any responsibility for the alleged obscurity of the 'Dream-Fugue', a strategy which itself further obscures the author. Having reiterated the concerns of the essay, underlining the fact that the 'grandest' feature of the mail system lay in its political mission (4: xiii), De Quincey, usually so careful to explain that his possible errors relate to illness, fatigue, lack of time, pressures of the Press and so forth, insists that he is in any event not to blame:

> If not – if there be anything amiss – let the Dream be responsible. The Dream is a law to itself: and as well quarrel with a rainbow for showing, or for *not* showing, a secondary arch (4: xiv).

This retreat from criticism reinforces the implicit absence of the writer from his autobiographical work. Signifier and signified function as one, the dream, 'a law unto itself', thwarts but also signifies infiltration. The dreamer is erased by dreaming, the writer by writing. De Quincey invests the loss of identity with positive significance, even if this is inevitably only localised. Artifice, the rainbow-like appearance of substantial being, gives the autobiographer a special immunity. The fact that the 'Dream-Fugue' can be revised between the publication of the criticisms and that of the author's explanatory gloss (the gloss itself constituting a revision, another criticism of the essay) belies De Quincey's denial of responsibility, but also reinforces his assertion that he is not in control, has perhaps never been in control. The revisions go no way towards asserting an extra-textual authority. On the contrary, the retouches are all aimed at embellishing the musicality of the prose: the momentum of the work is subtly and finely realised. Given that the text and the coach are connected metaphorically, the precedence of the vehicle over the subject it carries or embodies is emphasised. De Quincey's personality is not important here: true, it gives some form to the work, in so far as the constituents are in part 'personal', apparently results of individual choice; but the work of art has a social value as well – and it is this, the political, that concerns De Quincey.

The fabrication of the 'Dream-Fugue' confronts the unverifiable nature of the signified referents which go towards the composition of the autobiographical text. The absence of De Quincey from his writing, the singular estrangement of the autobiographer, is called into question and reasserted. Renza argues that the autobiographer

> cannot efface himself through a dream-narrative except [. . .] by a willful act that denotes itself as such as he writes; nor can he fully commit himself to writing about writing's inability to signify his life as he tries, nevertheless, to do so, for this would entail conceding his discursive act to the consciousness of "others".[19]

De Quincey's 'Dream-Fugue' is an apocalyptic dramatisation of effacement. The self changes into a blur swept along in a motion of 'flight and pursuit', from and towards the lost paradise of a past without a future which holds the illusion of a recognisable identity. Even in paradise, however, identity seems the product of motion – of a fall – and the dreamer must cope with this betrayal. In 'The Household Wreck' Hannah's son had been led into temptation, 'led astray' (*Blackwood's*, vol. XLIII, [January 1838], p. 13). In the *Confessions* the youthful De Quincey had been urged on by a desire for 'freedom' to quit school. Castlereagh had similarly wandered from the path 'and by one false step, irretrievably taken, had cancelled the merits of a life!' (*Tave* 283). Canning, Brougham, Wellington, Major Davie and others had, similarly, fatally erred. In the 'Dream-Fugue' the treachery of the self becomes the necessary connection between an entity and the motion which constitutes it. Writing, life, the 'warning' which makes no death truly sudden (unless one deliberately ignores it – 4: 335) is a process which betrays and fools De Quincey, but which he is obliged to embrace or at least to collude with, in so far as he continues to write. The dream, which connects, distorts, invents and revises experiences from which De Quincey is estranged, formally reflects its own content. In the 'Fugue' the betrayal in language is transformed by the possibilities of language into a victory, a celebration sounded in 'the voice of perfect joy' (4: 354; L 232).

This transformation, however, does not lack in ambiguities. Throughout 'The English Mail-Coach' the contingent possibilities of language are emphasised. The essay, punctuated with puns and riddled with word-play, asserts the duality of experience, the conscious and unconscious aspects of experience. The 'Dream-Fugue' is itself mirrored by the introduction of 'The Vision of Sudden Death' (4: 323–8; L 209–12), in that the accident recounted furnishes two texts (or, a text open at both ends). The details of the 'Fugue' rehearse those represented in the 'Vision' and in 'The Glory of Motion'. At the beginning of the essay, De Quincey alludes to 'the anarchies' of his dreams and characterises the publication of political news as 'apocalyptic' (4: 289, 290; L 183, 184), prefiguring the 'Dream Fugue''s mixture of chaotic strife and religious vision. More important than the obvious thematic links which De Quincey painstakingly underlines are the subtler connections which invest the essay with a curious coherence. A casual reading produces an impression of random, idiosyncratic references having been thrown together into a semblance of order. However, the whole is brilliantly conceived and executed, deliberately designed to engage and perplex simultaneously. The 'Dream-Fugue', most forcibly, in that it declares itself as private experience, prohibits analysis; but the rest of the essay similarly requires a great deal of application if it is to be understood: the reader must rehearse 'the original curse of labour' (4: 335; L 218) and make the connections that pull the parts of the essay together. The erasure of the writer redeems him. The language of the essay is suggestive of the forgery of connections; and it is through a series of puns in 'The Glory of Motion/Going Down with Victory' that De Quincey establishes the immediate necessity, but also the ambiguity, of this forging action. Thus, the sailor who sets fire to the Royal Mail is 'making light of the law' (4: 298; L 189); while the heading 'Going Down With Victory' itself contains a pun: the members of the 23rd Regiment do just that as De Quincey observes in his version of the charge at the Battle of Talavera (4: 320). This pun registers less as a joke than as a wry comment on the themes engaged in the essay as a whole. The facts of the matter beg a symbolic interpretation:

> They leaped their horses – *over* a trench where they could, *into* it, and with the result of death or mutilation when they could *not*. What proportion cleared the trench is nowhere stated.

Those who *did*, closed up and went down upon the enemy with such divinity of fervour (I use the word *divinity* by design: the inspiration of God must have prompted this movement to those whom even then he was calling to his presence), that two results followed (4: 320; L 207).

The trench here functions as a grave. Some are swallowed by the grave, some manage to avoid being swallowed. The survivors ironically 'close up' on the enemy, closing like the grave; but, later, having 'ascended the hill', they are represented as having 'fixed the gaze' of the French. The idea that the Anglo-French battles are both deadly and redemptive is subtly reinforced as the Christ-like position of the regiment holds the enemy fascinated. The death-defying leap (like that of the wit of the writer, the one who connects: 'Great wits jump' [4: 294; L 187]) prefigures the imaginative crossing of boundaries in the 'Dream-Fugue', and reinforces the nature of the trial faced by the autobiographer in his leap across 'a gulf of forty years' (4: 311) and his claim to divine inspiration implied in the dream.

De Quincey conceals the significance of the partial victory of Talavera from the woman he encounters on the journey described in this section. He lies to spare her the experience of mingled joy and grief, the horror inherent in victory. Again, the concerns dramatised in the 'Dream-Fugue' are prefigured, raising the question of the 'Vision"s meaning. Does De Quincey wake to horror? In that the 'Fugue' terminates the essay, the question remains unanswered – there is no waking, which again is suggestive of death, so leading back to the impenetrable ambiguity which the essay records. In 'Going Down With Victory' the political import of the dream is also prefiguratively glossed: De Quincey addresses 'Mother England' as he speaks to the 'fey' woman from whom he conceals the truth. She kisses him instead of her son. The connections made here suggest that England is doomed; that the writer is dead; and that the relation between the writer and the nation he so proudly supports is artificial. This sense of ambiguity informs the entire work: after all, it is only through 'the vicious habit of sleeping' (4: 332; L 216) that De Quincey can recover lost time. And will the reader make the connections, or will the reader fail through ignorance like the coach-driver who misunderstands De Quincey's hackneyed citation of Virgil (4: 299; L 189)?

That the narrative will overwhelm the reader is acknowledged early on in 'The English Mail-Coach'. The limits of writing are obliquely touched upon in the discussion of the right-of-way of the mail-coach. De Quincey emphasises that a certain immunity pertains to the seat on top of the coach, that 'Nobody can touch you there' (4: 297; L 188). The writer, absent from the autobiography, is out of reach. The mail is characterised as defying the law. What governs its behaviour is obscure, even alarming: 'Not the less impressive were those terrors, because their legal limits were imperfectly ascertained' (4: 299). Literature and power are explicitly linked:

> We, on our parts (we, the collective mail, I mean), did our utmost to exalt the idea of our privileges by the insolence with which we wielded them. Whether this insolence rested upon law that gave it a sanction, or upon conscious power that haughtily dispensed with that sanction, equally it spoke from a potential station; and the agent, in each particular insolence of the moment, was viewed reverentially, as one having authority (4: 300; *L* 190).

The bold connections forged in the essay reinforce the insolence referred to, especially in the 'Dream-Fugue': such complexity is both a self-conscious display and a challenge (and, given that De Quincey argues for self-conscious individualism as a political principle, it constitutes a challenge to explore self-consciousness itself). When the mail-coach is nearly beaten in a race against a Birmingham vehicle, the outside of which is plastered with an excessive number of signs, the driver of the mail allows the other to 'be full-blown before he froze it' (4: 302; *L* 192). The implications of this are complex. The action of the 'Dream-Fugue' involves a freezing, a checking of motion by the Dying Trumpeter. De Quincey goes to excessive lengths in his realisation of the dream vision, before and after this checking action. To continue *ad infinitum* at this excessive pitch, the essay implies, is to tempt death, is 'treason'. The race with the Birmingham (shoddy) coach symbolically asserts the claims to good taste of 'The English Mail-Coach'.[20] The just limits of this work are indicated. De Quincey is on the verge of leaving others behind, in his better past and better future. This movement into excess is avowedly dangerous: to advance means to risk one's life, as a joke on becoming the foremost lover of Fanny of the Bath Road indicates. De Quincey thinks that 'a few casualties amongst her lovers (and observe, they *hanged* liberally in those days) might have promoted me speedily to the top of the tree' (4: 309; *L* 197) – but whether or not he might be hanged from this tree himself remains uncertain. The possibility that writing will overwhelm De Quincey remains problematic, and the ironic realisation that it already has done so is revealed repeatedly in this essay.

In the 'Dream-Fugue' De Quincey is about to crash in a headlong collision with the female infant before the sudden checking of motion halts this potential disaster. The infant embodies the imminent collapse of language, of identity and of power: the incarnation of what De Quincey calls the 'effeminate collapse of your energies' (4: 327), she is nevertheless a figure who intercedes between De Quincey and God. As the 'ransom for Waterloo' (4: 352; *L* 230) she is the figure of the interdependence of resurrection and collapse (in that 'Waterloo', at once the 'secret word' which promises peace [4: 350; *L*

228] and the apocalyptic 'dreadful word, that rode before us' [4: 350; L 228] – secret like birth, dreadful like life – is the sign of resurrection). Voiceless and collapsing (4: 353; L 231) the female infant is repeatedly sacrificed. Mockery and false signs (the deceitful hand from the sky – De Quincey's God? or a mockery of God? [4: 349; L 227]) delude and bury her before she is revivified, allowing motion to be resumed. In this vision one may read the autobiographer's realisation that his necessary loss of identity, his estrangement, ironically links him to the rest of humanity. To be absent from one's autobiographical text is the common fate of all. The sacrifice of De Quincey's female infant, an innocent Eve, a symbol of original failure – his own – and of original life, images the autobiographer's collapse of energies, a collapse on which he founds the hoped-for resurrection. Infinite collapse, the reiterated deconstruction of the process of substitution ('God') is rehearsed; and De Quincey recreates this glimpse of the infinite in the 'Dream-Fugue'. Finally, he is absorbed, overtaken, perhaps even left behind, as the 'hosts of jubilation' (4: 354; L 232) – the human race stretching infinitely into the past and into the future – sweep around him.

The vision concludes with a positive acceptance of death, but is in itself the memorial of this acceptance. The translation of the dream (made conscious through the memory and thus invested with emotional meaning, felt 'as a thrilling' – 4: 304; L 194) expose it to scepticism. Its publication in a modern world of disconnection, of unsympathetic machinery, preserves it as a text but limits the connections which the narrative projects. The essay is, in this respect, like 'the eternal writing which proclaims the frailty of earth and her children' (4: 312). 'Visionary sympathy' is called for if horrific connections are not to overwhelm the positive implications of 'The English Mail-Coach'.

The possibility of a definitive reading of the work is deliberately prevented, not only by the revision of the essay, important though that is, but by a precise structuring of multiple ironic referents. The text thwarts definition, the confluent keys of horror and glory lending it a *tonal* contingency. Is the autobiography De Quincey's or that of 'unknown voices' (4: 354; L 231) – of his *class*?

If the essay does articulate a specific class response, and I suggest that it patently does, then De Quincey predicts for the middle-classes a crisis which can scarcely be averted, unless it be through the 'proper' use of language (by which is implied the use of language as a tool of power). 'The English Mail-Coach' signifies impending disaster for Britain. As such it reiterates the argument of virtually all of De Quincey's political commentaries. In 'The Prospects of Britain', the prefigurations of disaster are discussed in a way which suggests that the definite interpretation of such prefigurations can never be in time – the crisis will always overwhelm the interpreter:

> Every great crisis, which is such for a mighty and important section of the human race, comes heralded by many signs: these are large, vague, and ambiguous at a distance; and they first assume a general legibility when the dangers which they announce are close upon us: the signs cease to be disputed, when the things signified cease to be within control ('The Prospects of Britain', *Blackwood's*, vol. XXXI [April 1832], p. 581).

'The English Mail-Coach' is itself a sign of the generalised state of crisis, and of the obscure disaster which it heralds and contains. How one is to read the danger sign only becomes obvious when the crisis actually happens, when it is already *too late*. 'The English Mail-Coach' is, in this scheme of things, a privileged intervention, one which attests to the maintenance of a position of power. Its power relies upon a vision of reality in which doom is always about to destroy everything. This is an economically defined reality in which a special effort must always and for ever be maintained if 'the human race' – more correctly those privileged 'mighty and important' beings who define themselves as representing the human race – is to survive. For De Quincey the middle-classes are always threatened by 'others', by death. The exploration of the death-instinct is specifically useful for such a class. De Quincey's is a politics of fear and protective aggression, his writing grounded in death, 'stained with the guilt not merely of culture in particular but of History itself as one long nightmare'[21] – a nightmare from which, like that of the 'Dream-Fugue', there is no awakening.

CHAPTER SIX 153

The Logic of Political Economy
and related writings

Political economic theory preoccupied De Quincey on and off for a major part of his career as a professional journalist. Though critics, with some notable exceptions, have largely ignored the political-economic essays, they bear some investigation. In this chapter I analyse De Quincey's major political economic writings and relate them to analogous interventions. My analysis suggests that, far from being works that one can ignore, the essays on economy form an integral part of De Quincey's oeuvre.

As well as numerous short, fugitive items (for instance, the papers published in Tave's *New Essays* and several unrepublished items from *Blackwood's*), De Quincey wrote two extended works on economic theory. The first was the 'Dialogues of Three Templars', serialised in 1824 in *The London Magazine*. This was a popularist explanation of the new and important theories of David Ricardo, whose *On the Principles of Political Economy and Taxation* (published in 1819) De Quincey had hailed in the *Confessions of an English Opium-Eater* as the 'work of a profound understanding' (L 65). For the Opium-Eater, Ricardo had 'constructed what had been but a collection of tentative discussions into a science of regular proportions, now first standing on an eternal basis' (L 65). Twenty years later, in 1844, Blackwood published in book form De Quincey's major work on political economy, *The Logic of Political Economy*, basically a recast of a series of articles from *Blackwood's Edinburgh Magazine* called 'Ricardo Made Easy'.[1] As with the 'Dialogues' De Quincey's purpose in this work was primarily to elucidate the ideas of Ricardo. The *Logic*, however, is also thoroughly informed (as one might expect, given the content of those of De Quincey's essays for *Blackwood's* discussed in the previous chapter) by party political considerations.

Although these works demonstrate that De Quincey certainly had a thorough understanding of economics, for which he was respected and valued by *The London Magazine* and, subsequently, by *Blackwood's*, it cannot be said that he significantly advanced on the work of Ricardo. Rather, his essays popularised political economy in an eloquent and sometimes entertaining manner. More than this, De Quincey attempted to reconcile the 'scientific' elements of Ricardian economics with his own Tory principles. It is largely De Quincey's blatant *politicisation* of economic theory which forms the basis of the following analysis.

In his monograph 'Lonely Empires', Maniquis has usefully discussed De Quincey's relation to Ricardo. His comments on the pessimistic implications of the new 'science' underline the fascination that economics held for De Quincey:

> The cheaper the bread, the less an industrialist paid for labor and the more he earned in profits. The more he earned in profits, the more he reinvested in the economy and the more the economy grew. But it seemed to Ricardo that the beautiful forward movement of this spiral was being interrupted at each turn by the landowner who unjustly accumulated more and more of the wealth produced by industrialist and laborer. In Ricardo there is the suggestion, one that he would not clearly assent to, that expanding capitalism was a self-destructive machine. No economic theory could more easily attract the imagination of De Quincey, an expert in the patterns of self-destruction.[2]

In economics De Quincey finds a generalised version of an individual death-wish, for Ricardian theory implies that the human race will eventually be consumed in an inevitable movement towards inertia. This tendency in its relation to Ricardo's doctrine of rent (and the short-term solution to the problem) is simply and conveniently explained by Fine:

> By utilizing labour time as the source of value, Ricardo develops a theory of differential rent in which value for agriculture is determined by the labour-time of production on the worst land in use (or more exactly the last unit or dose of capital in use). The worst land pays no rent, but the better lands appropriate the surplus product relative to the worst land in use. With the movement onto worse land as accumulation proceeds, rents rise and profitability falls as the value of corn wages increases. The resulting movement towards and ultimately around a stationary state, for which the last land in use barely provides normal profit and subsistence wages, can only be postponed by exporting the margin of cultivation abroad, by importing corn. The existence of a tariff on corn raises rents and hastens the arrival of the stationary state.[3]

Foucault has analysed the ideological shift of classical economic theory. Crudely put, whereas Adam Smith's concern was with equivalences and simultaneity, Ricardo replaced simultaneity with historicity: labour forms part of a successive series of definitions;

The Logic of Political Economy

and value, in the Ricardian system, is defined not as a *sign*, but as a *product*. The implications of this shift are far-reaching:

> All labour gives a result which, in one form or another, is applied to a further labour whose cost it defines; and this new labour participates in turn in the creation of value, etc. This accumulation in series breaks for the first time with the reciprocal determinations that were the sole active factors in the Classical analysis of wealth. It introduces, by its very existence, the possibility of a continuous historical time, even if in fact [. . .] Ricardo conceives of the evolution ahead only as a slowing down and, at most, a total suspension of history.[4]

Furthermore, Foucault suggests, a realisation of the logical result of this slowing down – the petrification or immobilisation of History – impinges upon the present and throws human existence into relief:

> The tide of History will at last become slack. Man's *finitude* will have been *defined* – once and for all, that is, for an *indefinite* time.[5]

It is here, at an actual and ever-present moment of extremity, that De Quincey's fascination comes into play – at the point where the anxiety of composition coincides with a cultural and all-pervasive anxiety grounded in scarcity. *The Logic of Political Economy* (1844) indicates the ever-recurring problem which needs to be confronted:

> Our own social system seems to harbour within itself the germ of our ruin. Either we must destroy rent, *i.e.* that which causes rent, or rent will destroy *us*, unless in the one sole case where this destroying agency can be headed back uniformly as it touches the point of danger – that point where it would enter into combination with evil co-agencies. Now, this great case of reservation, this saving clause, (which, by the intervention of an *"unless,"* i.e. of an *"if not,"* entitled, of course, to the benefits of a Shakspearian *"if,"* defeats a dreadful tendency always lying *couchant* in our social mechanism,) being almost unnoticed by Ricardo, or not finding a systematic *locus* in his exposition, besides leaving room for a sort of wonderment not creditable to a severe science, has the further bad effect of inviting a malignant political disaffection. Both in France, Germany, and England, a dreadful class is forming itself of systematic enemies to property. As a wild, ferocious instinct, blind as a Cyclops and strong as a Cyclops, this anti-social frenzy has naturally but too deep a root in the predispositions of hopeless poverty (*Logic* 191–2).

The image of the Cyclops here prefigures the description of the coach-driver in 'The English Mail-Coach' (published in 1849, five years after the *Logic*), though here the Cyclops is blind rather than asleep. The raging energies of the poor are directed haphazardly against society, urged on by the inferences to be drawn from Ricardian economics. De Quincey diverges from Ricardo's doctrines, insisting upon the possibilities for increased sophistication in land-cultivation – a 'great pursuing counter-agency which travels after the tendency on land, overtakes it continually, and once at least in each century, like an *annus Platonicus*, restores the old relations of our system'(*Logic* 195), thereby halting the recourse to increasingly inferior grades of soil. Ricardian pessimism must be negated, yet De Quincey's assertion of (an admittedly vague) hope is grounded all the same in a gloomy view of society ever on the point of collapse.

De Quincey's adjusted revision of Ricardian economic theory indicates the contingent status of the discourse by means of which society is to be interpreted. Economics breaks down internally, Ricardo's system allowing for uncertain speculation – 'a sort of wonderment' – which suggests that society is doomed. It will either be wiped out historically according to Ricardo's doctrine of rent, or will be destroyed by the forces of radical political revolution. The logical theory proves inadequate, the 'detective' Ricardo flawed in his interpretation. Economics also breaks down when confronted with political reality in the shape of the irrational inclinations of the 'dreadful class', which suggest that the rational system the economist proposes is inapposite, if not misguided. De Quincey's criticism of Ricardo's failure underlines the hypothetical nature of the intervention, and its worrying contingency.

'Unless', 'if not' and 'if' appear synonymous at this juncture in the *Logic*: precision momentarily abandoned, De Quincey exposes economics as a manipulatable fiction necessarily informed by ideological considerations. So too, De Quincey's characterisation of the poor as an inhuman, mythical, monstrous Cyclops suggests that the 'scientific' theory of political economy need have little connection with actual social relations; and that the words in which the theory is grounded – words such as 'price', 'wealth' and 'value' – are no purer than any others. Economics, evidently, is open to subversion and disruption and is liable, like the society it purportedly represents, to collapse in ruin.

Ricardo had objected to the language used by his fellow political economists Smith and Malthus, and protested that his own consistent terminology was an essential prerequisite in the development of the discipline:

> I am told that I adopt new and unusual language, not reconcileable with the true principles of the science. To me it appears that the unusual and, indeed, inconsistent language, is that used by my opponents.[6]

The Logic of Political Economy

De Quincey in turn praises Ricardo's consistent use of language, remarking in the 'Dialogues of Three Templars' (1824, 1854) that he 'seems a model of perspicuity' (*London Magazine*, vol. IX, p. 344). Heinzelmann points out that De Quincey's approving comments nevertheless undermine economic representations:

> But in seeming to praise Ricardo through the speech of X.Y.Z., De Quincey actually attacks all economists at what seemed their point of safest shelter – in their claims for the immaterial "value" of language itself. De Quincey insists that we see the (Ricardian) shift in verbal counters not as "a mere dispute about words" but as an alteration in the intellectual "ground" of the argument.[7]

The shift from the inconsistent language of Smith or Malthus to the consistent language of Ricardo provokes in turn the subversion of consistency in the writings of De Quincey, whose intervention underlines the failure of political economy in its attempts to reconcile theory with reality. Where economics breaks down, morality and political belief intrude to throw into relief the economist's claims of accuracy. De Quincey's Tory sentiments call into question the rhetorical content of economics and indicate profound contradictions. These are compounded rather than analytically solved, which is not to suggest that any 'solution' would be any less expressive of a particular ideology: each (mis)interpretation opens itself for further (mis)interpretation. De Quincey repeatedly shifts the ground from political economy to politics, a shift which involves a pointedly perverse union of apparently mutually exclusive discourses. This apparent dissolution in his logical commentary was remarked by Mill, whose review of the *Logic* praised the text in general, but lamented De Quincey's 'ultra-Tory prejudices' which had 'deformed' it:

> It might make the angels weep for the pretensions of science and philosophy, when, even on the subject with which he is most scientifically conversant, they cannot inspire such a man with sufficient calmness, impartiality, and candour of judgment, to save him from the incessant use of such phrases as "corn traitors," "corn-law incendiaries," and the like, to designate those who think that the trade in food ought to be free; an opinion which the author himself is bound to hold, by every fair deduction from his own principles. We are quite unable to reconcile this wretched party invective with the respect we sincerely wish to feel for Mr De Quincey.[8]

Mill's criticism emphasises the contradictory tendency embodied in the *Logic*. Like so many of De Quincey's works, the *Logic* seems a synthesis of conflicting impulses, and Tyson's comment on 'Sir William Hamilton' could as well be applied here: 'Concepts are joined that are not merely exclusive, but actively repulsive: they violate the decorum of our perceptions'.[9] The 'horrid inoculation' (*L* 200) of opposing forces defeats the preconceptions of the reader of the De Quinceyan text. One is forced to revise one's predictions in the light of the writer's change of register.

The areas of politics and political economy are clearly differentiated by De Quincey. For example, in the newspaper article 'Political Economy, The Standard and the Edinburgh Saturday Post', published in 1827, he writes that 'political expedience, of a much higher character than any which belongs to political economy, raises doubts' over the wisdom of importing corn from abroad (*Tave* 176). Rational argument which follows specific principles is subject in De Quincey's view to irrational refutations: a separate principle may pre-empt the most complex theory and generate its own necessities.

De Quincey's efforts thus tend towards an admission of necessary and inevitable failure, though this tendency is tempered by a desire to overcome an apparently impossible situation of resourcelessness within the text. Hence, in addressing the problem of the relation of the elements which comprise exchange value, De Quincey provides an ironic gloss on his present-time dilemma as writer – as one whose work must, as it were, deliver the goods:

> It is a difficulty which seems, when stated, to include a metaphysical impossibility. You are required to do *that* which, under any statement, seems to exact a contradiction in terms. The demand is absolute and not to be evaded, for realizing an absurdity and extracting a positive existence out of a nonentity or a blank negation. To this next step, therefore, let us now proceed, after warning the reader that even Ricardo has not escaped the snare which is here spread for the understanding; and that, although a masculine good sense will generally escape in practice from merely logical perplexities, (that is, will cut the knot for all immediate results of practice which it cannot untie,) yet that errors "in the first intention" come round upon us in subsequent stages, unless they are met by their proper and commensurate solutions. Logic must be freed by logic: a false dialectical appearance of truth must be put down by the fullest exposure of the absolute and hidden truth, since also it will continually happen (as it *has* happened in the present case,) that a plausible sophism, which had been summarily crushed for the moment by a strong appeal to general good sense upon the absurd consequences arising, will infallibly return upon us when no such startling consequences are at hand (*Logic* 16–17).

The perplexity that De Quincey attempts to solve, the composition of 'exchange value' in economic theory, prefigures the difficulty explored at length in 'Sir William Hamilton' (discussed in Chapter

3). In the later essay, the absurd anxiety of composition demands that 'Art must thaw the dilemma which art has frozen together' (*Hogg's Instructor*, vol.IX, 1852), while in *The Logic of Political Economy* a similar 'fix' threatens to disrupt coherent thought and prevent progress. Here, 'Logic must be freed by logic'. The 'character' of political economy must be so used as to ward off any 'absurd consequences' generated by ignoring (or misinterpreting, misunderstanding) a fundamental error. But though he employs consistent language, in the manner of Ricardo, De Quincey does not articulate at this juncture the problem which pertains to his task as a writer, a problem 'Sir William Hamilton' finds insurmountable: can writing ever give 'hidden truth' in such a straightforward manner? or are attempts at representation errors in themselves which cannot be overcome, but must be embraced as so many absurdities, or quietly ignored for reasons of expediency? Behind the 'snare' he tries to evade lies yet another, more subtle one – the question of the exchange value of language. Writing would seem to extract a meaning from a 'blank negation', for writing as representation tends to negate the actuality that it seeks but fails to give. To let the argument proceed, De Quincey must ensure that the 'hidden truth' remain hidden. The solution would seem to be to indulge in the kind of fictional tactics that elsewhere De Quincey criticises as suspect. As in the *Confessions*, the reverberating error defies rectification. The writer's mistake is to (re)start writing, an inevitable action which is compounded by his reliance on another suspect exchange, namely the exchange of the textual figure of 'the reader' for an extra-textual entity which *might* exist. This exchange again assumes that the value of language need not be called into question (that is, that the word 'reader' does *give* an actual reader); but such an assumption is speedily subverted by the simultaneous realisation that writing must operate in the absence of a real reader; and that the text which posits a reader is a self-referring system, a short-circuit.

De Quincey acquiesces in this series of errors which comprise the written text. Indeed, were he to stop and question the various exchanges he assumes will occur, the *Logic* would collapse entirely. As it is, the text confronts its own potential dissolution in an uneasy conflation of the generation of meaning and the absence-of-meaning; or, which is as bad, between two plausible meanings which negate one another's implicit claim to truth.

In the *Logic* De Quincey asserts the validity of two distinct 'truths': on the one hand, an economic truth which suggests a state of gradual and inevitable decline; on the other hand, a political truth which rhetorically posits a potential resurrection from, or staving-off of, this decline. Political economy is found wanting: ironically enough the *Logic* attests *formally* to the scarcity of the society which it attempts to understand. In seeking to escape from the implications of Ricardian pessimism (and simultaneously from the promotion of free-trade, as Mill's criticisms underline), De Quincey merely betrays the inadequacies of the economic discourse. (Mono)Logicality breaks down, and De Quincey has recourse to the 'emotive' terms which subvert the 'scientific' text: the true traitors are not those concerned with the importation of corn, but the *words* by which these extra-textual entities are denoted in the writing.[10] By extension, De Quincey's 'Britain' (an imagined land which could be compared to the imagined Orient discussed in Chapter 5) may be understood as primarily a complex of potentially treacherous words. Language, with its contradictory impulses which allow for a macaronic literary intervention, reveals itself to be the state of unrest which De Quincey calls 'Great Britain'.

This seems perhaps a far-reaching assertion, and needs some qualification. The crux of my argument is that the 'traitors' in the land dramatically correspond to the traitors in the text. The emotive description which violates the scientific text provides an analogy of the supposed destroyers of the political equilibrium. In effect, the one 'proves' the other, making it impossible or at least extremely laborious for De Quincey to define the state of the nation in any terms other than those of 'betrayal' and 'treachery'. The conscious choice of vocabulary does not so much limit his options as determine that a particular imperative be explored, and proposed repeatedly as fact, in a single-minded fashion and to its obvious conclusion. Again, this tactic provokes a curious reaction: the pose of victim which I discussed in Chapter 5 is maintained here too, for the very same reasons; while the possibility of *blame* arises in conjunction with this position, affording De Quincey a means of expressing first a sense of the tendency of humanity towards self-destruction (a death-wish, then), and secondly, his own distance from this tendency (he represses it). In the 'traitor', the death wish and the fear of death coincide. By blaming a specific group of people, characterised by the term 'traitors', De Quincey subliminally expresses a fear of compounding a suicidal urge that political economy exposes but which Ricardian theory does not resolve. De Quincey's resolution (which at once accepts and rejects Ricardian pessimism) is to cordon off the area of responsibility. The blame devolves onto the traitors strategically inserted into the system. The traitor is an economic figure, a short-cut.

The fusing of the political and the economic discourses in the text attests to the absence of authority first in the De Quinceyan/Ricardian writing; and secondly, in the imagined nation of Britain. I would suggest that the first category here is primary, and that the view of a 'political reality' which De Quincey expresses may be understood as a by-product of textual problems: and it is on the text *per se* that I shall concentrate. The figures which will not work, will not obey their masters – these traitors suggest that *any* claims to authority by anyone must be spurious. Ricardo himself, the figure which initially authorises De Quincey's economic writing, proves flawed, like so many others (see the discussion of the 'flawed leader' type in Chapter 5). His failure allows De Quincey to intervene as a teacher, Ricardo having a 'natural inaptitude for the task of simplifying knowledge' (*Logic* 186). One of the 'Ricardian Protestants' (*Logic* 189n), De Quincey hones and enlivens portions of his predecessor's *Principles* to produce a hybrid text which at once accepts and subverts the authority of Ricardo. If De Quincey hints at his own status as victim of the traitors with whom he must engage, then he also betrays Ricardo (who in turn has been betrayed himself by his text). De Quincey attempts, indeed, to expose the system of betrayals which constitutes the economic text, but in doing so reveals that his own authority is invalid. As the figure of master-of-his-materials, 'De Quincey' (his name appears on the title-page of the *Logic*) fails necessarily. An exhausted parasite, De Quincey invests another figure – that of 'the capitalist' – with the power that he lacks himself. This transference of energy, from betrayed 'author' to potent 'conductor', requires some analysis, for it constitutes an economy grounded not in logic but in something approaching caprice, involving as it does the construction of a belief system – economics – from an apparent system of betrayals. Typically, De Quincey explores the ambiguity of his choice of figure: the capitalist not only affords a measure of security, but produces anxiety as well, while the obverse of this figure – the anti-social entity which appears in the guise of the Radical agitator or the murderer – also provides an object of fascination. Accompanied by an uncertain examination of alternatives, De Quincey's choice gradually disintegrates in perplexity. This process of disintegration requires further elucidation.

Capital

The authority of the Tory aristocracy (their power based in *landed* property) which informs De Quincey's political essays gives way in part to that of the monied industrial capitalist in the *Logic*. Towards the end of this text De Quincey discusses the principles which apply to the rate of profits in the employment of capital and the 'natural counteraction' to attempts to raise profits arbitrarily. In an absolutely crucial passage, he describes the 'continual transition' of energy which the capitalist system involves:

> Ricardo, who, as a stockbroker, stood in the very centre of the vast money machinery accumulated in London, had peculiar advantages for observing and for investigating the play of this machinery. If our human vision were fitted for detecting

agencies so impalpable, and if a station of view could be had, we might sometimes behold vast arches of electric matter continually passing and repassing between either pole and the equatorial regions. Accordingly as the equilibrium were disturbed suddenly or redressed, would be the phenomena of tropical hurricanes, or of auroral lights. Somewhat in the same silent arches of continual transition, ebbing and flowing like tides, do the re-agencies of the capital accumulated in London modify, without sound or echo, much commerce in all parts of the kingdom. Faithful to the monetary symptoms, and the fluctuations this way or that, eternally perceptible in the condition of every trade, the great monied capitalist standing at the centre of this enormous web, throws over his arch of capital or withdraws it, with the precision of a fireman directing columns of water from an engine upon the remotest quarter of a conflagration. It is not, as Ricardo almost *professionally* explains to us, by looking out for new men qualified to enter an aspiring trade, or by withdrawing some of the old men from a decaying trade, that the equilibrium is recovered. Such operations are difficult, dilatory, often personally ruinous, and disproportionately noisy to the public ear in the process of execution. But the true operation goes on as silently as the growth of light. The monied man stands equidistantly related to many different staple interests – the silk trade, the cotton trade, the iron trade, the timber and grain trade. Rarely does he act upon any one of them by direct interpolation of new firms, or direct withdrawals of old ones. An effect of this extent is generally as much beyond his power as beyond his interest.

Not a man has been shifted from his station; possibly not a man has been intruded; yet power and virtue have been thrown into vast laboratories of trade, like shells into a city. But all has been accomplished in one night by the inaudible agency of the post-office, co-operating with the equally inaudible agencies of capital moving through banks and through national debts, funded or unfunded. Such is the perfection of our civilization (*Logic* 227–9).

De Quincey places the figure of authority (first Ricardo, then the capitalist) in a central position from which the network of fluctuating relations may be comprehended. This figure corresponds roughly to the persona of the Opium-Eater, a procrastinatory detective or interpreter who has access to an apparently obscure and impenetrable system of hieroglyphics. But unlike the Opium-Eater, the capitalist seems stable and singular. The motionless assurance of the Opium-Eater gives way to anxious nightmares which the capitalist is spared (there is no shift from procrastination to a state of extremity for the idealised capitalist of the *Logic*). Here De Quincey hints at a different kind of order from that projected in his political essays and autobiographical writings. 'Equilibrium' is now grounded in permanent capital. A nameless paradigm provides a still centre. Flux and its upsets can be survived with little or no anxiety. Furthermore, the monied man remains 'faithful' – he maintains his principles and uses his skills accordingly. Betrayal barely features as a possibility, even though De Quincey hints at an irrational, anarchic impulse in the capitalist (namely, that profits may be raised arbitrarily – a logical inference which De Quincey deflects with reference to the inexplicable and unexplained 'natural counteraction' to such tendencies). In the 'play' of the 'money machinery', in the processes of political economy, De Quincey curiously asserts that the operations of capital are a mystery that can barely be understood: eventually, economy proves to be a metaphor of the transference of energy between antagonists (the poles), like electricity or warfare ('shells into a city'). A scarcity of knowledge becomes apparent in this quasi-mystical vision of capitalism: Ricardo only 'almost *professionally* explains' its workings; De Quincey opts for a variety of 'amateur' strategies to indicate 'the perfection of our civilization'. All in all, the economic intervention seems inadequate and falls short of its purpose. The text fails to complete its task. The silence of the capitalist's operations, the very lack of discourse, conceals rather than reveals the workings of the 'true operation'. The vision of completeness and of mastery expressed here is as imaginary as the 'Dream-Fugue''s anxious desires for deliverance from ruin, while the very stasis of the figure of the capitalist suggests that the 'perfection' De Quincey describes is that of the grave, of death, of oblivion (as well as of his God).

This ironic possibility is taken up in the autobiographical work 'Suspiria de Profundis', published in *Blackwood's* in 1845, a year after the *Logic*. A parallel to the image of the 'great monied capitalist' in the *Logic* occurs in the section of the 'Suspiria' entitled 'The Affliction of Childhood', where the all-powerful figure constitutes a threat rather than a source of hope and assurance. The context of the later work sheds a more sinister and disturbing light upon the operations of economic exchange. As a seven-year-old boy, De Quincey writes, he purchased the first volume of an apparently infinite text, the subject of which, the sea, seemed inexhaustible. The possibilities of being entrapped for ever in a formal obligation to purchase volume after volume of this work provoke a sickening fascination, a far less optimistic reaction than the persuasive and confident depiction of the capitalist given in the *Logic*. The narrative of this section of the 'Suspiria' constitutes a criticism, albeit veiled, of the capitalist order which De Quincey had supported. The obverse of his optimism – an optimism grounded in a post-Ricardian conviction that as a system capitalism can continue 'for ever' – is a sense of paranoia. Anxiety, the concomitant of his faith in the potential of capitalism, mingles with a hilarious horror when De Quincey realises that he has entered unwittingly on a silent contract. The semi-conscious awareness of the economically contrived/controlled world indicates that the *Logic* has provided only a partial vision of the effects of 'the vast money machinery.' Though De Quincey claims the experience was that of a child, the issue exposed here denotes an adult's perplexity:

> Certainly I had never heard of a work that extended to 15,000 volumes; but still there was no natural impossibility that it should; and, if in any case, in none so reasonably as one upon the inexhaustible sea. Besides, any slight mistake as to the letter of the number, could not affect the horror of the final prospect. I saw by the imprint, and I heard, that this work emanated from London, a vast centre of mystery to me, and the more so, as a thing unseen at any time by my eyes, and nearly 200 miles distant. I felt the fatal truth, that here was a ghostly cobweb radiating into all the provinces from the mighty metropolis. I secretly had trodden upon the outer circumference, had damaged or deranged the fine threads and links, – concealment or reparation there could be none. Slowly perhaps, but surely, the vibration would travel back to London. The ancient spider that sat there at the centre, would rush along the network through all longitudes and latitudes, until he found the responsible caitiff, author of so much mischief (*L* 133–4).

Earlier in the 'Suspiria', De Quincey had described how he wished to save from a maid's broom a spider, 'the poor doomed wretch', until he was told that the creature had committed 'many murders' and would carry on doing so if allowed to live ('This staggered me': *L* 126). In the dilemma, De Quincey the child opts out of the situation: in his perplexity, his efforts are negated – the fate of the spider is out if his hands. This situation De Quincey subtly echoes in the passage cited above, only now the position of resourcelessness proves far more extreme. Evidently there exists no way out of the web which has entangled him (the web of the ancient spider here is also the safety net of the *Logic*). Capital consumes the ignorant and the unwary, tracks them down, tortures and threatens the 'consumer' – 'all in profound silence' (*L* 134). In the face of this threat, De Quincey's reaction consists of a curious fascination once more. The horror is also a joke; the moment of confused loathing has passed and so can be handled at a distance, so that although he appears the perversely willing victim of the destructive system (a theme explored elsewhere, in writings such as 'The Household Wreck'), De Quincey also manages to remain oddly immune. Yet the text does not allow for any reductive appraisal, and the immunity implied by the placing of this consciousness of the negative aspects of capitalism in a myth of childhood is thoroughly undercut by the knowledge that the text itself exists as a commodity to be consumed. That is to say, our awareness of the machinery by which the text has been produced suggests that De Quincey is trapped within (not the text but) the 'unseen' machinery which goes to produce the published work, machinery unseen by the reader and which De Quincey does not explicitly elucidate. De Quincey himself has become the 'author of so much mischief' – of the autobiographical text which threatens to extend itself in proportion to the length of his life - provoked by his anxiety. The economic operation in which he 'accidentally' becomes involved (the buying of books, the writing of papers) generates horror; and, in the expression of this reaction, generates the text by means of which he can sustain himself and self-reproduce. As a victim of a potentially endless system (money generates anxiety, generates text, generates money, and so on), De Quincey can only collude with the forces which control him, never work round or outside them: that at least is the inference.

Capitalism serves the martyr who undergoes the painful and *valuable* tortures by which he is finally initiated into the adult world of the capital, London. De Quincey's acquiescence to the forces that close in around him and his acceptance of his own ineffectuality (whether his view is 'optimistic' or 'anxious') is powerfully expressed in his depictions of the capital. The solitary observer cannot maintain his identity in London, but instead finds he is consumed amid the crowds. His position is that of a nonentity who has lost the possibility of asserting his individuality. In the 'Autobiographic Sketches' De Quincey describes the state of the resourceless being, absorbed in the horror of others:

> Finally, for miles before you reach a suburb of London such as Islington, for instance, a last great sign and augury of the immensity which belongs to the coming metropolis forces itself upon the dullest observer, in the growing sense of his own utter insignificance. Everywhere else in England, you yourself, horses, carriage, attendants (if you travel with any), are regarded with attention, perhaps even curiosity: at all events you are seen. But, after passing the final post-house on every avenue to London, for the latter ten or twelve miles, you become aware that you are no longer noticed: nobody sees you; nobody hears you; nobody regards you; you do not even regard yourself. In fact, how should you, at the moment of first ascertaining your own total unimportance in the sum of things – a poor shivering unit in the aggregate of human life? Now, for the first time, whatever manner of man you were, or seemed to be at starting, squire or "squireen,"

lord or lordling, and however related to that city, hamlet, or solitary house, from which yesterday or to-day you slipped your cable, – beyond disguise you find yourself but one wave in a total Atlantic, one plant (and a parasitical plant besides, needing alien props) in a forest of America.

These are feelings which do not belong by preference to thoughtful people – far less to people merely sentimental. No man ever was left to himself for the first time in the streets, as yet unknown, of London, but he must have been saddened and mortified, perhaps terrified, by the sense of desertion and utter loneliness which belong [sic] to his situation. No loneliness can be like that which weighs upon the heart in the centre of faces never-ending, without voice or utterance for him; eyes innumerable, that have "no speculation" in their orbs which *he* can understand; and hurrying figures of men and women weaving to and fro, with no apparent purposes intelligible to a stranger, seeming like a mask of maniacs, or, oftentimes, like a pageant of phantoms (1: 185–6).

A kind of destruction of the self occurs in the capital, which swamps the individual and obliterates attempts at self-assertion. The position described here contrasts sharply with the privileged point of vantage occupied by the capitalist in the *Logic*. While the monied man can interpret the workings of the capital, the ignorant visitor can gain no purchase on the structure which threatens to obliterate him. The hideous immunity afforded by the destruction of identity arises from the sapping effect of the city. The identity of the city consists of the non-identity of its inhabitants; that is, the city is not a group of people, but an effect of numbers. The paranoia of the 'Suspiria' exists as a possible concomitant of the claustrophobia described here, but whereas debt affords a specific role – that of the miserable victim who cannot act but must collude with the money machinery – in the centre of the web the individual becomes a mere cipher, a non-entity unable to establish human relations with his fellows. This suggests that the 'monied man' of the *Logic* has established relations with others by turning the 'parasitical' situation of the city-dweller to advantage. Yet this manoeuvre remains 'mysterious' in De Quincey's view of things: it relies heavily on an unanalysed ability to read correctly the signs that threaten destruction (of the self in the environment of the city; of the race in the area of political economy). The interpretation of the capitalist transforms the 'mask of maniacs' into an intelligible system. By consciously removing himself from sight, the capitalist undergoes a kind of resurrection. It is as if the initiation which erases his identity has given way to a new identity grounded precisely in the distance afforded by the city's effect on individuals. De Quincey tacitly accepts the urban situation and explores its fascinating potential. He wonders how to exploit, rather than how to change the situation.

Three significant methods of exploitation are explored in his writings: first, the nightmarish voyeurism of the Opium-Eater who removes himself from the crowd; secondly, the tactics of the capitalist; and thirdly, the exploitation of the city by the murderer (see also Chapter 4). All three figures rely on a precise usage of the anonymity that the city affords. They maintain the disjunction between themselves and others, detecting (interpreting the figures of) the characteristics of others to create an identity, yet finally being identified purely by the method of detection – by their ability to *read* which pre-empts the efforts of others to read them. The exploitation of the crowd involves a continual shifting, the abandonment and displacement of the self in the struggle for self-reproduction. The ambiguities of 'insignificance' can be maintained so that the very lack of meaning may be filled: the individual absorbs the crowd, becoming a representative figure.

The economics of the murderer or Radical

The capitalist's position of power finds a direct analogy in that of the murderer. Whereas the capitalist's resurrection leaves him precisely centred, and thus open to threat, the murderer can move about at will and self-reproduce with the minimum of effort (and here the murderer contrasts with the Opium-Eater whose struggle to survive entails considerable pain). The murderer, whose labour is entirely negative, is a figure of the most efficient economic transaction: he obtains enormous power from next to nothing. In a note towards a paper on 'Murder as Fine Art' (published posthumously), De Quincey defines the murderer in terms of his utter immunity:

> The privilege of safe criminality, not liable to exposure, is limited to classes crowded together like leaves in Vallombrosa; for *them* to run away into some mighty city, Manchester or Glasgow, is to commence life anew. They turn over a new leaf with a vengeance. [. . .] Wealth is power; but it is a jest in comparison of poverty. Splendour is power; but it is a joke to obscurity. To be poor, to be obscure, to be a baker's apprentice or a tailor's journeyman, throws a power about a man, clothes him with attributes of ubiquity, *really* with those privileges of concealment which in the ring of Gyges were but fabulous. Is it a king, is it a sultan, that such a man rivals? Oh, friend, he rivals a spiritual power (*PW* 1: 79–80).

The murderer represents an ideal state in which the external resourcelessness of Ricardian economics may be overcome by recourse to an internal power. The murderer's effortless self-reproduction constitutes a defiant exploitation of the 'parasitical' relation to the crowd. By filling the common and easily-assumed form of the unskilled worker, the criminal remains quite obscure in the disguise of total anonymity. To exist without being identified may be both a horror and a delight.

Like the capitalist, the murderer spontaneously resurrects 'to commence life anew'. This resurrection involves the appropriation of the attributes of the crowd in which the individual had been hidden. This has political implications for De Quincey. In many of his political commentaries, the criminal coincides precisely with the figure of the Radical agitator: both have this chameleon quality which allows them to be defined as frauds. This characterisation, while it lends the fraud a certain charisma (using McLuhan's definition of charisma as a 'resemblance to a lot of other people'), also betrays the relative lack of political analysis in De Quincey's reaction to Radicalism. The Radicals, interpreted as an urban crowd in the control of a handful of criminals, are generally dismissed as 'anti-social'. They violate what De Quincey, citing Harrington as his authority, styles 'the very primal law of social institutions [. . .] – the gravitation of power to property' ('Conservative Prospects', *Blackwood's*, vol. XLIX [March 1841], p. 416). Revolutionary political tendencies De Quincey defines as 'temptation' fuelled by unprincipled agitators:

> Multitudes of those who have practised as mercenary orators on the question of slavery (not slave-trade) abolition, repeal of the corn-laws, &c., are not to be viewed as men that even erroneously had any such conscientious views as they professed. Generally speaking, they belong to the needy half-educated race, who crowd into great cities from obscure conditions of society, are troubled with no embarrassing principles upon any subject, with no scruples of conscience, with no accurate knowledge, all of which might operate as drags, or retarding forces upon the disposable value of their talent; but are ready at an hour's notice to undertake any career of public agitation in behalf of any possible opinions ('Conservative Prospects', *Blackwood's*, vol. XLIX, p. 417).

In effect, the criminal and the Radical 'scamp', motivated by 'spite and low-bred insolence' ('French Revolution', *Blackwood's*, vol. XXVIII [September 1830], p.551), are one and the same. Both represent the illegitimate transference of power. In a Britain in which power and property are linked together, the power of the poor may be equated to a kind of theft – an almost magical trick which throws into relief the economic theory that the *Logic* and similar interventions support. The criminal defies the system, taking the potentials of self-generating labour to an extreme which allows him to remain undetected and therefore unbetrayed.

De Quincey barely acknowledges labour as the ground of value in the *Logic*, a bias which informs many other essays as well.

The Logic of Political Economy 169

Instead he emphasises the power of the capitalist, the inference being that all labour tends necessarily towards the extreme *criminal* manifestation of labour: thus, the 'contagion of sympathy with his own class acting as a mob' draws the 'honest worker' into radical action ('Conservative Prospects', *Blackwood's*, vol. XLIX, p. 417). The criminal betrays others, leading them astray and prompting them to violence against the extant social order.[11] A figure of inevitable betrayal, of an unavoidable error in spite of all precautions (a familiar theme in De Quincey's writings), the criminal, Radical, or murderer – analogous figures in De Quincey's scheme – may be understood as expressing the ambiguity of the exchange value of language. That the power invested in any figure is open to question is exploited in De Quincey's essays, for it is precisely in the possibilities of doubt that his depiction of 'Great Britain' operates. The suggestion seems to be that if such figures were really eradicated, the political-economic discourse might function successfully: but this requires that the actual agitators who correspond to the words in the writings have the characteristics which De Quincey attributes to them, characteristics which articulate a specific ideological bias and which have been predetermined to serve the requirements of the political-economic belief system. De Quincey's arguments, whether from the Tory viewpoint or from the political-economist viewpoint (Ricardo was a Whig), suggest that there can be no solution to the problem of 'fixing' reality. At best one may propose a contingent 'truth' and include as part of the programme a definite scapegoat (the poor, the criminal, and so forth) – a figure within the system whose formulated destruction serves to legitimise it. The necessary fault in the system, the flaw in the hypothesis, is exposed and limited: its definition reinforces the coherence of the system.

In his attempt to wrest from the Radicals the doctrines of Ricardo, De Quincey places his faith in the figure of the capitalist, and suggests in the *Logic* that the professional manipulator of money will suffice as an authority. Already, the political disillusionment of 'The English Mail-Coach' is suggested in that the 'flawed leader' figure – the Prime Minister – has been replaced by an anonymous, 'mysterious' monied man. Though Mill decries De Quincey's Tory prejudices, read in the light of the rest of De Quincey's writings the *Logic* indicates the absence of any solid belief in the possibilities of political change for the (Tory) better. The capitalist, whose identity is constituted in his central position, and there alone, stabilises an otherwise chaotic society. For better or worse, De Quincey opts for this figure, even though in many ways it corresponds to the 'flawed leader' type. Ironically enough, the capitalist also corresponds to the figure of the murderer, in that the general characteristics of both figures are similar. Where the capitalist differs from his opposite lies, crucially, in the property that he 'legitimately' owns. The Radicals,

Chartists, and other 'anti-social' criminals in De Quincey's vision of Britain simply desire to take such property as does not belong to them. The capitalist structure, penetrated from without by the Radical whose example contaminates the poor, seems constantly under threat. By introducing the figure of the criminal into the economic discourse, De Quincey attempts, not entirely unsuccessfully, to merge the possible oblivion for the human race that Ricardo's theories suggest with the possible obliteration of the hierarchical power-system that the actions of labour-based political movements seem to promise.

This conflation indicates De Quincey's suspicious attitude towards democratic tendencies and towards the de-centring of power that extra-parliamentary agitation implies. Just as the 'Chinese' represent loss of identity and personal oblivion for the Opium-Eater, so too the democrats (all alike, as it were, much as the Orientals are for De Quincey) suggest a kind of death. The criminal or Radical engages in the theft of another's identity. His ability to assume the station of a poor labourer in the urban environment prefigures the possibility that he will assume the identity of the capitalist. This penetration of the capitalist order suggests that the authority of the capitalist is provisional and open to subversion. As complementary figures with the potential to serve as one (the property of the capitalist may be stolen by the criminal), the capitalist and criminal suggest a simultaneous acceptance and suspicion of authority on De Quincey's part. The wish for a legitimate, pre-determined and static centre of power based in the figure of the capitalist corresponds to a wish for a similarly reliable monologicality in language; yet this desire indicates an absence in actuality. De Quincey makes it quite plain that no true centre exists – the capitalist is a fantasy figure of eternal renewal, of resurrection – and that writing will always carry with it its own contradictions, not least of which will be the lack of communication between the writer and the reader that the text necessarily expresses. The mutually defining figures of capitalist and criminal suggest that any writing will be open to a disruptive reading, that the property of the author may be appropriated by the reader in an effortless, 'instinctive' fashion, unless this tendency to consume be refuted by strategies which prevent misinterpretation. Given that any reading will tend towards misinterpretation, these protective strategies will try to make the text difficult to read. That this seems perverse indicates the state of extremity which pertains to the De Quinceyan text, while also calling into question the nature of value which attaches to the commodity.

The figure of the capitalist suggests that a proper, literal meaning which writing embodies can be reappropriated by the reader without misapprehension, while that of the criminal suggests that this transaction (which posits a precise identity shared by the text-as-written and the text-as-read, rather than the one *producing* the other via disjunction) does not take place. Rather, the text-as-written may well be obliterated entirely by being read (the criminal erases the 'text' of his own past and destroys both his own identity and that which he appropriates). In employing these figures, De Quincey explores the limits of direct communication. If metaphor 'is what is proper to man' (Derrida),[12] then the improper theft of property by the criminal calls into question the claims of the 'economic' figure of the capitalist. The immediate and efficient translation of energy between two forces can always be disrupted and there will always be distortion – distortion by writing in the economic discourse, by the criminal in the imaginary flow of the political-economic 'reality'. De Quincey laments this inevitable disruption and seeks to suppress its effect; but he also acknowledges it and even explores *its* possibilities (for instance, in 'Sir William Hamilton', discussed in Chapter 3, and in the 'Dialogues', discussed below), possibilities which run counter to those of direct communication. Indeed, 'direct communication' is nothing other than one manifestation of these disrupted efforts at writing, one in which the fiction of singular identity is claimed to be useful. The assumption of another's identity which characterises the criminal/radical agitator fits into the economic discourse because it too suggests that singular identity is possible, that an 'economic' transaction can occur, even though the criminal subverts the transaction implied by the capitalist.

In the *Logic* De Quincey confronts the failure of the economic discourse to conduct singular meaning. The 'flawed' text in which 'the perfection of our civilization' is imagined attests to the imperfection of the economic transaction which it (the text) comprises. As the figure of intervention between writer and reader, the text constitutes a figure of disruption, of death, even as it conducts energy. That which conducts, seeks to re-establish the flow of energy; but it always falls short since as a medium it will assert itself, as 'writing', as much as the version(s) of reality it carries.

Economics and Mesmerism

The possibility of an exchange of energy that bypasses language comes under consideration in De Quincey's review article on 'Animal Magnetism' (1834).[13] Mesmerism provides a link between the 'external' and 'internal' worlds. It overcomes a sense of inner resourcelessness (the lack of self) where political economy ought to overcome the resourcelessness of external reality. In Mesmerism De Quincey sees offered the possibility of a harmonious order, a vital equilibrium, which even so may yet be liable to subversion. His comments on the implications of Mesmerism provide an interesting gloss on what may be termed the abbreviated or abridged economic exchange – that is, the imaginary transaction by which the potentially ambiguous quality of language may be suppressed in order to give reality in a precise manner. Excited by the prospect of 'functional transfiguration', where one organ may serve to do the work of another (for example, the stomach for the eye), De Quincey defines Mesmerism as a revolutionary discipline:

> *Appalling*, we have called the case; for it relates not merely to nature, to physical truth, but to our own *human* nature – to that part and section of physical truth with which chiefly we are concerned; and we are bold to affirm, that not the first solar eclipse visible to man, not the original, and as yet enigmatic earthquake, when the steadfast earth was perceived to rock like the waters beneath his feet, – not the sudden treachery and desertion of the mariner's compass at a critical point in the first voyage of Columbus, when an ancient law of nature, by suddenly giving way, seemed to argue an entrance within some new system of natural forces and laws, or, possibly, of utter lawlessness, – the anarchy of chaos and old night, – not any, or all of these cases, are fitted to excite awe so profound, or a thrill of horror so startling as the sudden transfiguration of parts in the human system, by which one organ takes upon itself the duties of another, by which a blank surface is lit up into an organization the most exquisite; and a communication suddenly opened with the external world, without apparent means or organs for communicating (*Tait's* vol. IV [January 1834], p. 464).

The extra-linguistic transference of energy constitutes a precise exchange. The disjunction which defines its economy (the opposition of 'external' and 'internal') can be waived so that a singular identity grounded in the general flux of 'animal magnetism' may serve for both worlds.

Whereas Ricardian political economic theory implies that a scarcity of resources requires intensive labour in order for the human race to survive, Mesmerism suggests that a secret pool of energy may be drawn upon. For De Quincey, animal magnetism remains a mysterious discipline to be developed for the common good, and above all provides a fascinating and dangerous instance of effortless communication between discrete entities. The language in which he couches the description of the capitalist at the end of the *Logic* indicates that political economy ought to function along similar lines: an 'electric' transference of money should take place: capital should be conducted with a kind of silent grace. Yet if Mesmerism provides the ideal model for such a system of exchange, even in its very perfection De Quincey notes that a special ambiguity arises. 'Utter lawlessness' and 'some new system of natural forces and laws' are both contained within the discovery and occupy the same mental space – as antagonists.¹⁴ Just as, in De Quincey's view, Ricardian economics can be subverted, so too the dream of perfect communication, of communication without recourse to communicating organs, may become a nightmare of paranoid anxiety, much as the capitalist network proves in the 'Suspiria' to be a spider's web.

Towards the end of 'Animal Magnetism' De Quincey cites the case of an epileptic called Cazot who, in a mesmeric trance, can predict the dates of his attacks and thus confine their effects. Cazot predicts that he will murder his wife in a frenzy to occur on a future date, but is killed by a horse before the time arrives. De Quincey comments that 'the epilepsy, and the madness, and the murder, were all intercepted and confounded' by the sudden death of the man (*Tait's*, vol. IV, p. 472). The figure of death penetrates the field of energy and puts into perspective the possibilities that Mesmerism seems to hold. Instead of the *crisis* – technically speaking the point at which the sickness terminates in Mesmerism – an accidental death occurs, erasing as much as interrupting the process. The unavoidable intervention which nevertheless does not *contradict* the prediction, conditional as it is on the epileptic being alive to have the fit, &c., comes from 'without': it is not communicated to the entranced man. As the reality of death throws into relief the system of animal magnetism here, so too in political economy the figure of the criminal interrupts the otherwise hypothetically 'flawless' process of capitalism, suggesting that the political economic intervention (the economic discourse generally, the *Logic* in particular) itself constitutes a highly ambiguous figure, one which may be understood as both a figure of crisis (cure) and a figure of death (negation). The economic text fills a space of extremity. The *Logic* has the status of a quotation of the activity which constitutes life for *homo oeconomicus* – namely, the staving off of oblivion. It is an intervention which fills out the moment between life and death, and as such is typical of De Quincey's oeuvre rather than an anomaly.

I have argued elsewhere that the moment of extremity in De Quincey's autobiographical pieces is analogous to the moment of composition of the text; and with the *Logic* also, I suggest that there is a relation between the present-time of composition and the sense of cultural extremity which Foucault describes. The 'autobiographical' impulse of De Quincey's writings expresses a reaction to the environment which the economic discourse tries to delineate. Foucault's definition may serve to underline the connection:

> What makes economics possible, and necessary, then, is a perpetual and fundamental situation of scarcity; confronted by a nature that in itself is inert and, save for one very small part, barren, man risks his life. It is no longer in the interplay

of representation that economics finds its principle, but near that perilous region where life is in confrontation of death.[15]

Given that Ricardian economics implies a state of perpetual extremity which requires a struggle for survival, one may understand how the Tory commentator De Quincey manages to conflate the imperatives of the economic theory with his party political bias. The cultural crisis is matched not only by the compositional crisis, but by a recurrent political crisis; the lament for a lost order – the coherent reality centred round Waterloo (the decisive 'cure') – serves a special purpose, for it is in the state of ruin, De Quincey's post-apostasy Britain, that his commentary is useful. One might even hypothesise that were the Waterloo idyll an actuality, De Quincey would have little or nothing to write about in the political context. It is certainly the case that his message throughout *Blackwood's* and beyond constantly predicts revolution, anarchy, and social upheaval. The crisis *per se* allows for quite contradictory opinions, fugitive projections that can be either hopeful or fearful. Thus, a decade before the optimism of the *Logic*, De Quincey voices a sense of disillusion in the possibilities of the present:

> Mechanical discoveries, by which the call for human labour is continually abridged, have proved at length a fatal snare to England. We read in romantic legends of meddlers with forbidden arts of demonology, who have gradually become alarmed by their own unlawful powers, who have revolted in horror from the meshes which their own spiritual ascendency was multiplying around their paths, and who have prayed, with rueful anguish, that it might be possible for them to exchange their criminal power and knowledge for the most pitiable imbecility unembittered by guilt. That is the condition of England. Means have concurred with opportunity to tempt her forward on a road, where at length there is no retreat and no advance, neither regress nor progress, and where every step brings up the bitter penalties of that system which has been made the paramount spring of her policy ('The Prospects of Britain', *Blackwood's*, vol. XXXI [April 1832], p. 582).

Here, the sense of impotence and of the uselessness of even trying tends paradoxically to fuel the commentary. The despairing, defiant filling-out of the moment of extremity provokes the textual strategies, over-riding any considerations for the contradictory imperatives of Tory belief and Ricardian theory mixed in the macaronic text of the *Logic*. The imperatives of writing are primary.

"[. . .] beyond retrieve"

De Quincey's conclusion to the *Logic* emphasises the contingent status of the economic intervention. The work ends on a cryptically hopeful note: 'Our fate [. . .] rests very much in our own hands' (*Logic* 260). It resolves little, and if De Quincey hints at human possibilities that might solve the dilemmas delineated in his argument, then he nevertheless closes at the point of ruin – ruin to be overcome precisely by a special effort, an effort akin to that which in many of his writings De Quincey claims he has invested in the text. By abandoning the enterprise 'unfinished' (that is, open-ended; in actuality the text finishes deliberately as my argument will shortly demonstrate), De Quincey lends his writing a peculiar relevance to the ever-revolving state of 'crisis': the point of ruin may be filled out again and again by the reading of the *Logic*. In so far as a reading, the revision of countless moments of present-time compositional crises, revivifies the textual figures, the vast filled moment of extremity which is the text can, potentially at least, be used repeatedly. The element that is lacking in this approach to the *Logic* is the fact that political expedience and historical actuality *do* overwhelm the economic intervention. As a product of its times, the *Logic* has a limited use. Two points suggest themselves in spite of this inevitable and obvious limitation. First, one may hypothesise that De Quincey's persistent reiteration of a Tory political policy (certainly up to and including 'The English Mail-Coach' of 1849; while later essays do little to modify such a criticism) constitutes an attempt to suspend historical time – for it is under conditions of suspended time that the *Logic* could be read *ad infinitum* (that is, as long as the precise conditions apply, then the text is relevant and useful). Secondly, in common with many of De Quincey's writings, the very abandonment of the *Logic* lends the work a special glory – one arising out of a sense of the monumental nature of apparently futile works.

This sense of futility, as I have already suggested, interfaces with a sense of self-betrayal. De Quincey as author, having embarked upon writing, must eventually abandon it to function outside his jurisdiction. And in fact this is always the case and goes to constitute the extremity of composition. The recurrent conflated crises I have outlined in this chapter demand bravado strategies which counteract the oppressive tendency of writing to erase the figure of the writer-as-controller. Writing not only abridges labour, but also replaces the labourer. It obliterates the author even as he attempts to stay in control. The 'fatal snare' is inscribed in De Quincey's attempts at representing a fugitive, 'dead' political reality.

Derrida's description of writing in 'Signature Event Context' has relevance here:

To write is to produce a mark that will constitute a kind of machine that is in turn productive, that my future disappearance in principle will not prevent from functioning and from yielding, and yielding itself to, reading and rewriting. When I say "my future disappearance," I do so to make this proposition more immediately acceptable. I must be able simply to say my disappearance, my nonpresence in general, for example the nonpresence of my meaning, of my intention-to-signify, of my wanting-to-communicate-this, from the emission or production of the mark.[16]

De Quincey discloses some unease about how his machine will function. Non-presence is hyperbolically underlined in several instances in which De Quincey wishes to stress the coherence and 'truth' of a particular argument. Estranged from the writing, he exploits in a dramatic fashion his own 'death' so as to insist that an imagined reality actually exists. An interesting example of this strategy occurs in 'On the Approaching Revolution in Great Britain' (1831), in which De Quincey describes 'in a letter to a friend' his own (imaginary) destruction by political upheavals:

> Let me then, professing to be a good interpreter of political signs and aspects, speaking to you as a bad one, but otherwise as agreeing with you in situation and capital interests, lay before you the grounds upon which I believe those interests to be something more than threatened. For you, however, that word *threatened* may still, I would hope, express the whole extent of the evil. You perhaps have it in your power to *act* upon the sense of danger which I may succeed in impressing. For myself, I repeat, *that* is impossible. I am a ruined man beyond retrieve (*Blackwood's*, vol. XXX, [August 1831], pp. 314–5).

De Quincey characterises non-presence as 'ruin' for strategic reasons. By recourse to the figure of a destroyed entity, one in the control of chaotic forces which are implicitly figures of destruction, he posits a reality which is adrift – a reality analogous to the authorless/unauthorised mark. This tactic allows for a characterisation of the 'infatuated government' (*Blackwood's*, vol. XXX, p. 316) and, simultaneously, a characterisation of a rebellious country made up of Radical agitators, &c. Between these antagonists stands the political commentator, 'beyond retrieve', whose very failure to act effectively constitutes the proof of his vision.

This strategy proves rather efficient. De Quincey's 'ruin' underlines the proposition that the government, a figure of authority analogous to the writer, is self-destructive and non-productive. The government must overcome its non-presence (its relation to the 'text' of Great Britain) *always* if it is to work at all. The figure of authority (and if possible the crucial authority-figure that is Waterloo) needs to be eternally resurrected. That is, the government must produce that mark which 'naturally' maintains itself, namely the figure of the Constitution which unprincipled actions have erased. De Quincey's depiction of the political scene consists of a dramatic examination of the relation between an 'author' (the government) and a 'text' (Great Britain/the country). This relation constitutes the fugitive political reality, and any question as to how Britain functions may be translated into the question, What is the relation of the text to its author?

Writing functioning in the necessary and complete non-presence of the writer translates into a vision of a country ungoverned and adrift, defined by De Quincey as a state of anarchy. The ruined land similarly proves analogous to the unread text; to writing without a reader or addressee who might figure as author. By making his reader a 'bad' interpreter, De Quincey reinforces his commentary, in that the unread writing continues to function and to provide a precise version of an imagined reality (chaotic Britain) even if no attention at all is paid to it. It is necessary to add that this strategy, though crucial, has a primarily local effect: even an illiterate interpreter constitutes some kind of (mis)reader whose potential existence is posited, if not in the text, then in the the context of the market. That is to say, the reader's existence incorporates an economic supposition; because an essay is bought (by *Blackwood's*; by the consumer), then that essay is assumed to be read; or, by virtue of its publication, it is assumed to be in a state where it may be readable. Perhaps the most one can say here is that the essay has been consumed as a commodity. The reader, as the quotation of the economically possible convergence of entities within the market (which is, in Heinzelmann's words, the 'verbal nexus by which we may say that supply and demand coincide'[17]), is imaginary, a figure of desire, of the lack of a reader – of the author's lack of control over the reader and how the writing is to be read; and, secondly, of the absence of any meaningful purchase on the social relations which contextualise the published work. De Quincey's commentary expresses a distinct sense of impotence. His political advice has a severely limited practical use. He can only suggest that the reader somehow defer the inevitable ruin, and seeks to persuade others to engage in the fundamental act of filling-out time.

I have already remarked the importance of this activity as it is defined by Foucault. The generalised attempt to stave off oblivion is of primary importance:

> *Homo oeconomicus* is not the human being who represents his own needs to himself, and the objects capable of satisfying them; he is the human being who spends, wears out, and wastes his life in evading the imminence of death. He is a finite being.[18]

De Quincey's evasive tactics evince precisely a fundamental recognition of the 'imminence of death'. But his perception of the Ricardian definition of reality focuses uncritically on the form of specific social relations and proves barely able to cope with the possibilities of change. A basically anxious fascination with the death-in-life which impinges on his perceptions provokes a mildly hysterical, sometimes weary, insistence upon the validity of a belief system which offers little hope and seems to deny the possibility of 'action'.

Deferment of ruin, of oblivion, of *finity*, then, proves problematic. De Quincey desires to survive destruction. Writing constitutes his means of attempting to do so – both locally, in that the published essay, bought in the market, allows him to self-reproduce by providing him with money for sustenance; and generally, in that the written word 'acts' as an index of trans-generational reproduction (notational rather than biological). The filling-out of the moment of extremity interfaces with a wish to conquer death. For De Quincey, this goal, resurrection, proves elusive. He is obliged to infer the possibility of success, to predict as an act of faith eventual fulfilment. Political economy and orthodox Christianity have a similar status for him in that both hold the promise of more than they reveal. In the *Logic*, De Quincey makes the link between the two apparent. On the Christian faith, he writes:

> There is no necessity that all things should be at the earliest stage understood – in part they will never be understood in a human state, because they relate to what is infinite for an intellect which is finite (*Logic* 41).

Political economy, he adds, is analogous to Christianity in this respect. The importance of a part which implies a greater whole (of a finite unit that implies infinity: something which has to be 'completed') lies in the sense of deferment which that part allows, on the one hand (the process has yet to be completed); and in the sense of integrity (completeness, not completion) which the part as index of the whole suggests. De Quincey's early delight with political economy, as expressed in the *Confessions*, underlines its usefulness and the desire it seems to satisfy:

> [. . .] and political economy offers this advantage to a person in my state, that though it is eminently an organic science (no part, that is to say, but what acts on the whole, as the whole again re-acts on each part), yet the several parts may be detached and contemplated singly (*L* 64).

The Opium-Eater's experience of expanded time recorded in the *Confessions* correspondingly suggests the possibility of infinity-within-finity, the interaction of contradictory experiences – a paradoxical defiance of 'reality':

> Space swelled, and was amplified to an extent of unutterable infinity. This, however, did not disturb me so much as the

vast expansion of time; I sometimes seemed to have lived for 70 or 100 years in one night; nay, sometimes had feelings representative of a millenium [sic] passed in that time, or, however, of a duration far beyond the limits of any human experience (L 68).

This appropriation of time from the imminence of death is analogous to the seizing of time from the *work* which, as the means of self-reproduction, is conflated with death in the capitalist system De Quincey attempts to support. Opium affords a special kind of disposable time even if this disposable time is grounded in the knowledge of work-time (thus, the 'pleasures' and the 'pains' of opium – freedom and restriction – infinity and finity – interact; and the leisure-time in which the *Confessions* is consumed is that which is 'spare' after work). Resurrection means in part at least the reappropriation of time from the demands of work. This might go some way towards explaining De Quincey's mistrust of Radicalism; his shallow attitude towards labour (by turns viewed sentimentally, paranoiacally and mathematically); and above all the strategies which go to comprise his own work, the writing of essays.

De Quincey's reliance on figures such as the autobiographical persona whose error leads to a form of martyrdom expresses an acceptance of what may be styled the 'religion of work'. That is, the sacrifice (with its quasi-religious overtones) and suffering undergone by the pariah figure reflect and strengthen a society which defines labour as the source of value. Though he reacts recalcitrantly towards the Ricardian emphasis on labour, De Quincey nevertheless does not analyse (and so break down) the theoretical system. Instead, he undertakes a conservative revision of it which focuses on capital. His interest here, one might say, is in the figure of resurrection and not in the figure of death, though the two are necessarily mutually supportive. The ground of value for De Quincey lies not so much in continual (homogeneous) labour, as in the consolidation of the processes of past labour – at those points where past labour may withstand any attempt to destroy it. In economic terms, this means the difference between circulating capital, which cannot be re-used, and fixed capital, which may be re-used. In terms of De Quincey's literary theory, it is the difference between the 'literature of knowledge' and the 'literature of power' (9: 5). Every De Quinceyan text will in practice be a complex of circulating and fixed capital.

No text will be exclusively an example of fixed capital: it will always require 'human vigilance, direction, and sometimes very considerable co-operation' (*Logic* 114). That is, to function as a self-reproduction machine, it will need a reader – often with De Quincey an *indulgent* reader (as discussed in Chapters 2 and 3). In this respect, the writing is akin to De Quincey's definition of the land as 'a *natural* machine' (*Logic* 85), something which is limited and cannot be reproduced, or an artificial machine whose secret has not been revealed – which is viewed as 'a cause equal to certain effects' (*Logic* 85) rather than an effect which may be easily reproduced. Writing requires an input of labour on the part of the reader in proportion to the preponderance of fixed capital which goes to comprise it. De Quincey attempts as far as possible to reduce to a minimum the element of circulating capital. He desires that the writing never be used up; that it always holds something in reserve; that the crisis be postponed; that payment be deferred. He guiltily desires a form of *credit* from the reader.

Maniquis has argued that De Quincey's 'principles and ideas, even economic and racial ideas, serve deeply personal fears, above all the fear of an imposed and unjust guilt'.[19] He suggests that political economy offers a semblance of order and that for De Quincey such oppositions as guilt and innocence, and debit and credit, 'are in equivalence in a circle of language where anything in fragmentation or of blurred identity is pushed away into the symbolism of pollution and guilt, anything of wholeness and completion is associated with purity and innocence'.[20] I wish to suggest that the problem of guilt in many of De Quincey's writings may be understood as a problem of exchange, and more specifically as a problem of the questionable, and often questioned, exchange-value of language: that the sense of guilt is grounded in the necessary failure of language to satisfy its promise of giving 'reality'. Maniquis questions Nietzsche's assertion that 'the categories of debit and credit precede those of guilt and innocence'.[21] If guilt is grounded in the lack of respect which informs exchange, in the feeling that one never surrenders enough of oneself, then we may readily understand De Quincey's exploration of guilt primarily as an expression of his textual concerns rather than of his psychological requirements as a living being (though the two are of course related). His basic fear is of not being read correctly, of being misinterpreted, of not being given credit by the actual reader who it is hoped will after all correspond to the figure of the sympathetic reader posited in the text. His anxiety is grounded in the possibility that the reader, like the writer, will not give up enough of him/herself. The 'imposed guilt' is that created in/by writing, which suggests an exchange at best partial in the extreme.

The literary transaction holds the promise of 'certain effects' which are not immediately delivered. In the autobiographical essays, then, the 'self' appears slowly and partially (if at all: it is rather the effect of a self – remains, as it were). In a text like the *Logic* a coherent structure builds up sequentially over a period of time represented by writing. There are no guarantees: witness De Quincey's lengthy argument in support of a proposed law of binomial price founded on the relation of supply and demand, speedily dismissed by Mill in a few lines as 'without meaning or reason'.[22] The possibility that the promise might be betrayed – might betray itself as empty – provokes expressions of anxiety and explanatory glosses. De Quincey is the example *par excellence* of an author who would have a special allowance. In 'Sortilege and Astrology' (1848), a curious, whimsical essay written for the *Glasgow Athenaeum Album*, he underlines his requirements:

> I am not one of those people who, in respect of bread, insist on the discretionary allowance (*pain à discrétion*) of Paris *restaurants*; but, in respect to time, I *do*. Positively, for all efforts of thought I must have time *à discrétion* (9: 261).

De Quincey wishes for time, but not pain (the pun links bread, sustenance for life, with suffering or death), in order to do his work successfully. A chain of sufferance is established, of doubtful value (will the effort involved prove worth while?). The reader must bail out the writing, as is the case in 'Sortilege' where assistants retrieve De Quincey's essays from a bath of texts, and must sacrifice his/her own time reading the often verbose De Quinceyan text. De Quincey strives to pay off this debt, but can never complete his task: he requires yet more credit to invest in his attempt to fulfil payment. Only localised 'pay-offs' are possible. Thus in the 'Dialogues of Three Templars' (1824) De Quincey's mouthpiece X.Y.Z. reaches a point in his argument where he can resort to hyperbole and challenge the very possibility of inadequacy in theatrical fashion:

> No! – hammer away, like Charles Martel: "fillip me with a three-man beetle:" be to me a *malleus haereticorum*: come like Spencer's Talus – an iron man with an iron flail, and thresh out the straw of my logic: rack me: put me to the question: get me down: jump upon me: throttle me: put an end to me any way you can (*London Magazine*, vol. IX [1824] p. 547).

Here De Quincey's sense of adequacy – the ability to survive destruction, to self-resurrect – provides a temporary guarantee. This proves delusive, as it must, for the text leaves off eventually and does not provide an adequate version of the reality that political economy proposes: indeed, how could it? Instead, the 'Dialogues' breaks down. It is not merely that this work is a fragment which might possibly have been continued, to be completed at another time. More than this, the 'Dialogues' seems formally to involve its own imminent irrelevance (and as such provides an interesting contrast to the *Logic*). The writer's intention, to 'spread the knowledge [. . .] in the plainest and most effectual manner' (*London Magazine*, vol. IX, p. 310), is prohibited by the form of the composition. The dialogues not only require a restrictive amount of leisure-time (it goes without saying that De Quincey's is a bourgeois intervention); but the chatty patter in which De Quincey couches Ricardo's scientific ideas blurs his intention. An unstated theme, as so often, starts to emerge, that of contradiction, of paradox. From the beginning, the absurdity of the task impinges upon the effort to enter *in media res*. The Introduction exemplifies my point. De Quincey writes:

> In August and September 1821 I wrote *The Confessions of an English Opium-Eater*: and in the course of this little work I took occasion to express my obligations, as a student of Political Economy, to Mr. Ricardo's 'Principles' of that science. For this as for some other passages I was justly attacked by an able and liberal critic in the New Edinburgh Review – as for so many absurd irrelevancies: in that situation no doubt they were so; and of this, in spite of the haste in which I had written the greater part of the book, I was fully aware (*London Magazine*, vol. IX, p. 309).

Unsurprisingly De Quincey removed this passage when he came to include the 'Dialogues' in the *Selections*, since the revised *Confessions*, in keeping with the style of much of his later work, kept and expanded the 'absurd' details. This apologetic admission of 'irrelevancies' in the *Confessions* itself constitutes an irrelevancy in the 'Dialogues'. A digression 'before the fact', the Introduction sets the tone of the text to which it has been appended: much extraneous matter is introduced into the argumentative conversation between *X.Y.Z.*, *Phaedrus*, and *Philebus*, the 'Three Templars' of the title. The form seems entirely inapposite and at least undermines the alleged intention of lucid communication. The disjointedness is augmented by the fact that the 'Dialogues' runs through several issues of the journal of its original publication.[23] Thus, the Second Dialogue, subtitled *Reductio ad Absurdum*, appears in the same issue as the First (*London Magazine*, vol. IX, [April 1824]) but is separated from it by some seventy pages. As well as carrying an explanation which emphasises that it 'seems necessary for the elucidation of the principle advanced in Dialogue 1' (*ibid*., p. 427), this sequel includes a formal joke of the kind that often occurs in De Quincey's essays, where the medium generates subversive asides. A rudimentary example of the kind of strategy developed more fully in, for instance, 'Sir William Hamilton', the joke is brief, innocuous, but significant. It opens the Second Dialogue, thus:

> *Phil*. X., I see, is not yet come: I hope he does not mean to break his appointment, for I have a design upon him (*London Magazine* vol. IX, p. 427).

Philebus's remark comments on the 'delay' between the First and Second Dialogues, as experienced by the reader of the journal; and also serves as a jest, the butt of which is De Quincey's failure to deliver the sequel in time. The form both hinders communication

The Logic of Political Economy   183

(the logical sequence is interrupted) and, on a different level, provokes it. On the one hand, the possibilities of an efficient, 'economic' language, that of Ricardian theory, prove elusive; on the other, the potential for self-parody lurks as an ever-present concomitant, as though all language is a type of pun. Just as there may be localised manifestations of apparently unassailable logic which attest to the adequacy of the discourse, so too there are those instances which reveal a generalised inadequacy. Furthermore this 'inadequacy' may prove more efficient, since more suggestive, than the perspicuous terminology of a monological language such as that proposed by Ricardian economics. *Philebus*'s observation in the Second Dialogue communicates more than a single sense. X has of course 'come' in that it is De Quincey who writes; nor can X not arrive – at least the title 'Second Dialogue' promises that he will do so. Yet 'De Quincey' is absent from the writing: dead, non-present, even as the reader must be up until the elusive present of reading, of re-composition. The joke that seems to say 'I am here/I am not here' indicates the process of self-reproduction, which I have argued is an essential concern, cannot be accomplished in a straightforward manner (there is no equivalence between X and De Quincey; or between the writing and the author or the figure-of-the-author: one *produces* the other). It also provides an image of a tendency towards procrastination, familiar in all De Quincey's writings. The deferment of the figure who will continue the dialogue constitutes a threat: the delay might be indefinite. The discourse may never communicate at all. *Philebus* could go on waiting.

Points like this suggest a breakdown of sense. Value now arises out of the sheer difficulty of producing the 'correct' meaning. But the choice will always deny one of the meanings bound up in the joke. As with the pun on 'pain/*pain*' in 'Sortilege', the reader is presented with insufficient data – too few words in spite of the procrastination. In the case of the pun, one word contains contradictory and exclusive meanings, a 'horrid inoculation' of parasites. Economics would maintain the disjunction between forces to provide an 'identity'. A pun, in Heinzelmann's words is an example of 'failed perspicuity', and in it language paradoxically comes across as anti-economic.[24] The metaphors used in economic theory reveal the partial nature of the contingent text they comprise, whether in the case of an Adam Smith who, confusing an alteration in the quantity of labour and an alteration in the value of labour, is unable to distinguish two separate categories; or in the case of a De Quincey, with his distinctions where none are needed (i.e. the binomial price argument dismissed by Mill).[25]

At either extreme, the economic discourse threatens to reveal its lack of knowledge about the conditions it seeks to describe, and its lack of power to intervene effectually to alter those conditions. At best, perhaps, it can offer some modicum of entertainment, as De Quincey himself suggests in 'Hints for the Hustings' (1840), where he indulges in *play* in order to make palatable his potentially wearying reiteration of the perennial argument against the advisability of importing corn:

> Next comes a subject which, even by its name, is fitted to alarm all readers and all hearers. We need not say that it is the *Corn Question* of which we speak. We figure to ourselves the shy public under the image of a horse, roaming freely on some spacious plain, which his groom is vainly seeking to catch. The bridle or the halter is kept out of sight, and he holds out some pretence or some reality of what may allure the animal to risk his liberty; but with this difference in favour of the groom as compared with ourselves, that the corn, if he really has any to offer, will prove a real temptation; whereas for us that unhappy article of corn is the supreme repellent of this world. Anarcharsis Clootz styled himself "the spokesman of the human race;" and this modern subject of corn may be styled by preference "the bore of the human race." The moment we present this fatal ally of apoplexy to the attention of our coy suspicious public, instantly we figure to ourselves that same many-headed public, under the image we have selected, as galloping off in widening circles – standing for a moment – then whinnying – throwing up its heels – and turning irreclaimable upon our hands.
>
> But, reader, fear us not; stand a minute; *woho*, then, poor fellow. We shall not bore you (*Blackwood's*, vol. XLVIII [September 1840], p. 302).

De Quincey here exploits the conflation of 'pretence' and 'reality' that the writing seems to offer. Corn, which threatens to sweep away the human race (punning on 'bore' in the sense of a tidal wave: see the revised *Confessions* [5: 99]), in reality might tempt the wandering horse; in writing, the very word repels the horse whimsically selected as an image of the public. By opting for the horse metaphor, De Quincey confronts the risk of losing his public. Reality and metaphor stand here in opposition to one another, and the amusement derived from the 'ill-chosen' figure (a horse repelled by the subject of corn) embraces the contradiction. So too, having dispensed with the 'the reader' and having substituted a horse, De Quincey begs the (absent figure of) the reader to 'stand a minute': to stay put and to hold up for an instant, to allow the writing some purchase on the reality in which it attempts to intervene. The machine that is writing threatens to grind to a halt when the question of corn (a corny problem provoking corny jokes as above) is raised. A word, a phrase, endangers De Quincey's entire effort and expresses a tendency towards the negation of his labour: even without deliberately punning on 'corn' the word becomes suspect, as every word gradually seems to in De Quincey's writings. Words go haywire and defeat the wish for clarity of communication. Notwithstanding laborious, often tedious, investment in his task, De Quincey repeatedly uncovers a sub-text which intrudes and disrupts his writings (and which can be expressed by the cliché 'Or words to that effect . . .'). This occult sub-text suggests that, as communication along the lines of the work discussed in this chapter, writing is somehow superfluous – an excessive secretion which strangely proves insufficient: something 'beyond retrieve'.

Notes

Introduction

1. Thomas De Quincey, *Selections Grave and Gay, from Writings, Published and Unpublished, of Thomas De Quincey, Revised and Arranged by Himself*, 14 vols (Edinburgh: James Hogg, 1853-60).
2. Even the *Selections* is not perfect: the final, posthumously published volume of the *Selections* (vol. 14) contains 'Traditions of the Rabbins', a paper written by Rev. Dr. Croly and not by De Quincey at all.
3. *The Collected Writings of Thomas De Quincey*, ed. David Masson, 14 vols. (Edinburgh: Adam and Charles Black, 1896-97).
4. William E. A. Axon, 'The Canon of De Quincey's Writings, with references to some of his Unidentified Articles,' in *Transactions of the Royal Society of Literature*, 2nd Series, vol. XXXII (1914) p. 5.
5. *Writings*, vol. III, p. 286.
6. *New Essays by De Quincey: His contributions to the* Edinburgh Saturday Post *and the* Edinburgh Evening Post *1827-1828*, ed. Stuart M. Tave (Princeton, New Jersey: Princeton University Press, 1966).
7. *Confessions of an English Opium-Eater and Other Writings*, ed. Grevel Lindop (London: Oxford University Press, 1985); *The Stranger's Grave*, ed. Edmund Baxter (London: Aporia Press, 1988); *The Caçadore: a Story of the Peninsular War*, ed. Edmund Baxter (London: Aporia Press, 1988).
8. Robert M. Maniquis, 'Lonely Empires: Personal and Public Visions of Thomas De Quincey', in *Literary Monographs*, vol. 8, ed. Eric Rothstein and Joseph Anthony Wittreich Jr (Madison: University of Wisconsin Press, 1976), pp. 47–127; Albert Goldman, *The Mine and the Mint: Sources for the Writings of Thomas De Quincey* (Carbondale: Southern Illinois University Press, 1965); Kurt Heinzelmann, *The Economics of the Imagination* (Amherst: University of Massachusetts Press, 1980).
9. *Thomas De Quincey Bicentenary Studies*, ed. Robert Lance Snyder (Norman and London: University of Oklahoma Press, 1985).
10. Robert Lance Snyder, 'Editor's Introduction', *Bicentenary Studies*, p. xxiii; p. xxiv.
11. Charles L. Proudfit, 'Thomas De Quincey and Sigmund Freud' in Snyder, *Bicentenary Studies*, p. 101.
12. David Sundelson, 'Evading the Crocodile: De Quincey's "The English Mail-Coach"' in *Psychocultural Review*, vol. I (New York, 1977), p. 16.

Notes

13. Sundelson, 'Evading the Crocodile', p. 10.
14. Sundelson, 'Evading the Crocodile', p. 20.
15. Michael Haltresht, 'The Meaning of De Quincey's "Dream-Fugue on ... Sudden Death"' in *Literature and Psychology*, vol. XXVI (New Jersey, 1976), p. 32.
16. Haltresht, 'De Quincey's "Dream-Fugue"', p. 36.
17. John W. Bilsland, 'De Quincey's Opium Experiences' in *Dalhousie Review*, vol. LV (Halifax, Nova Scotia, 1975), p. 422.
18. V. A. De Luca, *Thomas De Quincey: The Prose of Vision* (Toronto: University of Toronto Press, 1980), p. 118.
19. Robert Lance Snyder, 'Klosterheim: De Quincey's Gothic Masque' in *Research Studies*, vol. XXXXIX (Pullman, 1981) p. 135.
20. Snyder, 'Editor's Introduction', *Bicentenary Studies*, p. xix.
21. Snyder, 'Editor's Introduction', *Bicentenary Studies*, p. xix.
22. Thomas S. Szasz, *The Manufacture of Madness: A Comparative Study of the Inquisition and the Mental Health Movement* (New York: Harper and Row, 1977), p. 141n.
23. Robert Christison, *A Treatise on Poisons, in Relation to Medical Jurisprudence, Physiology, and the Practice of Physic* (Edinburgh: Adam Black, 1829), p. 528.
24. Isaac Ray, *A Treatise on the Medical Jurisprudence of Insanity* (Boston: Charles C. Little and James Brown, 1838), p. 418.
25. Virginia Berridge, 'Victorian Opium Eating: Responses to Opiate Use in Nineteenth-Century England' in *Victorian Studies*, vol. XXI (Indiana, 1978), p. 437.
26. Szasz, *The Manufacture of Madness*, p. 209.
27. For example, an actor who took the part of the late Sid Vicious, the punk rock star who died of a heroin overdose, apparently took De Quincey as a 'father figure' when he set about 'getting into character': 'His research for the part of Sid Vicious included reading Thomas de Quincey's *Confessions of an Opium-Eater* and taking Sid's mum out for a champagne dinner' (Sarah Spankie, 'He did it Sid's Way' in *The Sunday Times Magazine* [London, 27 July 1986]). Ludicrous as it may seem, this may be taken as a symptomatically important piece of evidence of the place occupied in the popular imagination by De Quincey.
28. Alethea Hayter, *Opium and the Romantic Imagination* (London: Faber, 1968), p. 35.
29. William C. Spengemann, *The Forms of Autobiography: Episodes in the History of a Literary Genre* (New Haven and London: Yale University Press, 1980), p. 95.
30. Spengemann, *The Forms of Autobiography*, p. 168.
31. Spengemann, *The Forms of Autobiography*, p. 94; p. 108.
32. John C. Whale, '"In a Stranger's Ear": De Quincey's Polite Magazine Context' in Snyder, *Bicentenary Studies*, p. 42; Michael Cochise Young, '"The True Hero of the Tale": De Quincey's *Confessions* and Affective Autobiographical Theory', in Snyder, *Bicentenary Studies*, p. 57; Martin Bock, 'De Quincey's Retrospective Analogues of Intoxication in the Opium-Eater's "Nursery Exeriences"' in Snyder, *Bicentenary Studies*, p. 84.
33. F. Samuel Janzow, 'The English Opium-Eater as Editor' in *Costerus*, New Series, vol. I (Amsterdam, 1974), p. 60.

34. Virginia Woolf, 'De Quincey's Autobiography' in *The Common Reader* Second Series (London: The Hogarth Press, 1935), p. 138.
35. Virginia Woolf, 'Impassioned Prose' in *Granite and Rainbow* (London and Toronto: Hogarth Press, 1958), p. 36.
36. John C. Whale, *Thomas De Quincey's Reluctant Autobiography* (London and Sydney: Croom Helm, 1984), p. 125.
37. Woolf, *Granite and Rainbow*, p. 32.
38. V. A. De Luca *Thomas De Quincey: The Prose of Vision* (Toronto: University of Toronto Press, 1980), p. x.
39. De Luca, *The Prose of Vision*, p. 9.
40. De Luca, *The Prose of Vision*, pp. ix-x.
41. Robert M. Maniquis, review of V. A. De Luca's *The Prose of Vision* in *Studies in Romanticism*, vol. XXIII (1984), pp. 139-47; Robert M. Maniquis, 'Lonely Empires: Personal and Public Visions of Thomas De Quincey,' in *Literary Monographs*, vol.8, ed. Eric Rothstein and Joseph Anthony Wittreich Jr (Madison: University of Wisconsin Press, 1976), p. 49.
42. Albert Goldman, *The Mine and the Mint: Sources for the Writings of Thomas De Quincey* (Carbondale: Southern Illinois University Press, 1965), p. 53.
43. E. Michael Thron, 'A New Introduction for Thomas De Quincey' in *Prairie Schooner*, vol. LV (Nebraska: University of Nebraska, 1981), p. 210.

Chapter 1

1. *Confessions of an English Opium-Eater* (London: Taylor and Hessey, 1822).
2. Rogan P. Taylor, *The Death and Resurrection Show: From Shaman to Superstar* (London: Anthony Blond, 1985).
3. Sir James George Frazer, *The Golden Bough*, Abridged Edition (London: Macmillan, 1957), p. 906.
4. Letter of Thursday, 18 September 1856 in *De Quincey at Work*, ed. Willard Hallam Bonner (Buffalo, New York: Airport Publishers, 1936), p. 69.
5. Tait is certainly referring to De Quincey's apology in the middle of 'Walking Stewart' (October 1840), even though his letter says that the interpolation is for the September paper. No paper of De Quincey's was published in September 1840 in *Tait's Edinburgh Magazine*.
6. J. Hillis Miller, *The Disappearance of God: Five Nineteenth Century Writers* (Cambridge: Harvard University Press, 1963), p. 53.
7. On the self as process, see James Olney, 'Autobiography and the Cultural Moment: a Thematic, Historical, and Bibliographical Introduction' in *Autobiography: Essays Theoretical and Critical*, ed. James Olney (Princeton, New Jersey: Princeton University Press, 1980), p. 25.
8. Philippe Ariès, *The Hour of Our Death*, trans. Helen Weaver (London: Allen Lane, 1981), p. 604.
9. Ariès, *The Hour of Our Death*, p. 609.
10. On extremity, see John Woolford, 'Dramatic Idyls: The Case-Law of Extremity' in *Browning Society Notes*, vol. VI (London, 1976), pp. 18-28.

11. Jacques Derrida, *Of Grammatology*, trans. Gayatri Chakravorty Spivak (Baltimore and London: The Johns Hopkins University Press, 1976), p. 142.
12. Derrida, *Of Grammatology*, p. 17.
13. On the relationship of the money-lender and the reader – 'a relationship of tantalising complementarity' – see Joshua Wilner, 'Autobiography and Addiction: The Case of De Quincey' in *Genre*, vol. XIV (Winter 1981), pp. 493–503.
14. John Locke, *Two Treatises of Government*, ed. Peter Laslett (New York: New American Library, 1965), p. 329.
15. 'self-preservation and self-production': the production and preservation of the self is a *struggle*. The revised *Confessions*, with its corrections of impressions given in the original alongside errors allowed to stand, exemplifies the contradictory tendencies of the De Quinceyan text in general. Self-preservation and self-production entail a measure of self-destruction or self-consumption. De Quincey touches upon this directly in the 'Suspiria', where he imagines the possibility of Brunell-Brown (the lawyer whose London house the young De Quincey shares) publishing a parallel volume of *Confessions* – an act which would necessitate him having to cope with what he calls 'a supplement to mine – printed so as exactly to match' (*L* 172). The idea of 'seeing a refutation of himself, and his own answer to the refutation, all bound up in one and the same self-combating volume' (*L* 172) fills De Quincey with horror. The revised *Confessions* is such a 'self-combating' work.
16. The connection between De Quincey – the fugitive self – and the woman – the figure of resolution – is made in a state of *extremity*. The threat of the Bore fuels a sense of danger that provokes De Quincey into communicating. Extremity brings the woman and De Quincey together. This scene on the Cop prefigures that in London, where Ann saves the Opium-Eater, and also the dreams which form the climax of the *Confessions*. This prefiguration has an ironic force which is underlined by the realisation that Ann does not survive the flood of faces in De Quincey's dreams: she is swept away in the nightmarish cataclysm.

Chapter 2

1. The seven 'Sketches' from the *Tait's* sequences are, from vol. I, 'Sketches of Life and Manners; from the Autobiography of an English Opium Eater' (introductory sketch) (February 1834); 'London' (March 1834); 'Dublin' (April 1834); 'The Irish Rebellion' (May 1834); 'Premature Manhood and consequent struggles' (August 1834); 'Travelling' (Supplementary volume, December 1834); and from vol. V, 'Pink' (March 1838).
2. See J. Hillis Miller, *The Disappearance of God: Five Nineteenth Century Writers* (Cambridge, Massachusetts: Harvard University Press, 1963, p. 17: 'Conscious life begins at the moment when life is finished'.
3. See Jacques Derrida, *Margins of Philosophy*, p. 316: 'This essential drifting, due to writing as an iterative structure cut off from all absolute responsibility, from *consciousness* as the authority of the

last analysis, writing orphaned and separated at birth from the assistance of its father, is indeed what Plato condemned in the *Phaedrus*'. De Quincey is a wanderer cut off from his father, from authority – an orphan, unassisted. The 'hero' of his work, one might say, is not opium, but writing, digression. De Quincey's revisions digress from their sources: he (or at least the earlier writings which he revises) is his own 'father' – and he is severed from this authority. Self-influence entails an acknowledgment of this severance. On De Quincey's digressive method, see sketch vi of 'A Sketch from Childhood' ('Literature of Infancy') (*Hogg's Instructor*, vol. VIII, p. 273).

Bruss argues that 'entrance into his life is ultimately denied' (Elizabeth W. Bruss, *Autobiographical Acts: The Changing Situation of a Literary Genre*, [Baltimore and London: The Johns Hopkins University Press, 1978], p. 121) – but entrance into De Quincey's method of writing is surely not. And what is De Quincey's life but his writing? The 'life' we cannot get access to is all past or dormant – the extant De Quincey is the being who reads, writes and *interrupts* his text.

4. 'cataphysical': for De Quincey's use of this term see 1: 337. Cataphysics has its roots in memory, in self-consciousness: death announces life and prefigures one's existence. One's being terminates before it happens – as though the future were a past thing; and as though the past were a future under the power of memory. De Quincey repeatedly suggests that a pre-existent scenario *creates* the person: one fits into the extant action. Occasionally this cataphysical reversal of cause and effect is a subject of amusement: see 1: 223, where De Quincey argues that the appearance of a teapot announced breakfast time, rather than the time determining when the teapot was brought to the breakfast-room.

5. Roland Barthes, 'Literature according to Minou Drouet', in *The Eiffel Tower and other Mythologies*, trans. Richard Howard (New York: Hill and Wang, 1979), pp. 114-15.

6. Miller writes that De Quincey cannot experience 'a Wordsworthian presence in nature. The literary strategy of De Quincey, and of the Victorians who come after him, must consequently be more extreme, more extravagant, as the gap between man and the divine power seems greater' (*The Disappearance of God*, p. 15). The simulation of authority attests to the writer's lack of control even as the extravagant strategies to visualise God attest to the absence of God. This is a question not so much of religious conviction as of De Quincey's lack of control over his materials – over the means of production by which his work appears in the world (in the case of the 'Suspiria', the rules, demands and restrictions of *Blackwood's*).

7. Walter Benjamin, *Charles Baudelaire: A Lyric Poet in the Era of High Capitalism*, trans. Harry Zohn (London: NLB, 1973), p. 140n.

8. Philippe Ariès, *The Hour of Our Death*, trans. Helen Weaver (London: Allen Lane, 1981).

9. On De Quincey's plagiarism of the chapters on Irish history from the Rev. James Gordon's *History of the Rebellion in Ireland*

in the Year 1798, see Albert Goldman, *The Mint and the Mint*.
10. See 'On Christianity as an organ of political movement' (1846) in which De Quincey writes that, but for lack of space, he would 'have attempted to show, that from the same mighty influence [the Christian idea of man's relation to God] had grown up a *social* influence of woman, which did not exist in Pagan ages, and will hereafter be applied to greater purposes' (12: 267).
11. See 'Style' in which De Quincey argues that women produce the most 'natural' – and therefore 'best' – writing, especially if, as amateurs, they do not come into contact with the machinery by which the work of professional writers is determined (11: 171). For an interesting discussion of 'Style' and 'The English Mail-Coach' see Arden Reed, '"Booked for Utter Perplexity" on De Quincey's *English Mail-Coach*' in *Thomas De Quincey Bicentenary Studies*, ed. Robert Lance Snyder (Norman and London: University of Oklahoma Press, 1985), pp. 279–307.
12. See Elizabeth Bruss, who comments that in the 'Suspiria' De Quincey is concerned not with 'a particular female, but the "receptive" female principle itself' (*Autobiographical Acts*, p. 124).

Chapter 3

1. The 'Sketches' I have in mind as constituting a 'biographical' body are as follows (all references to *Tait's*): from vol. I (1835), the papers for September, October and November (on Coleridge); from vol. II (1835), the paper for January (Coleridge); from vol. IV (1839), the papers for January, February, April (all on Wordsworth), July (Wordsworth and Southey), September (Recollections of Grasmere), November (Southey, Wordsworth and Coleridge) and December (The Saracen's Head); from vol. VII (1840), the papers for January (Westmoreland and the Dalesmen), March (Lloyd *et al*), June (Miss Smith), August (Wilson *et al*), October (Walking Stewart *et al*) and December (Talfourd *et al*).
2. See NLS MS 1670 fo. 27, where De Quincey writes of 'my Lake reminiscences, which (you, will soon see) are by much the most interesting chapters of my Autobiography'.
3. James Gillman, *The Life of Samuel Taylor Coleridge*, vol. 1 (London: William Pickering, 1838), p. 250.
4. cf. the comments on Coleridge in Robert M. Maniquis, 'Lonely Empires: Personal and Public Visions of Thomas De Quincey' in *Literary Monographs*, vol. 8, ed. Eric Rothstein and Joseph Anthony Wittreich, Jr (Madison: University of Wisconsin Press, 1976), p. 78.
5. See also *PW* 2: 16.
6. cf. Spector's remarks on Wordsworth in Stephen J. Spector; 'Thomas De Quincey: Self-effacing Autobiographer' in *Studies in Romanticism*, vol. XVIII (Boston University, 1979), p. 508.
7. John E. Jordan, *De Quincey to Wordsworth: A Biography of a Relationship* (Berkeley and Los Angeles: University of California Press, 1962), p. 31.
8. The major deletions are from the 'Sketches' in *Tait's* for January, February and April 1839.

9. cf. *Tait's*, vol. VII, p. 632; *Tait's*, vol. VIII, p. 527; 6: 235; 12: 184–5, &c.
10. cf. 6: 235.
11. See J. Hillis Miller, *The Disappearance of God: Five Nineteenth Century Writers* (Cambridge, Massachusetts: Harvard University Press, 1963).
12. cf. Bryan Guy Tyson, 'Thomas De Quincey and the Unconsuming Fire: a Study in Irony and Narcissism' in *Dissertation Abstracts International* (Ann Arbor, Michigan: University Microfilms International), vol. XXXX, no. 12 (June 1980).
13. 'questions of their own generation': it would be easy to miss this pun. 'Sir William Hamilton' deals at length with the problem of generating the putative subject, the expected commodity, &c. De Quincey himself is invariably concerned with questions of *his own generation*, with the production of his autobiographical self.
14. Miller, *The Disappearance of God*, p. 53.
15. Jameson has written: 'We have implied [. . .] that the social contradiction addressed and "resolved" by the formal prestidigitation of narrative must, however reconstructed, remain an absent cause, which cannot be directly or immediately conceptualised by the text. It seems useful, therefore, to distinguish, from this ultimate subtext which is the place of social *contradiction*, a secondary one, which is more properly the place of ideology, and which takes the form of the *aporia* or the *antinomy*: what can in the former be resolved only through the intervention of praxis here comes before the purely contemplative mind as logical scandal or double bind, the unthinkable and the conceptually paradoxical, that which cannot be unknotted by the operation of pure thought, and which must therefore generate a whole more properly narrative apparatus – the text itself – to square its circles, and to dispel, through narrative movement, its intolerable closure' (Frederic Jameson, *The Political Unconscious* [London: Methuen, 1981], pp. 82–3). On *aporia* see also Tyson's excellent essay 'The Frightful Co-Existence of the *To Be* and the *Not To Be*: Antinomy and Irony in De Quincey's 'Sir William Hamilton"' in *Philosophical Approaches to Literature*, ed. William E. Cain (London and Toronto: Associated University Presses, 1984), pp. 81-2.

Chapter 4

1. *The Stranger's Grave* (London: Aporia Press, 1988); *Walladmor: Freely translated into German from the English of Sir Walter Scott and Now Freely Translated from the German into English* (London: Taylor and Hessey, 1825), 2 vols; *Klosterheim: or The Masque* (Edinburgh: William Blackwood, 1832); 'The Peasant of Portugal' in *The Literary Souvenir: or Cabinet of Poetry and Romance*, ed. Alaric Watts (London: Longman, Rees, Orme, Brown and Green, 1827); *The Caçadore* (London: Aporia Press, 1988). On 'The Curse', see my introduction to *The Stranger's Grave*.
2. Judson S. Lyon, *Thomas De Quincey* (New York: Twayne, 1969), p. 146.

3. V. A. De Luca, *Thomas De Quincey: The Prose of Vision* (Toronto: University of Toronto Press, 1980); Horace A. Eaton, *Thomas De Quincey* (London: Oxford University Press, 1936), p. 348.
4. Eaton, *Thomas De Quincey*, pp. 348-9.
5. Albert Goldman, *The Mine and the Mint: Sources for the Writings of Thomas De Quincey* (Carbondale: Southern Illinois University Press, 1965), p. 156.
6. Goldman, *The Mine and the Mint*, p. 157 (letter of 6 March 1858).
7. Grevel Lindop, 'Innocence and Revenge: The Problem of De Quincey's Fiction' in *Thomas De Quincey Bicentenary Studies*, ed. Robert Lance Snyder (Norman and London: University of Oklahoma, 1985), pp. 213-14.
8. On the status and significance of *Walladmor* see Jan B. Gordon, 'De Quincey as Gothic Parasite: The Dynamic of Supplementarity' in *Thomas De Quincey Bicentenary Studies*, ed. Robert Lance Snyder (Norman and London: University of Oklahoma Press, 1985), pp. 239-62.
9. Lindop, 'Innocence and Revenge', p. 213.
10. Financial motivations need no comment here: see any of the biographies of De Quincey for details of his numerous debts, dependants, &c. The psychological motivations articulated in De Quincey's fictions perhaps deserve some further comment. It is all too easy to read De Quincey's work as expressions of a particular psychological 'type'. There is also a suggestion that feelings of 'guilt' for letting down his wife – and being responsible for her death – inform De Quincey's fictions. Yet *The Stranger's Grave*, 'The Peasant of Portugal' and 'The Caçadore' were written before Margaret De Quincey's death in 1837. Though it would be foolish to claim that no element of the real experience of her death informs 'The Household Wreck' and 'The Avenger', I would argue that the female who is destroyed in De Quincey's fictions and autobiographical works is a figure of the text (see Chapter 2).
11. Barrett J. Mandel, 'Full of Life Now' in *Autobiography: Essays Theoretical and Critical*, ed. James Olney (Princeton, New Jersey: Princeton University Press, 1980), p. 64.
12. Evidently it was Blackwood who opted for this aptly ambiguous title: De Quincey wrote that the tale might be called 'either *Household Desolation, a Tale*: or *The Household Wreck*' (NLS MS 4717 fo. 36: letter of 19 December 1837).
13. On the possibilities of engulfment and self-dissolution, complementary to the states of entrapment and madness, see Robert M. Maniquis, 'Lonely Empires: Personal and Public Visions of Thomas De Quincey' in *Literary Monographs*, vol. 8, ed. Eric Rothstein and Joseph Anthony Wittreich, Jr (Madison: University of Wisconsin Press, 1976).
14. De Luca makes the following accurate observation on 'The Household Wreck': 'It is not immediately clear whether this travesty of romance conventions is intended as some kind of joke. Whatever the intent, De Quincey appears relentless in disrupting such conventions while evoking and toying with them' (*The Prose of Vision*, p. 53).

15. Louis A. Renza, 'A Theory of Autobiography' in Olney, *Autobiography*, p. 294.
16. The verse at the end of the narrative, a recast of 'A Slumber did my Spirit Seal' (from the *Lyrical Ballads*), is as follows:

    No motion has he now, no force;
    He neither hears nor sees;
    Roll'd round in earth's diurnal course,
    With stocks, and stones, and trees   (SG 305).

    'He', which substitutes for 'she' in the original, refers to Stanley; the 'stocks' are those in which he has been confined by the Spanish magistrate in the novel: while he is trapped Emily and their baby die.

    Lindop's comment on this misquotation, to the effect that it is 'regrettable' and typical of De Quincey, ignores the distinct possibility that it is deliberate (Lindop, 'Innocence and Revenge', p. 223).
17. See too William Wordsworth, *The Prelude* Book V ('There was a Boy', &c). (*The Prelude: A Parallel Text*, ed. J. C. Maxwell [Harmondsworth: Penguin Books, 1971, 1972]).
18. *Klosterheim* has pronounced political overtones and would doubtless merit a lengthy study in the light of De Quincey's political papers. Some indication of these overtones may be gleaned from, for instance, 'Political Anticipations' (1830), in which De Quincey comments upon the state of Europe: 'Now, in 1830, all this is changed; Europe is overshadowed, as by some great Hercynian forest, with a rank growth of anti-social desires and disorganizing principles' (*Blackwood's*, vol. XXVIII [November 1830], p. 720).
19. In 'The Somnambulist' De Quincey announces 'a most excellent hoax with which we design to hoax all our dear brother contributors to the QUARTERLY MAGAZINE' (*Knight's Quarterly Magazine*, vol. III, No.4 [1824], p. 463). This reference to *Walladmor* substantiates Axon's attribution of this tale to De Quincey. See William E. A. Axon, 'The Canon of De Quincey's Writings, with Reference to some of his Unidentified Articles' in *Transactions of the Royal Society of Literature of the United Kingdom*, 2nd Series, vol. XXXII (London, 1914), p. 34. For a comparison between the German text and De Quincey's recast, see Goldman, *The Mine and the Mint*, pp. 93-102.
20. For De Quincey's opinion of the German *Walladmor*, see 'Recollections of Charles Lamb' (*Tait's*, vol. V [September 1838]). De Quincey's cagey attitude towards the success or failure of his version is articulated in the Dedication of the novel (*Walladmor*, 1: xi–xxi).
21. On the term 'rifacimento' see Goldman, *The Mine and the Mint*, p. 92. The necessity of recasting – rather than simply translating – preoccupied De Quincey before he had read Gillies's volume: in his review of the German *Walladmor* he claims that he has 'endeavoured to translate not merely *from* the German – but also *into* English, a part of their task which translators are apt to forget' (*London Magazine*, vol. X. [October 1824], p. 355).
22. Goldman, *The Mine and the Mint*.

23. See Goldman, *The Mine and the Mint*, p. 185 (note 72); and NLS MS 4046 fo. 142 (21 June 1838): 'I have no author's vanity connected with any one part whatsoever,' De Quincey writes to Blackwood about a paper being 'corrected' by the publisher. Probably this paper was 'The Avenger', which was one of only two papers published by Blackwood in this year (the other being 'The Household Wreck'). See also NLS MS 4048 fo. 220, in which De Quincey writes of an article published in *Tait's* which includes the phrase 'written in this present year of our Lord 1838'. This interpolation, De Quincey claims, was Tait's: 'It was written 8 months ago'.
24. For attribution of 'The Caçadore' see my edition of this story (London: Aporia Press, 1988).
25. For De Quincey's generally dismissive views of the novel-reading public, see especially 'Oliver Goldsmith' (6: 204-5; 6: 224). See also *PW* 1: 199; *PW* 1: 300-5; and *Blackwood's*, vol. XX, p. 858; and *London Magazine*, vol. X, p. 380).

Chapter 5

1. 'Imbecility' is defined by Isaac Ray in his *Treatise* as 'an abnormal deficiency either in those faculties that acquaint us with the qualities and ordinary relations of things, or in those which furnish us with the moral motives that regulate our relations and conduct towards our fellow-men' (Isaac Ray, *A Treatise on the Medical Jurisprudence of Insanity* [Boston: Charles C. Little and James Brown, 1838], p. 77).
2. cf. 'The Present Cabinet', *Blackwood's*, vol. XXIX [February 1831], p. 155.
3. Hopkins has suggested that 'War' be read as an introduction to 'The English Mail-Coach' (Robert Hopkins, 'De Quincey on War and the Pastoral Design of "The English Mail-Coach" in *Studies in Romanticism*, vol. VI no. 3, Spring 1967). The entire body of the political essays is where the concerns of this paper are prefigured.
4. F. S. Janzow: '"Philadelphus": A New Essay by De Quincey', in *Costerus*, vol. X, 1973), p. 43.
5. See Maniquis, 'Lonely Empires'; De Luca, *The Prose of Vision*, p. 116; Tave, *New Essays*.
6. 'the only true supporter': see William Tait's footnotes to De Quincey's 'A Tory's Account': 'We can only sincerely regret that Mr De Quincey, and the Tories who, with him, understand what he concludes, their "own creed," form so very small a minority at the present time, that there cannot be a half dozen such Tories in Great Britain' (*Tait's Edinburgh Magazine*, New Series, vol. III [1836], p. 3n).

Working for both Tait and Blackwood undoubtedly caused some problems for De Quincey: at least, a letter to Blackwood suggests that he was not happy to contribute to a publication, the political views of which were anti-Tory. In it De Quincey writes: 'It is, and always has been, a feeling of mine – that, without being positively dishonourable, it is not handsome or in the spirit of a gentleman – whilst maintaining a connexion with one journal – to correspond with a hostile one; so long at least as the first does not decline to receive one's contributions' (NLS MS 4717 [n.d.] fo. 61). It is worth pointing out that De Quincey was probably seeking some assurance from Blackwood that his papers would continue to be accepted even though he was providing much work for Tait. The letter, then, must be read *cum grano salis*. Doubtless financial pressures took precedence over 'gentlemanly' principles.

7. De Quincey's fear of the 'natural catastrophe' of spontaneous combustion in the revised *Confessions* (5: 237–8) provides an analogous possibility to this 'burning out'. (See Chapter 2.)
8. Warnings to the reader about the treachery of Orientals forms an integral part of De Quincey's characterisation of the East. A key feature lies in the 'fact' that Orientals are invariably treacherous *translators*: their use of language prevents proper communication. See, for examples of this attitude, 'The Dourraunee Empire' (*Blackwood's*, vol. XLIX [March 1841], p. 293); 'Foreign Politics', where sweeping generalisations are passed, such as: 'All Oriental nations exaggerate upon impulse' (*Blackwood's*, vol. XLVIII [October 1840], p. 560); 'Sir Robert Peel's Position' (*Blackwood's*, vol. L [September 1841], pp. 408–9); and letter to Robert Blackwood dated 15 August 1844 (NLS MS 4070 fo. 215).
9. Curiously enough, De Quincey apparently spent some time counting waves, according to the rogue footnote to 'The Pagan Oracles' (8: 185n).
10. cf. Maniquis, who asserts that 'racial thinking served his need for a symbolic innocence and wholeness' ('Lonely Empires', p. 52).
11. Davie's actions are paralleled by those of two other military commanders, Lieutenant Eyre, criticised in 'Affghanistan' (*Blackwood's*, vol. LVI [August 1844], pp. 133-52) and Captain Elliot, the villain of the 'Canton Expedition and Convention' (*Blackwood's*, vol. L [November 1841], pp. 677-88).
12. *China* (Edinburgh: James Hogg, 1857).
13. On the composition and publication of *China*, see Willard Hallam Bonner, *De Quincey at Work* (Buffalo, New York: Airport Publishers, 1936).
14. De Quincey asserts as much in the 'Autobiography' (1: 294).
15. William Barrett, 'The Flow of Time' in *The Philosophy of Time*, ed. Richard M. Gale (New Jersey: Humanities Press, 1968), p. 370.
16. Baudelaire, a writer greatly influenced by De Quincey, asserts that musical prose is a product of urban living, of people gathered together in great numbers: 'Who among us has not dreamt, in moments of ambition, of the miracle of a poetic prose, musical without rhythm and without rhyme, supple and staccato enough to adopt to the lyrical stirrings of the soul, the undulations of dreams, and the sudden leaps of consciousness? This obsessive ideal is above all a child of the experience of giant cities, of the intersecting of their myriad relations' (Charles Baudelaire, *Oeuvres*, ed. Yves-Gérard Le Dantec [Paris: Bibliothèque de la Pléïade, 1931-2]; quoted in Walter Benjamin, *Baudelaire: A Lyric Poet in the Era of High Capitalism*, trans. Harry Zohn [London: NLB, 1973], p. 69.)

17. In the revised version of 'The English Mail-Coach' De Quincey sits between the infinity of the open sky and the enclosing box of the coach, the interior of which seems to be nothing less than a coffin: those inside do not feature in 'The Vision of Sudden Death'. This definition of the inside of the coach is, however, only strictly accurate in the context of the revised version of the essay. In the original version of 'The English Mail-Coach' De Quincey writes that a representative of the 'vermin' class travelled in the coach, but alighted before the crisis. See L 214.
18. Stephen J. Spector, 'Thomas De Quincey: Self-effacing Autobiographer' in *Studies in Romanticism*, vol. XVIII, no. 4 (1979), p. 517.
19. Louis A. Renza, 'A Theory of Autobiography' in *Autobiography: Essays Theoretical and Critical*, ed. James Olney (Princeton, New Jersey: Princeton University Press, 1980), pp. 294-5.
20. Note too that the showy but shoddy coach represents the forces of Radicalism, or at least an unthinking, irreflective, anti-social political movement which is opposed to the self-conscious individualism of the Tory party.
21. Fredric Jameson, *The Political Unconscious* (London: Methuen, 1981) p. 299.

Chapter 6

1. Thomas De Quincey, *The Logic of Political Economy* (Edinburgh and London: William Blackwood and Sons, 1844). 'Dialogues of Three Templars' in *The London Magazine* (London: Taylor and Hessey), vol. IX (1824).
2. Robert M. Maniquis, 'Lonely Empires', pp. 116-7.
3. Ben Fine, *Economic Theory and Ideology* (London: Edward Arnold, 1980), pp. 144-5.
4. Michel Foucault, *The Order of Things: An Archaeology of the Human Sciences* (London: Tavistock, 1970), p. 255.
5. *Ibid.*, p. 259.
6. David Ricardo, *On the Principles of Political Economy and Taxation*, ed. Piero Sraffa with the collaboration of M.H. Dobb (Cambridge University Press, 1951), p. 19. (Hereafter *Principles*).
7. Kurt Heinzelmann, *The Economics of the Imagination* (Amherst: University of Massachusetts Press, 1980), pp. 89-90.
8. John Stuart Mill, review of De Quincey's *Logic of Political Economy*, *Westminster Review*, vol. XLIII (June 1845), pp. 330-1.
9. Bryan Tyson, "The Frightful Co-existence of the *To Be* and the *Not To Be*": Antinomy and Irony in De Quincey's "Sir William Hamilton"' in *Philosophical Approaches to Literature*, ed. William E. Cain (London and Toronto: Associated University Presses, 1984), p. 79.
10. 'Monologicality': see Tyson, 'Antinomy and Irony', p. 80.
11. In several instances, De Quincey suggests that the Radical channels a 'natural' human impulse. See his comments in 'Political Anticipations' on the 'native jacobinism lurking in all human hearts, – a hatred, in the abstract, to authority seated in weak human administrators, and a wish to see the distinctions of merit, originally created by nature, supplanting those which are created by law and arbitrary institutions' (*Blackwood's*,

vol. XXVIII [November 1830], p. 720); and his description of the 'personal Jacobinism of that sort which is native to the heart of man' in the 'Introduction to the World of Strife' (1: 51–2).

12. Jacques Derrida, *Margins of Philosophy*, trans. Alan Bass (Chicago and Brighton: The Harvester Press, 1982), p. 246. Derrida writes of 'the concept which seems to support literal, proper meaning, the propriety of the proper, Being' (*Margins of Philosophy*, p. 291). Being is metaphoric: it seems to support 'proper meaning' – which is a figure grounded in the metaphor of Being. To expose the metaphoric nature of Being is necessarily 'improper', a disruption which points to an essential lack of the ground of meaning. See Chapter 1.

13. This paper is in the main a review of J.C. Colquhoun's translation of the *Report of the Experiments on Animal Magnetism made by a committee of the Medical Section of the French Royal Academy of Sciences* (Edinburgh, 1833). In 1836 Colquhoun incorporated this text into *Isis Revelata*, a lengthy study of Animal Magnetism – 'the Philosophy of Superstition' (*Isis Revelata*, vol. 2, p. 184). De Quincey seems to have originally offered this review to Blackwood (NLS MS 4717 fo. 14 [Letter of 11 May 1834]).

14. Mesmerism provided a useful vehicle for both radical and reactionary ideas in 19th century Europe. See Robert Darnton, *Mesmerism and the End of the Enlightenment in Europe* (Cambridge, Massachusetts: Harvard University Press, 1968); and Maria M. Tatar, *Spellbound: Studies in Mesmerism and Literature* (Princeton, New Jersey: Princeton University Press, 1978).

15. Foucault, *The Order of Things*, pp. 256–7.
16. Derrida, *Margins of Philosophy*, p. 316.
17. Heinzelmann, *The Economics of the Imagination*, p. 99.
18. Foucault, *The Order of Things*, p. 257.
19. Maniquis, 'Lonely Empires', p. 51.
20. Maniquis, 'Lonely Empires', p. 126.
21. Maniquis, 'Lonely Empires', p. 126.
22. Mill, 'De Quincey's Logic of Political Economy', p. 327.
23. *The London Magazine*, vol. IX (1824), pp. 341–55 (First Dialogue) and pp. 427-8 (Second Dialogue).
24. 'The pun is the most economical of linguistic transactions in which the verbal values may be exchanged, but to the economist-grammarian, it is also the most flagrant example of failed "perspicuity"' (Heinzelmann, *The Economics of the Imagination* pp. 74–5).
25. Smith, in De Quincey's view, creates what amounts to an unintentional macaronic or pun. He comments:
    > Adam Smith uniformly takes it for granted that an alteration in the quantity of labor [sic], and an alteration in wages (i.e. the value of labour), are the same thing and will produce the same effects: and hence he never distinguishes the two cases, but every where uses the two expressions as synonymous [. . .] There is not a chapter in the Wealth of Nations in which it is not made redundantly clear that Adam Smith adopts both laws as

mere varieties of expression for one and the same law. This being so, how could he possibly make an election between two things which he constantly confounded and regarded as identical? The truth is, Adam Smith's attention was never directed to the question: he suspected no distinction: no man of his day, or before his day, had ever suspected it (*London Magazine*, vol. IX [1824] p. 353).

Select Bibliography

Primary sources

Books

De Quincey, Thomas, *Selections Grave and Gay, from Writings, Published and Unpublished. of Thomas De Quincey, Revised and Arranged by Himself*, 14 vols (Edinburgh: James Hogg, 1853–60).
De Quincey, Thomas, 'The Somnambulist' (after Schulz) in *Knight's Quarterly Magazine*, vol. III (1824).
De Quincey, Thomas, *Walladmor: Freely translated into German from the English of Sir Walter Scott and now Freely Translated from the German into English* (London: Taylor and Hessey, 1825), 2 vols.
De Quincey, Thomas, 'The Peasant of Portugal' in *The Literary Souvenir; or, Cabinet of Poetry and Romance*, ed. Alaric Watts (London: Longman, Rees, Orme, Brown and Green, 1827).
De Quincey, Thomas, *Klosterheim; or, The Masque* (Edinburgh: William Blackwood, 1832).
De Quincey, Thomas, *The Logic of Political Economy* (Edinburgh and London: William Blackwood and Sons, 1844).
De Quincey, Thomas, *China* (Edinburgh: James Hogg, 1857).
Hogg, James (ed.), *Uncollected Writings of Thomas De Quincey* (London: Swan Sonnenschien, 1890).
Japp, Alexander H. (ed.), *The Posthumous Works of Thomas De Quincey*, 2 vols (London: William Heinemann, 1891).
Masson, David (ed.), *The Collected Writings of Thomas De Quincey*, 14 vols. (Edinburgh: Adam and Charles Black, 1896–97).
Page, H. A. (ed.), *Thomas De Quincey: His Life and Writings, with Unpublished Correspondence*, 2 vols (London: John Hogg, 1877).
Japp, Alexander H. (ed.), *De Quincey Memorials*, 2 vols (London: William Heinemann, 1891, 1893).
Eaton, Horace A. (ed.), *A Diary of Thomas De Quincey* (London: Noel Douglas, n.d.).
Bonner, Willard Hallam, *De Quincey at Work* (Buffalo, New York: Airport Publishers, 1936).

Select Bibliography

Musgrove, S. (ed.), *Unpublished Letters of Thomas De Quincey and Elizabeth Barrett Browning* (Auckland: Auckland University College Bulletin no. 44, 1954).

Tave, Stuart M. (ed.), *New Essays by De Quincey: his contributions to the* Edinburgh Saturday Post *and the* Edinburgh Evening Post *1827–1828* (Princeton, New Jersey: Princeton University Press, 1966).

Janzow, F. S., '"Philadelphus": A New Essay by De Quincey' in *Costerus*, vol. IX (Amsterdam, 1973).

Lindop, Grevel (ed.), *Confessions of an English Opium-Eater and other Writings* (London: Oxford University Press, 1985).

Baxter, Edmund (ed.), *The Caçadore* (London: Aporia Press, 1988).

Baxter, Edmund (ed.) *The Stranger's Grave* (London: Aporia Press, 1988).

Journals

From the *London Magazine*:

'Confessions of an English Opium-Eater: Being an Extract from the Life of a scholar', vol. IV (1821), pp. 292–312, 353–79.

'Dialogues of Three Templars, on Political Economy', vol. IX (1824): Introduction, pp. 309–10.
  Advertisement, Introductory Dialogue, pp. 341–7.
  I. 'On the Elementary Principle of Political Economy', pp. 347–55.
  II. 'Reductio ad Absurdum', pp. 427–8.
  III. 'Principle of Value', continued, pp. 547–50.
  IV. 'Theory of Value', pp. 550–7
  V. 'On the Immediate Uses of the New Theory of Value', pp. 557–61.
  VI. 'On the Objections to the New Law of Value', pp. 561–6.

'Walladmor: Sir Walter Scott's German Novel', vol. X (1824), pp. 353–82.

From *Tait's Edinburgh Magazine*:

'Mrs Hannah More', vol. IV (December 1833), pp. 293–321.
'Animal Magnetism', vol. IV (January 1834), pp. 456–74.

From *Tait's Edinburgh Magazine* (New Series):

'Sketches of Life and Manners; from the Autobiography of an English Opium Eater', vol. I (February 1834), pp. 18–30.

'Sketches of Life and Manners; from the Autobiography of an English Opium Eater (continued)', vol. I (March 1834), pp. 83–96.

'Sketches of Life and Manners; from the Autobiography of an English Opium Eater (continued)', vol. I (April 1834), pp. 196–204.

'Sketches of Life and Manners; from the Autobiography of an English Opium Eater: The Irish Rebellion', vol. I (May 1834), pp. 263–73.
'Sketches of Life and Manners; from the Autobiography of an English Opium Eater (continued)', vol. I (August 1834), pp. 482–7.
'Samuel Taylor Coleridge', vol. I (September 1834), pp. 509–20.
'Samuel Taylor Coleridge (continued)', vol. I (October 1834), pp. 588–96.
'Samuel Taylor Coleridge (continued)', vol. I (November 1834), pp. 685–90.
'Travelling in England Thirty Years Ago: from the Autobiography of an English Opium Eater', vol. I (Supplementary [December] 1834, pp. 797–802.
'Samuel Taylor Coleridge (continued)', vol. II (January 1835), pp. 3–10.
'Sketches of Life and Manners: from the Autobiography of an English Opium Eater: Oxford', vol. II (February 1835), pp. 77–83.
'Sketches of Life and Manners; from the Autobiography of an English Opium Eater: Oxford (continued)', vol. II (June 1835), pp. 366–77.
'Sketches of Life and Manners; from the Autobiography of an English Opium Eater: Oxford (continued)', vol. II (August 1835), pp. 541–56.
'A Tory's Account of Toryism, Whiggism, and Radicalism. In a Letter to a Friend in Bengal', vol. II (December 1835), pp. 769–76.
'A Tory's Account' (continued), vol. III (January 1836), pp. 1–10.
'Autobiography of an English Opium-Eater (continued)', vol. III (June 1836), pp. 350–60.
'Autobiography of an English Opium-Eater: Literary Connexions or Acquaintances', vol. IV (February 1837), pp. 65–73.
'Autobiography of an English Opium-Eater: Literary Connexions or Acquaintances' (continued), vol. IV (March 1837), pp. 169–76.
'Sketches' &c. (continued), vol. V (March 1838), pp. 152–63.
'Recollections of Charles Lamb', vol. V (April 1838), pp. 237–47.
'Recollections of Charles Lamb. No.ii', vol. V (June 1838), pp. 355–66.
'Recollections of Charles Lamb' (continued) [Walladmor], vol. V (September 1838), pp. 559–63.
'Lake Reminiscences, from 1807 to 1830. No. I – William Wordsworth', vol. VI (January 1839), pp. 1–12.
'Lake Reminiscences, from 1807 to 1830. No. II – William Wordsworth', vol. VI (February 1839), pp. 90–103.
'Lake Reminiscences, from 1807 to 1830. No. III – William Wordsworth', vol. VI (April 1839), pp. 246–54.

Select Bibliography 203

'Lake Reminiscences, from 1807 to 1830. No. IV – William Wordsworth and Robert Southey', vol. VI (July 1839), pp. 453–64.
'Lake Reminiscences, from 1807 to 1830. No. VI – Southey, Wordsworth, and Coleridge', vol. VI (August 1838), pp. 513–17.
'Sketches' &c. (continued): 'Recollections of Grasmere', vol. VI (September 1839), pp. 569–81.
'Sketches' &c. (continued): 'The Saracen's Head', vol. VI (December 1839), pp. 804–8.
'Sketches' &c. (continued): 'Westmoreland and the Dalesmen', vol. VII (January 1840), pp. 32–9.
'Sketches' &c. (continued) [Lloyd], vol. VII (March 1840), pp. 159–67.
'Sketches' &c. (continued) [Miss Smith *et al*], vol. VII (June 1840), pp. 346–56.
'Sketches' &c. (continued) [Wilson *et al*], vol. VII (August 1840), pp. 525–32.
'Sketches' &c. (continued) [Stewart *et al*], vol. VII (October 1840), pp. 629–37.
'Sketches' &c. (continued), vol. VII (December 1840), pp. 765–76.
'Sketches' &c. (continued) [Duelling], vol. VIII (February 1841), pp. 97–109.

From *Blackwood's Edinburgh Magazine*:

'Gillies's German Stories', vol. XX (December 1826), pp. 844–58.
'The Duke of Wellington and Mr Peel', vol. XXV (March 1829), pp. 294–302.
'French Revolution', vol. XXVIII (September 1830), pp. 542–58.
'France and England', vol. XXVIII (October 1830), pp. 699–718.
'Political Anticipations', vol. XXVIII (November 1830), p. 719–36.
'The Late Cabinet', vol. XXVIII (December 1830), pp. 960–81.
'The Present Cabinet in Relation to the Times', vol. XXIX (February 1831), pp. 143–58.
'On the Approaching Revolution in Great Britain, and its proximate consequences', vol. XXX (August 1831), pp. 313–29.
'The Prospects of Britain', vol. XXXI (April 1832), pp. 569–91.
'Dilemmas on the Corn Law Question', vol. XLV (February 1839), pp. 170–6.
'The Opium and the China Question', vol. XLVII (June 1840), pp. 717–38.
'Postscript on the China and the Opium Questions', vol. XLVII (June 1840), pp. 847–53.
'Lord Stanley's Irish Registration Bill', vol. XLVIII (July 1840), pp. 135–44.
'Hints for the Hustings', vol. XLVIII (September 1840), pp. 289–315.

'Foreign Politics', vol. XLVIII (October 1840), pp. 546–62.
'The Dourraunee Empire', vol. XLIX (March 1841), pp. 280–302.
'Conservative Prospects', vol. XLIX (March 1841), pp. 406–22.
'Sir Robert Peel's Position on next resuming power', vol. L September 1841), pp. 393–409.
'Canton Expedition and Convention', vol. L (November 1841), pp. 677–88.
'Sir Robert Peel's Policy', vol. LI (April 1842), pp. 537–52.
'Anti-Corn-Law Deputation to Sir Robert Peel', vol. LII (August 1842), pp. 271–80.
'Ricardo Made Easy Part I', vol. LII (September 1842), pp. 338–53.
'The Riots', vol. LII (September 1842), pp. 410–18.
'Ricardo Made Easy Part II', vol. LII (October 1842), pp. 457–69.
'The Last Session of Parliament', vol. LII (October 1842), pp. 538–50.
'Ricardo Made Easy Part III', vol. LII (December 1842), pp. 718–39.
'The Aristocracy of England', vol. LIV (July 1843), pp. 51–66.
'The Repeal Agitation', vol. LIV (August 1843), pp. 264–74.
'The Game Up with the Repeal Agitation', vol. LIV (November 1842), pp. 679–86.
'Ireland', vol. LV (April 1844), pp. 518–32.
'Affghanistan', vol. LVI (August 1844), pp. 133–52.
'Coleridge and Opium-Eating', vol. LVII (January 1845), pp. 117–32.
'Suspiria de Profundis' (Part I), vol. LVII (March 1845) pp. 269–85.
'Suspiria de Profundis' (Part I continued), vol. LVII (April 1845) pp. 489–502.
'Maynooth', vol. LVII (May 1845), pp. 647–56.
'Suspiria de Profundis' (Part I concluded), vol. LVII (June 1845) pp. 739–51.
'Suspiria de Profundis' (Part II), vol. LVIII (July 1845) pp. 43–55.

From *Hogg's Instructor*:

'A Sketch from Childhood':
no. I, vol. VI (1851), pp. 145–51.
no. II, vol. VI (1851), pp. 232–7.
no. III, vol. VIII (1852), pp. 1–4.
no. IV, vol. VIII (1852), pp. 97–9.
no. V, vol. VIII (1852), pp. 177–9.
no. VI, vol. VIII (1852), pp. 273–7.
no. VII, vol. VIII (1852), pp. 337–9.
'Sir William Hamilton, Bart.' vol. VIII (1852), pp. 401–4.
'Sir William Hamilton, with glance at his logical reforms', vol. IX (1852), pp. 273–7 (First Paper); 291–5 (Second Paper).

Select Bibliography

Manuscripts

All manuscript references are from the collection in the National Library of Scotland (cited by volume and folio, e.g. 4789 fo. 1). Here I list only those which have a specific bearing on this study. I have provided a brief description of the MS contents.

3112 fo. 288 [Concerning 'The Avenger'].
4032 fo. 179 [Concerning a review of Christison on Poisons].
4046 fo. 142 [De Quincey's work being 'corrected' by Blackwood].
4048 fo. 219–20 [On 'a Tale' i.e. 'The Curse'].
4060 fo. 258 [On the poor].
4060 fo. 262 [The working class as a revolutionary force].
4065 fo. 193 [On 'Ceylon'].
4065 fo. 196 [On 'Ceylon'].
4070 fo. 215 [Concerning the treachery of Chinese translators].
4717 fo. 14 [On 'Animal Magnetism'].
4717 fo. 18 [On 'The Avenger'].
4717 fo. 21 [On 'Medical Jurisprudence' i.e. Christison's book].
4717 fo. 36 [On 'The Household Wreck'].
4717 fo. 38 [On Christison].
4717 fo. 52 [On 'Klosterheim'].
4717 fo. 57 [On the burning of the MS of 'Klosterheim'].
4717 fo. 61 [On working for two hostile journals].
4717 fo. 67 [On Christison].

1670 (material relating to *Tait's*):
    fo. 27 [De Quincey's Lake Reminiscences].
    fo. 39 [A Psychological Curiosity to feature in the 'Sketches'].
    fo. 40–1 [De Quincey 'winding up' the Autobiography].
    fo. 63–4 [Difficulty in correcting proofs].
    fo. 73–5 [Letter from William Tait to Mrs Johnstone about De Quincey].
    fo. 83–4 [Complains of proofs lost or unused by the Press].

4789 [volume containing MS of 'The English Mail-Coach' and some unpublished articles].

4892, pp. 27–8 (*Blackwood's* Contributor's Book [typed]).
Acc 1424A Box 44, pp. 42–43 [*Blackwood's* Contributor's Book (MS)].
Acc 5644 (Blackwood's Cash Book).

Secondary Sources

Abrams, Meyer Howard, *The Mirror and the Lamp*, (London, Oxford & New York: Oxford University Press, 1953).

Anderson, N.A. and M.E. Weiss (eds.), *Interspace and the Inward Sphere: Essays on the Romantic and Victorian Self* (Macomb, Illinois: Western Illinois University Press, 1978).

Ariès, Philippe, *The Hour of our Death*, trans. Helen Weaver (London: Allen Lane, 1981).

Axon, William E.A., 'The Canon of De Quincey's Writings, with Reference to some of his Unidentified Articles' in *Transactions of the Royal Society of Literature of the United Kingdom*, 2nd Series, vol. XXXII (1914) pp. 1–46.

Barrett, William, 'The Flow of Time' in *The Philosophy of Time*, ed. Richard M. Gale (New Jersey: Humanities Press, 1968), pp. 355–77.

Barthes, Roland, *The Eiffel Tower and Other Mythologies*, trans. Richard Howard (New York: Hill and Wang, 1979).

Benjamin, Walter, *One Way Street and other writings*, trans. Edmund Jephcott and Kingsley Shorter (London: NLB, 1970).

Benjamin, Walter, *Charles Baudelaire; A Lyric Poet in the Era of High Capitalism*, trans. Harry Zohn (London: NLB, 1973).

Berridge, Virginia, 'Victorian Opium Eating: Responses to Opiate Use in Nineteenth-Century England' in *Victorian Studies*, vol. XXI (1978), pp. 437–61.

Bilsland, John W., 'De Quincey's Opium Experiences' in *Dalhousie Review*, vol. LV, no. 3 (1975), pp. 419–30.

Black, Joel D. 'Confession, Digression, Gravitation: Thomas De Quincey's German Connection' in *Thomas De Quincey Bicentenary Studies*, ed. Robert Lance Snyder (Norman and London: Oklahoma University Press, 1985), pp. 308–34.

Blake, Kathleen 'The Whispering Gallery and Structural Coherence in De Quincey's Revised Confessions of an English Opium-Eater' in *SEL: Studies in English Literature, 1500–1900, vol. XIII* (1973), pp. 633–42.

Bock, Martin, 'De Quincey's Retrospective Analogues of Intoxication in the Opium-Eater's "Nursery Experiences"' in *Thomas De Quincey Bicentenary Studies*, ed. Robert Lance Snyder (Norman and London: Oklahoma University Press, 1985), pp. 72–87.

Boyle, Andrew, *An Index to the Annuals, vol. 1 (1820–1850): The Authors* (Worcester: Andrew Boyle Ltd, 1967).

Bruss, Elizabeth W., *Autobiographical Acts: The Changing Situation of a Literary Genre* (Baltimore and London: The Johns Hopkins University Press, 1978).

Byrne, Richard R., 'Some Unrepublished Articles of De Quincey's in "Blackwood's Magazine"', in *Bulletin of Research in the Humanities*, vol. LXXXV (1982), pp. 344–51.

Christison, Robert, *A Treatise on Poisons, in Relation to Medical Jurisprudence, Physiology, and the Practice of Physic* (Edinburgh: Adam Black, 1829).

Colquhoun, John Campbell, *Report of the Experiments on Animal Magnetism made by a committee of the Medical Section of the French Royal Academy of Sciences* (Edinburgh: Robert Cadell, 1833).

Colquhoun, John Campbell, *Isis Revelata* 2 vols (Edinburgh: Maclachlan and Stewart, 1836).

Darnton, Robert, *Mesmerism and the End of the Enlightenment in Europe* (Cambridge, Massachusetts: Harvard University Press, 1968).

De Luca, V. A., *Thomas De Quincey: The Prose of Vision* (Toronto: University of Toronto Press, 1980).

De Man, Paul, *Allegories of Reading* (New Haven and London: Yale University Press, 1979).

Dendurent, H. O., *Thomas De Quincey: A Reference Guide* (Boston: G. K. Hall, 1978).

Derrida, Jacques, *Of Grammatology*, trans. Gayatri Chakravorty Spivak (Baltimore and London: The Johns Hopkins University Press, 1976).

Derrida, Jacques, *Margins of Philosophy*, trans. Alan Bass (Chicago and Brighton: The Harvester Press, 1982).

Devlin, D. D., *De Quincey, Wordsworth and the Art of Prose* (London and Basingstoke: Macmillan Press Ltd, 1983).

Eaton, Horace A., *Thomas De Quincey* (London: Oxford University Press, 1936).

Fetter, Frank Whitson, 'The Economic Articles in *Blackwood's Edinburgh Magazine*; and their Authors, 1817–1853' in *Scottish Journal of Political Economy*, vol. VII (1960), pp. 85–107, 213–231.

Fine, Ben, *Economic Theory and Ideology* (London: Edward Arnold, 1980).

Foucault, Michel, *The Order of Things: An Archaeology of the Human Sciences* (London: Tavistock, 1970).

Frazer, Sir James George, *The Golden Bough: A Study in Magic and Religion*, Abridged Edition (London: Macmillan, 1957).

Freud, Sigmund, *The Interpretation Of Dreams*, trans. James Strachey (Harmondsworth: Penguin Books, 1976).

Gillies, Robert P., *German Stories, selected from the works of Hoffman, De La Motte Fouqué, Pichler, Kruse, and others*, 3 vols (Edinburgh: William Blackwood, 1826).

Gillman, James, *The Life of Samuel Taylor Coleridge*, vol.1 (London: William Pickering, 1838).

Goldman, Albert, *The Mine and the Mint: Sources for the writings of Thomas De Quincey* (Carbondale: Southern Illinois University Press, 1965).

Green, J. Albert, *Thomas De Quincey, a Bibliography based upon the De Quincey Collection in the Moss Side Library* (Manchester, 1908).

Haltresht, Michael, 'The Meaning of De Quincey's "Dream-Fugue on . . . Sudden Death"' in *Literature and Psychology*, vol. XXVI, no. 1 (1976), pp. 32–6.

Hayden, John O., 'De Quincey's "Confessions" and the Reviewers' in *Wordsworth Circle*, vol. VI (1975), pp. 273–9.

Hayter, Alethea, *Opium and the Romantic Imagination* (London: Faber, 1968).

Heinzelmann, Kurt, *The Economics of the Imagination* (Amherst: University of Massachusetts Press, 1980).

Holstein, Michael E., '"An Apocolypse of the World Within": Autobiographical Exegesis in De Quincey's "Confessions of an English Opium-Eater" (1822)' in *Prose Studies 1800–1900*, vol. II (1979), pp. 88–102.

Hopkins, Robert, 'De Quincey on War and the Pastoral Design of "The English Mail-Coach"', in *Studies in Romanticism*, vol. VI, no. 3 (1967), pp. 129–51.

Jameson, Fredric, *The Political Unconscious: Narrative as a Socially Symbolic Act* (London: Methuen, 1981).

Janzow, F. Samuel, 'The English Opium-Eater as Editor' in *Costerus*, New Series, vol. I (1974), pp. 47–82.

Jordan, John E., *De Quincey to Wordsworth: A Biography of a Relationship, with the Letters of Thomas De Quincey to the Wordsworth Family* (Berkeley and Los Angeles: University of California Press, 1982).

Lever, Karen M., 'De Quincey as Gothic Hero: A Perspective on "Confessions of an English Opium-Eater" and "Suspiria de Profundis"' in *Texas Studies in Literature and Language*, vol. XXI, no. 3 (Austin, 1979), pp. 33–46.

Lindop, Grevel, *The Opium-Eater: A Life of Thomas De Quincey* (London: J. M. Dent, 1981).

Lindop, Grevel, '"Pursuing the Throne of God": De Quincey and the Evangelical Revival' in *Charles Lamb Bulletin*, New Series, no. 52 (1985), pp. 97–111.

Lindop, Grevel, 'Innocence and Revenge: The Problem of De Quincey's Fiction' in *Thomas De Quincey Bicentenary Studies*, ed. Robert Lance Snyder (Norman and London: University of Oklahoma Press, 1985), pp. 213–38.

Locke, John, *Two Treatises on Government*, ed. Peter Laslett (New York: New American Library, 1965).

Lyon, Judson S., *Thomas De Quincey* (New York: Twayne, 1969).

Mandel, Barratt J., 'Full of Life Now' in *Autobiography: Essays Theoretical and Critical*, ed. James Olney (Princeton, New Jersey: Princeton University Press, 1980), pp. 49–72.

Maniquis, Robert M., 'Lonely Empires: Personal and Public Visions of Thomas De Quincey' in *Literary Monographs*, vol. 8, ed. Eric Rothstein and Joseph Anthony Wittreich, Jr (Madison: University of Wisconsin Press, 1976), pp. 47–127.

Select Bibliography 209

Maniquis, Robert M., 'The Prose of Vision by V. A. De Luca' in *Studies in Romanticism*, vol. XXIII (1984), pp. 139–47.

Marx, Karl, *Grundrisse*, trans M. Nicolaus (Harmondsworth: Penguin Books, 1973).

Mill, John Stuart, 'De Quincey's Logic of Political Economy' in *Westminster Review*, vol. XLIII (June 1845), pp. 319–31.

Miller, J. Hillis, *The Disappearance of God: Five Nineteenth Century Writers* (Cambridge, Massachusetts: Harvard University Press, 1963).

Murray, James G., 'Mill on De Quincey: Esprit Critique Revoked' in *Victorian Newsletter*, no. 37 (1970), pp. 7–12.

Olney, James (ed.), *Autobiography: Essays Theoretical and Critical* (Princeton, New Jersey: Princeton University Press, 1980).

Park, Roy, *Hazlitt and the Spirit of the Age* (London: Oxford University Press, 1971).

Pollitt, Charles, *De Quincey's Editorship of the Westmoreland Gazette, July 1818 to November 1819* (London and Kendal, 1890).

Praz, Mario, *The Hero in Eclipse in Victorian Fiction*, trans. Angus Davidson (London: Oxford University Press, 1956).

Proctor, Sigmund K., *De Quincey's Theory Of Literature* (Ann Arbor: University of Michigan Press, 1943).

Proudfit, Charles L., 'Thomas De Quincey and Sigmund Freud: Sons, Fathers, Dreamers – Precursors of Psychoanalytic Developmental Psychology' in *Thomas De Quincey Bicentenary Studies*, ed. Robert Lance Snyder (Norman and London: Oklahoma University Press, 1985), pp. 88–108.

Ramsey, Roger, 'The Structure of De Quincey's "Confessions of an English Opium-Eater"' in *Prose Studies 1800–1900*, no. 1 (1978), pp. 21–9.

Ray, Isaac, *A Treatise on the Medical Jurisprudence of Insanity* (Boston: Charles C. Little and James Brown, 1838).

Redfern, Walter, *Puns* (Oxford: Basil Blackwell, 1984).

Reed, Arden, '"Booked for Utter Perplexity" on De Quincey's "English Mail-Coach"' in *Thomas De Quincey Bicentenary Studies*, ed. Robert Lance Snyder (Norman and London: University of Oklahoma Press, 1985), pp. 279–307.

Renza, Louis A., 'A Theory of Autobiography' in *Autobiography: Essays Theoretical and Critical*, ed. James Olney (Princeton, New Jersey: Princeton University Press, 1980), pp. 268–95.

Ricardo, David, *On the Principles of Political Economy and Taxation* ed. Piero Sraffa with the collaboration of M. H. Dobb (Cambridge University Press, 1951).

Rosenbaum, Barbara and Pamela White, *Index of English Literary Manuscripts*, vol. 4, 1800–1900, Part 1 (London and New York: Mansell, 1982).

Sackville-West, Edward, *A Flame in Sunlight: The Life and Work of*

Thomas De Quincey, ed. John E. Jordan (1936; London: Bodley Head, 1964).

Snyder, Robert Lance, '*Klosterheim*: De Quincey's Gothic Masque' in *Research Studies*, vol. XXXXIX, no. 3 (Pullman, 1981), pp. 129–42.

Snyder, Robert Lance (ed.), *Thomas De Quincey Bicentenary Studies* (Norman and London: University of Oklahoma Press, 1985).

Sundelson, David, 'Evading the Crocodile: De Quincey's "The English Mail-Coach"' in *Psychocultural Review* vol. I, no. 1 (1977), pp. 9–20.

Strout, A. L., *A Bibliography of Articles in Blackwood's Magazine 1817-1825* (Lubbock, Texas: Texas Technical College Library Bulletin no. 5, 1959).

'The Source and Remedy of the National Difficulties Deduced from Principles of Political Economy in a Letter to Lord John Russell' (London: Rodwell and Martin, 1821).

Spankie, Sarah, 'He did it Sid's Way' in *The Sunday Times Magazine* (London: 27 July 1986).

Spector, Stephen J., 'Thomas De Quincey: Self-effacing Autobiographer' in *Studies in Romanticism*, vol. XVIII (1979), pp. 501–20.

Spengemann, William C., *The Forms of Autobiography: Episodes in the History of a Literary Genre* (New Haven and London: Yale University Press, 1980).

Szasz, Thomas S., *The Manufacture of Madness: A Comparative Study of the Inquisition and the Mental Health Movement* (New York: Harper and Row, 1977).

Tatar, Maria M., *Spellbound: Studies in Mesmerism and Literature* (Princeton, New Jersey: Princeton University Press, 1978).

Taylor, Rogan P., *The Death and Resurrection Show: From Shaman to Superstar* (London: Anthony Blond, 1985).

Thron, E. Michael, 'A New Introduction for Thomas De Quincey' in *Prairie Schooner*, vol. LV (1981), pp. 210–25.

Tyson, Bryan Guy, 'The Frightful Co-Existence of the *To Be* and the *Not To Be*: Antinomy and Irony in De Quincey's "Sir William Hamilton"' in *Philosophical Approaches to Literature*, ed. William E. Cain (London and Toronto: Associated University Presses, 1984), pp. 73–90.

Tyson, Bryan Guy, 'Thomas De Quincey and the Unconsuming Fire: a Study in Irony and Narcissism' in *Dissertation Abstracts International* (Ann Arbor, Michigan: University Microfilms International), vol. XXXX, no. 12 (June 1980).

Watson, J. R., 'Thomas De Quincey: The Opium Eater and the Other Selves' in *Critical Quarterly*, vol. XXIV (1982), pp. 13–17.

Wellek, René, 'De Quincey's Status in the History of Ideas' in *Philological Quarterly*, vol. XXIII (1944), pp. 248–72.

The Wellesley Index to Victorian Periodicals 1824–1900, vol. 1, ed.

Walter E. Houghton (London & Toronto: Routledge & Kegan Paul/University of Toronto Press, 1966).

Whale, John C., *Thomas De Quincey's Reluctant Autobiography* (London and Sydney: Croom Helm, 1984).

Whale, John C., '"In a Stranger's Ear": De Quincey's Polite Magazine Context' in *Thomas De Quincey Bicentenary Studies*, ed. Robert Lance Snyder (Norman and London: Oklahoma University Press, 1985), pp. 35–53.

White Jr, Robert B., *The English Literary Journal to 1900: A Guide to Information Sources* (Detroit: Gale Research Company, 1977).

Wilner, Joshua, 'Autobiography and Addiction: The Case of De Quincey' in *Genre* vol. XIV (1981), pp. 493–503.

Winters, Warrington, 'De Quincey and the Archetypal Death Wish (a note on *The English Mail-Coach*)', in *Literature and Psychology*, vol. XIV, no. 2 (1964) pp. 61–3.

Woolford, John, 'Dramatic Idyls: The Case-Law of Extremity' in *Browning Society Notes*, vol. 6, no. 2 (1976), pp. 18–28.

Woolf, Virginia, 'De Quincey's Autobiography' in *The Common Reader* Second Series (London: Hogarth Press, 1935), pp. 132–9.

Woolf, Virginia, 'Impassioned Prose' in *Granite and Rainbow* (London and Toronto: Hogarth Press, 1958), pp. 32–40.

Wordsworth, William, *The Prelude: A Parallel Text*, ed. J. C. Maxwell (Harmondsworth: Penguin Books, 1971, 1972).

Young, Michael Cochise, '"The True Hero of the Tale": De Quincey's *Confessions* and Affective Autobiographical Theory' in *Thomas De Quincey Bicentenary Studies*, ed. Robert Lance Snyder (Norman and London: Oklahoma University Press, 1985), pp. 54–71.

Index

Aberrance. *See* Error
Abscondence, from school, De Quincey's, 12; and characterisation of text, 15, 23. *See also*, Error
Accident, 140, 144. *See also* Press, in relation to De Quincey's text
Addiction, 4, 5–9; as disease and vice, 7–8; irrelevance of, in criticism of De Quincey, 9
Adulthood, 14, 43–5, 134; (manhood), 61; *See also* Childhood
Afterlife. *See* Resurrection
Alienation. *See* Estrangement
Animal Magnetism. *See* Mesmerism
Ann, in the *Confessions*, 9, 32, 60–62, 80, 130
Anxiety: caused by desire for eternity, 27; and economics, 155, 163–64; and guilt, 180; of influence, 65, 71, 83; and politics, 121, 134; caused by possibilities of reinterpretation, 24; recurrence of, 79, 99, 159; produced by writing, 73, 83, 89, 91, 159. *See also* Extremity
Apology, De Quincey's use of, 14–15, 19–20, 29, 43, 86, 88, 90, 182
Ariès, Philippe, 27, 52
Asia. *See* East
Authority, 40–43, 57, 69, 76, 103, 114, 118, 126, 142, 147, 160–62, 170, 176; of influences, 82; of text, 82, 120. *See also* De Quincey, William; Flawed Leader
Axon, William E. A., 1, 194n

Barrett, William, 142
Barthes, Roland, 45
Baudelaire, Charles, 196n
Benjamin, Walter, 51
Bennett, J. W., (author of *Ceylon and its Capabilities*), 132, 134
Berridge, Virginia, 7
Betrayal: political, 125–27, 132, 136, 147, 160; of self, 129, 175;

by words, 159–63, 181; of Wordsworth and Coleridge, by De Quincey, 82–3. *See also* Britain; England
Bilsland, John W., 6
Biography, chapter 3 *passim*
Blackwood's Edinburgh Magazine, 2, 36, 56, 57, 69, 126, 132, 153, 163, 174, 177, 195–96n
Blackwood, Robert, 2, 18, 93, 127; letters from De Quincey to, 196n, 198n; corrections to 'The Avenger' by, 195n
Bock, Martin, 8–9
Bourgeoisie, 45, 56, 62, 136, 151–52. *See also* Politics
Brougham (flawed minister), 147
Bruss, Elizabeth W., 190n
Britain, as figure, 160, 169, 176–77

Canning (flawed minister), 122, 132, 147
Capital, 17, 61, 161–67, 172–73, 179
Capitalist, figure of the, 161–63, 166, 168–69, 172
Castlereagh (flawed minister), 122, 147
Ceylon: as paradise, 133–34, 136; as site of fascination, 133. *See also* China; Davie, Major; De Quincey, Thomas: Works, 'Ceylon'; East; Flawed Leader; Orientals
Childhood, 13, 30, 38, 44, 53, 61; and death, 55–6; Barthes on, 45. *See also* Adulthood
China: as site of death-wish, 128–31; real and imaginary status of, 130–31. *See also* Ceylon; Crocodile; East; Orientals
Choice, 83, 134, 144, 147; and contradiction, 23–6. *See also* Error
Christ, 38, 58, 60, 70–1, 80–1
Christianity, 58–61, 128–30, 133, 178
Christison, Robert, 7

Index

Chronology, disruption of, in De Quincey's writings, 22, 46–7, 58, 87–8
Coach, image of, 123–25, 138–40, 147, 150, 197n
Coleridge, Mrs (wife of Samuel Taylor Coleridge), 67–8
Coleridge, Samuel Taylor, 36, 64, 65, 76, 78–82, 85, 119, 129; as doppelganger, 66–7; 71–3; as failure, 70; as figure of extremity, 65–74; and opium, 68–70; and his relationship to his wife, 67–8; as victim, 71
Communication: difficulties of, 17–18, 20, 32, 47, 76, 170, 182–83; and publication, 56, 62, 85
Composition, present of, in autobiographical writings, 29–30, 39, 57; and cultural moment, 173–75; and De Quincey's fictions, 96, 98, 103, 111, 114; in 'Sir William Hamilton', 83, 89; and time, 138–39; and use of figure of Coleridge, 71. *See also* Extremity
Contradiction, 24, 37; as cataphysical process, 40; and truth, 48. *See also* Choice
Corn, 158, 184–85
Credit, 28–9; 181–82
Crisis. *See* Extremity
Criticism, of De Quincey's writings, 3–11, 93–5
Crocodile: and autobiographical text, 129–30: in De Quincey's Orient, 128, 145–46; as figure of finity, 128: and self-identity, 128–29
Croly, Rev. Dr., essay of, mistaken for De Quincey's, 186n
Cyclops, as figure of political control, 124, 155–56

Davie, Major (flawed military leader), 134–36; and deathwish, 135; as Adam, 135–36
Death: of authority, 40; and beauty, 51–2; and class perspective, 151–52; defiance of, 133–34, 149; of De Quincey, 26–7, 29–30, 36–9, 88–90, 176; of equilibrium, 137; in De Quincey's fictions, 101–103, 112–14; and influence, 65, 82; of the self, 52–6, 79, 141; text as figure of, 171, 173; of woman in De Quincey's writings, 62; of Wordsworth, formulated by De Quincey, 77. Sudden death, 139, 144–45. *See also* Extremity; Resurrection Death-wish, 27, 39, 67, 71, 96, 99, 119–20, 135, 145–46, 154, 160. *See also* China; Davie, Major; Death
De Luca, V. A., 6, 10, 94, 126, 152
De Quincey, Elizabeth (sister), 36, 38, 40; as figure of pre-textuality, 38–9, 61–2; as figure of redemption, 32
De Quincey, Emily (daughter), on originality of 'The Avenger', 94
De Quincey, Thomas: editions of writings of, 1–2, 21; own edition of writings of, 21–2. Works: 'Alexander Pope', 64; 'Animal Magnetism', 3, 171–73; 'Autobiographic Sketches', 21, 22, 32, 36–40, 42–51, 53, 56–61, 125, 165–66; 'The Avenger', 93–4, 108–113, 193n, 195n; 'The Caçadore', 2, 93, 118–19, 193n; 'The Caesars', 131; 'Ceylon', 132–36; *China*, 136; 'Coleridge and Opium-Eating', 69–71; *Collected Writings* (ed. Masson), 1, 2, 4; *Confessions of an English Opium-Eater*, 1, 2, 5–9, 12–6, 18–35; 37–9, 43–5, 57, 60–63, 68–70, 74, 79–80, 83, 96, 100–101, 105, 111, 126–30; 133, 145, 147, 153, 178–79, 182, 184, 189n, 196n; 'Conservative Prospects', 168–69; 'The Curse', 93; 'Dialogues of Three Templars', 153, 157, 171, 181–83; 'The Duke of Wellington and Mr Peel', 125; 'The English Mail-Coach', 2, 5, 96, 101, 123–52, 155, 169, 175; 'France and England', 126–27; 'French Revolution', 121; 'Gillies's German Stories', 94, 117; 'Hannah More', 1, 9; 'Hints for the Hustings', 125, 184; 'The Household Wreck', 93–108, 110, 113, 147, 164, 193n; 'Judas Iscariot', 80–1; *Klösterheim*, 93–5, 114–6, 120; *The Logic of Political Economy*, 153, 155–71;

173–81; 'The Ministry', 122–24; 'Modern Superstition', 66; 'Murder as Fine Art' (posthumous), 167; 'The Opium Question with China in 1840', 131–32; 'On Murder Considered as One of the Fine Arts', 3; 'On the Approaching Revolution in Great Britain', 176–77; 'The Pagan Oracles', 196n; 'The Peasant of Portugal', 93, 118–20, 193n; 'Philadelphus, on Mr Clarkson's Letter', 124; 'Political Anticipations', 124–25, 194n, 198n; 'Political Economy, The Standard and the Edinburgh Saturday Post', 158; *Posthumous Works*, 66, 103–104, 137, 167; 'The Prospects of Britain', 151–52, 174; 'Protestantism', 77; 'Ricardo Made Easy', 154; *Selections Grave and Gay*, 1, 12, 22, 36, 75; 'Sir William Hamilton', 2, 43, 64–5, 83–92, 130, 157–59, 171, 182; 'Sketches of Life and Manners', 20–21, 36, 40, 45–7, 57, 65–9, 71–2, 75–82, 100, 117, 128, 133; 'A Sketch from Childhood', 6, 21, 36–8, 40–3, 47–8, 50, 57, 113; 'The Somnambulist', 194n; 'Sortilege and Astrology', 181, 183; *The Stranger's Grave*, 2, 93, 112–14, 134, 193n; 'Style', 191n; 'Suspiria de Profundis', 2, 15, 21, 36–45, 47, 51–8, 60–1, 70–1, 83, 89, 96, 116, 163–66, 173; 'Toilette of the Hebrew Lady', 131; 'A Tory's Account', 195n; *Uncollected Writings*, 131, 136; 'Walking Stewart', 19–20; *Walladmor*, 93, 116–17, 194n; 'War', 195n

De Quincey, William (brother), 6, 37, 40–2, 51
Derrida, Jacques, 28, 171, 175, 198n
Digression, 11, 37, 47, 58, 86–7, 182
Dreams, 16, 36, 60, 99–100, 129, 140, 142, 145, 147–48

East, the, as imagined by De Quincey, 127–32, 136, 145; compared to Britain, 160. *See also* Ceylon; China; Orientals
Eaton, Horace A., 94

Economics, 153–61, 183; and De Quincey's Tory politics, 157–58. *See also* Capital; Capitalist; Murderer; Mesmerism; Ricardo; Value
Edinburgh Evening Post, 122
England, image of Fey woman as, 149. *See also* Betrayal; Britain
Equilibrium, 73, 79, 108, 121, 123, 137, 163, 171
Error: in de Quincey's writings, 12–16, 23–5, 37, 81, 86, 101, 111, 122, 126, 134, 146–7, 154; and growing up, 12, 43, as inevitable false step, 122–25, 132–6; and productivity, 15, 24–5, 86; and publication, 17, 19, 88–9. *See also* Press; Writing
Estrangement, 13, 17, 32, 34, 44, 50, 123, 147, 176
Extremity, 27–8, 32, 139–41, 145, 170; and acclimatisation to death, 39, 54, 110–11, 114–15; and class-based fears, 151–52, 155–56; and cultural moment, 155–56, 170–71; and De Quincey's influences, 65, 70, 74–7, 82–4; and desire for resurrection, 92; and economic text, 173–75, 177–78; and memory, 89–90; moment of decision as instance of, 134–35; and production of text, 100–101; and revelation, 52. *See also* Composition; Death; Error

False step. *See* Error, characterised as inevitable false step
Failure: of De Quincey's text, differentiated from flawed text as implied by previous critics, 11 (*see also* Flaws); figures of, 70, 74, 135–36, 144, 151, 156, 161, 163, 171, 176–79, 182, 184; inevitability of, 21, 62, 80, 158, 169, 176, 184–85; and politics, 137–38, 146, 156. *See also* Error; Flawed Leader
Fascination, 27, 34, 53, 55, 71, 92, 126, 133, 143, 145, 149, 155, 161, 178
Fictions, 2, chapter 4 *passim*; and autobiography, 95–6
Fine, Ben, 154

Flaws, supposed in De Quincey's writings, 4, 9–11, 46. *See also* Failure
Flawed Leader, figure of the, 122–24, 126, 169, 196n; and the Opium-eater, 123, 161–63; the capitalist as, 161–63, 166; Major Davie as, 134–36, 147; Ricardo as, 161–63. *See also* Murderer
Footnotes, De Quincey's use of, 15, 86, 87, 89–90, 116–17
Foucault, Michel, 154–55, 173, 177
Freud, Sigmund, theories of. *See* Psychoanalysis

Glasgow Athenaeum Album, 181
God, 141, 151, 163, 190n
Goedrich (flawed minister) 122
Goldman, Albert, 3, 11, 94, 117, 118
Gordon, Rev. James, 190n

Hamilton, Sir William, 64, 87, 88, 92. *See also* De Quincey, Thomas: Works, 'Sir William Hamilton'
Haltresht, Michael, 5–6
Hayter, Alethea, 7–8
Heinzelmann, Kurt, 3, 157, 177, 183
Hogg's Instructor, 6, 36, 43, 85–6
Huskisson (Canningite minister), 123

Identity, 31, 51, 65, 98, 103, 104, 115, 150, 169, 171, 183; complex nature of, for De Quincey, 13, 32, 39–40, 73, 126–27, 129, 147, 158; evident lack of, 29, 65, 112–13, 128, 138, 142, 146–47, 165–66; and memory, 16, 82; and production of self through text, 18, 21, 26, 45, 73, 110. *See also* Self
Imbecility: of political leaders, 122–26; Ray's definition of, 195n
Infinity, 23, 114–15, 123, 145, 151, 163–64, 175, 178–79. *See also* Time
Influence, 18–19, Chapter 3 *passim*; as threat to self, 79, 81–2; as contamination, 64–5, 84–5. Self–influence, 39–40, 72–4, 85

Janzow, Samuel F., 9
Jameson, Fredric, 192n

Johnstone, Mrs (correspondent of William Tait), 19
Judas, 80–1. *See also* Pariah
Judea, 130–31. *See also* East

Knowledge, literature of, 179

Lamb, Charles, 133
Language: ambiguities of, 13, 17–8, 21, 156–57; and artifice, 137, 148; collapse of, 150–51, 160; and potentiality, 87, 132–33, 148; relation of truth to, 47–8, 49; uncanny feel of, 104–5; unreliability of, 160, 170–72, 183
Life of Samuel Taylor Coleridge, vol. 1 (James Gillman), 69
Lindop, Grevel, 2, 94, 95
Literature of power, De Quincey's formulation of, 22; and literature of knowledge, 179
Lloyd, Charles, 100
Locke, John, conception of Nature of, 30, 34
London Magazine, 12, 21, 153, 182
Lyon, Judson S., 93

Madness, 99–101; and social upheaval, 101; and the East, 128
Malthus, Thomas, 156, 157
Mandell, Barrett J., 95
Manhood, *See* Adulthood
Maniquis, Robert M., 3, 10–11, 126, 127, 133, 154, 180
Manuscripts, 2, 20, 94
Massey, Lord, in the *Confessions*, 59–60
Masson, David, 1, 9; edition of De Quincey's *Writings of*, 1, 2, 4
McLuhan, Marshall, 168
Memory, 16, 19, 25, 50–1; 58, 60, 65, 73, 78–9, 82, 84, 89, 104, 108, 112, 117, 138, 140, 142, 190n
Mesmerism: ambiguities inherent in, 172–73; and communication, 173; and crisis, 173; and economics, 171–73; and singular identity, 172
Middle–classes. *See* Bourgeoisie
Mill, John Stuart, on De Quincey's *Logic*, 157, 160, 181, 183
Miller, J. Hillis, 20, 88, 190n
Milton, John, 70, 78, 122
Misreading, 12–15, 81, 92, 96, 98, 112–13, 118, 132, 157, 170

Motion, 68, 71, 74–5, 77, 84, 87, 115, 128–29, 137, 138–45, 147, 150, 151; and stasis, 145–46
Murder, 71, 90, 96, 109, 118–9
Murderer (or Radical), figure of the, 110, 112, 167–71
Music, 33, 142, 146

Nature, 30, 34
Nietzsche, Friedrich, 180
Nightmare. *See* Dream

Opium, 6–9, 16, 23, 34, 43; and Coleridge, 68–70; De Quincey's attitudes towards, 23–4, 27; and self-possession, 33–5; and value, 16
Opium-Eater, the: ambiguous character of, 75; as charismatic, 34; as deciphering figure, 22; as detective, 22, 57, 80, 162, 167; as distinct from Coleridge, 69–73; as English, 127–28; figurative status of, 22, 72; as martyr, 129–30, 132, 143–44; as philosopher, 80; as shaman, 16
Opium-eating, 8–9, 16, 69–71, 127–28; depiction of pagan practice of, 128
Orientals: De Quincey's depiction of, 128, 130–33, 136, 170; indecipherable faces of, 130; paradoxical characterisation of, 131–32; supposed untrustworthiness of, 131; as treacherous translators, 196n. *See also* East

Paradise Lost (John Milton), 70, 122
Paranoia. *See* Anxiety
Pariah, figure of the, 57, 101, 102, 123, 179; De Quincey's fascination for, 80; and inevitable victimisation, 49–51. Pariah woman as text, 63. *See also* Coleridge, Samuel Taylor; Press, the: De Quincey as martyr to
Passion, 44–6; and 'impassioned prose', 45–7, 56. *See also* Violence
Payment, 28–9, 62, 158, 180–81
Plagiarisms: by Coleridge, 68, 80; by De Quincey, 190n
Poetry, De Quincey's writings incoherently defined as, 10

Political Economy. *See* Economics
Politics, De Quincey's, 121–26, 132, 136, 146–47, 150, 154, 156, 160, 168, 174, 194n, 195n. *See also* East; Economics; Orientals
Poole, Thomas, 65–6
Power, 17–18, 22, 150, 168–70; literature of, *see* Literature of power
Prefiguration, 15, 50–51, 57, 79, 82, 100
The Prelude (William Wordsworth), 76–7
Presence, 33–4; 39, 90, 128–29. *See also* Composition
Press, (the machinery of) the: and choice, 20, 23, 43; as control, 17, 19, 21, 23, 42–3, 87–8, 90–1, 165; De Quincey as martyr to, 16–17, 18, 23, 146, 165; and error, 14, 15, 19, 20; and politics, 126–27, 140; post-office as, in the *Confessions*, 33; and power relations, 17–18, 23, 44, 55–6, 61; relation of De Quincey's text to: 2, 14, 15, 16–23, 61–2, 65, 88, 117–18, 140, 151, 165; and resurrection, 22; and revision, 21–2; and the self, 21, 65
Prime Minister. *See* Flawed Leader
Private, experience characterised as, 18, 44–7, 55–6; the 'Dream-Fugue' as, 148. *See also* Publication; Reader, the: De Quincey's relation to
Procrastination, 27–8, 134, 137, 139, 141, 162; of Christ, 81; of De Quincey, 82, 89, 92, 115–16; in 'The Household Wreck', 102; of Charles Lloyd, 100
Proofs (printer's sheets), 2, 64, 80, 89, 91, 94–5; difficulties of correcting, 19–20
Propaganda, 126; De Quincey's 'Ceylon' as, 132–34
Property, 28–30, 47, 170–1; Locke on, 30, 34; and propriety, 29; and the self 26, 28–9, 46; and truth, 48
Psychoanalysis, 4–5
Proudfit, Charles L., 4
Publication, process of, 2, 18–20, 23, 56, 65, 85–6, 145, 146, 148, 151. *See also* Press; Reader; Writing

Index 217

Punctuation, 1–2
Puns, 81–3, 148, 198n

Radical, figure of the. *See* Murderer
Radicalism, 156, 168–71, 179, 197n, 198n
Ray, Isaac, 7, 195n
Reader, the: attitudes of, in relation to quasi-autobiographical fiction, 95–6, 104; characterised as in danger from Orientals, 131; De Quincey as, 13, 32, 75, 80, 82, 85, 101, 112, 131, 140–41, 144, 177; and disorder of text, 22, 58; status of, 75, 81–2, 159, 179–80; and God, 141; production of, in text, 13–14, 16, 29, 75, 117, 159, 177; relation of De Quincey to, 18, 58, 72, 82, 85, 89, 90, 112, 118, 140–41, 149, 159, 170, 181. Wordsworth, as absent reader, 75
Reading, potentially definitive, in De Quincey's writings, 96, 98–9, 100, 102, 110, 112–16, 118, 134, 151
Rebirth. *See* Resurrection
Rent, doctrine of, 154
Renza, Louis A., 147
Representation, 13, 15, 23–5, 50, 65, 83, 86, 91, 108, 119, 138–39, 156–57, 159, 184
Resourcelessness. *See* Extremity
Resurrection, 16–17, 26, 56, 129–30, 143; and collapse, 150; enabled via writing, 30, 89–91; figures of, 166, 168, 170, 179; opium as agent of, 34; and the past, 52; and posterity, 21–2; of pre-text, 38–40; and revision, 21, 56, 61; and self, 29; as theme in De Quincey's writings, 47, 59–60, 62, 70–71, 106, 108, 115, 120, 145. *See also* Revision
Revision, 14, 20–1, 23–4, 41, 43, 64, 75–7, 82–3, 87, 89–92, 101, 104, 141, 147, 175; and contradiction, 26; Cop episode in the *Confessions* as figure of, 31–3; difficulty of, 17; as erasure, 128; principle of, 58–9, 61, 117, 133; and 'the proper', 29–30; of purported autobiography, in De Quincey's fictions, 112–13; and the self, 31, 37–8, 44–5, 80.

See also Resurrection; Text, as self-consumption; Translation
Ricardo, David, 153–57; 159; 169; as authority figure, 162–63; De Quincey's divergence from theories of, 156–57, 161, 178, 179, 182; significance to De Quincey of economic theories of, 155–60, 164, 170, 172, 174, 183; and language, 156–57, 183

Saviours, female, in De Quincey's writings, 32, 40, 60–61, 105–106
Scarcity, in political economics, 155. *See also* Economics; Extremity
Selections Grave and Gay. *See* De Quincey, Thomas: Works, *Selections*
Self, the: preservation of, 31–5, 69, 78, 99; production of, 28–35, 40, 46, 62, 64, 71–4, 82–3, 85, 99, 123, 126–27, 130, 138–39, 142–43, 147, 180–81, 195n. Self-consciousness, 13, 27, 30, 33, 50–51, 84, 190n; revision as, 37 (*See also* Memory).
Self-destruction: *see* Suicide.
Self-effacement, 147–48.
Self-reproduction, 27, 30, 69, 128, 167, 178–79, 182–83
Selfhood (state of being), 13, 20–21, 26, 31, 33, 39, 50. *See also* Self 'A Slumber did my Spirit Seal' (William Wordsworth), 113
Smith, Adam, 154, 156–57, 183, 198–99n
Snyder, Robert Lance, 4, 6
Southey, Robert, 36
Spector, Stephen J., 144
Spengemann, William C., 8
Stasis. *See* Motion, versus stasis
Substitution, 64–5, 82, 86, 90, 139, 145. *See also* Motion
Suicide, 13, 39, 71, 82, 90, 113, 129, 150, 160, 166; threat of by Coleridge, 68. *See also* Death-Wish
Sunday Times Magazine, 187n
Sundelson, David, 5
Szasz, Thomas, 6, 7

Tait's Edinburgh magazine, 2, 36, 57, 65, 77, 188n, 195–96n
Tait, William, 2, 19, 36, 127; letter

about De Quincey's proofs, 19–20; letter to, from De Quincey, 19; corrections to De Quincey's proofs by, 195–96n
Tave, Stuart, 2, 121, 126, 153
Taylor, Rogan P., 16
Text, De Quincey's: correction of, by other hands, 1–2, 19–20; functional failure of, 11; generation of, 15, 85, 111; problematic nature of, 1–2, 61, 62; status of, 16, 19, 20–1, 26, 61–3, 72–3, 75, 82, 87, 107, 113, 118, 130, 138, 160–61, 165, 170–71, 177; as self-consumption, 28, 34, 85, 112–13; supposed flaws of, 9–11, 46
Thomas De Quincey Bicentenary Studies (Robert Lance Snyder), 4
Thron, E. Michael, 11
Time, 21–3, 36–7, 91–2, 129, 138, 142, 175, 178–79, 181
Titan, 136
Traitors. *See* Betrayal
Translation, 87–8, 93, 96, 104, 112, 116–18, 140, 143, 194n, 196n; idea of De Quincey's fictions as examples of, 94–5
Truth, 49, 82, 92, 102–103, 107, 109–10, 112, 119, 127, 136, 159, 169; as method, 58. *See also* Language
Tyson, Bryan Guy, 157–58

Unity: individual's lack of, 46; political, 124–27

Value, 108, 155, 168, 170, 181, 183; and error, 81; exchange-value, 158–59, 169, 180; production of, by De Quincey, 16, 24–5, 115
Vice, 6–7
Vicious, Sid, 187n
Victim. *See* Pariah.
Violence, 45–6, 49–50, 102, 119, 169; valorised as passion, 45–6

Waterloo, Battle of, as figure, 121, 174, 176
Wellington, Duke of, 122–24, 147
Westmoreland Gazette, 9, 124
Whale, John C., 8, 10

Wilkins, Bishop, 49
Woman, De Quincey's idea of, 33, 59–63; 105–106, 191n, 193n; and Christianity, 59; and writing, 33, 38, 53, 59. *See also* De Quincey, Elizabeth; Saviours, female
Woolf Virginia, 10
Wordsworth, William, 19, 36, 64–5, 79, 80–82, 85, 113, 128; as absent reader, 75; as figure complementary to Coleridge, 73–4; as figure of coherent self, 73–4, 76–7, 83; formulation of death of, by De Quincey, 75–9; quotation of works of, by De Quincey, 76–7; as threat, 74, 77
Works, De Quincey's: neglect of, by critics, 2; lack of clarity in defining bodies of, 36; interdependence of, 12, 21, 22, 37, 42, 48
Writing: as catastrophe, 30, 98 (*see also* Extremity); characteristics of De Quincey's, 9–11, 86–7, 107, 142, 159, 177, 179, 181–82, 184–85; and commodity form, 18–9, 21, 23, 56, 91, 165, 170, 177–78; contingent status of De Quincey's, 20–21, 99, 101, 103–104, 108, 112, 116, 134, 151, 156, 175; and disfigurement, 38, 113; and entertainment, 183–5; and error, 12–15; and labour, 12–13, 61, 148, 175; primary importance of, 5, 8, 9, 11, 13, 59–60, 62, 83, 88, 91, 93, 95, 100, 117, 120, 126, 141, 147–48, 159, 171, 174, 178, 196n; and production process, 20–1, 56, 62, 65, 86, 90, 113; and reading, 20, 82, 89, 98, 106, 177; and representation, 13, 67, 119; and the self, 32, 35, 39–40, 65, 67, 79, 85, 86, 112–14, 136, 140, 146, 150; and woman, 33, 38, 61–3, 105–106, 191n, *See also* Text
Writings, (ed. Masson). *See* De Quincey, Thomas: Works, Collected
Writings. *See also* Masson, David

Young, Michael Cochise, 8